Women Against the Raj

Women Against the Raj

Female Freedom Fighters in the Struggle for India's Independence and Partition

Chloë Gardner

First published in Great Britain in 2024 by
Pen & Sword History
An imprint of
Pen & Sword Books Ltd
Yorkshire – Philadelphia
Copyright © Chloë Gardner 2024
ISBN 9781399066211

The right of Chloë Gardner to be identified as Author of this work has been asserted by her in accordance with the Copyright, Designs and Patents Act 1988.

A CIP catalogue record for this book is
available from the British Library.

All rights reserved. No part of this book may be reproduced or transmitted in any form or by any means, electronic or mechanical including photocopying, recording or by any information storage and retrieval system, without permission from the Publisher in writing.

Set in Aldine 401 13/16.75
Printed in the UK on paper from a sustainable source by CPI Group (UK) Ltd, Croydon, CR0 4YY

Pen & Sword Books Limited incorporates the imprints of After the Battle, Archaeology, Atlas, Aviation, Battleground, Discovery, Family History, History, Maritime, Military, Politics, Select, Transport, True Crime, Fiction, Frontline Books, Leo Cooper, Praetorian Press, Seaforth Publishing, Wharncliffe and White Owl.

For a complete list of Pen & Sword titles please contact
PEN & SWORD BOOKS LIMITED
George House, Beevor Street, Off Pontefract Road, Hoyle Mill, Barnsley, South Yorkshire, England, S71 1HN
E-mail: enquiries@pen-and-sword.co.uk
Website: www.pen-and-sword.co.uk
Or
PEN AND SWORD BOOKS
1950 Lawrence Rd, Havertown, PA 19083, USA
E-mail: Uspen-and-sword@casematepublishers.com
Website: www.penandswordbooks.com

For Rabia and Bharati

'I wonder why there should be any distinction between males and females in a fight for the cause of the country's freedom? If our brothers can join a fight for the cause of the motherland why can't the sisters? Instances are not rare that the Rajput ladies of hallowed memory fought bravely in the battlefields and did not hesitate to kill their country's enemies. The pages of history are replete with high admiration for the historic exploits of these distinguished ladies. Then why should we, the modern Indian women, be deprived of joining this noble fight to redeem our country from foreign domination?'

—Suicide Note of Pritalata Waddedar, 1932.

Contents

Abbreviations	12
Introduction	13

Chapter one: Ranis and Revolutionaries — 43
- Ahilya Bai Holkar (1725–1795) — 44
- Rani Velu Nachiyar (1730–1796) — 46
- Rani Kittur Chennamma (1778–1829) — 48
- Maharani Jindan Kaur (c.1817–1863) — 50
- Rani Avantibai Lodhi (1831–1858) — 58
- Rani Lakhsmibai of Jhansi (c. 1828–1858) — 61
- Jhalkaribai (1830–1858) — 69
- Begum Hazrat Mahal (c. 1820–1879) — 71
- Uda Devi Pasi (1830–1857) — 77
- Mahabiri Devi (died 1857) — 79
- Asghari Begum (died. 1857) — 81
- Nanibala Bandyopadhyay (1888–1967) — 82
- Bhogeshwari Phukanani (1885–1942) — 84
- Bina Das (1911–1986) — 86
- Pritilata Waddedar (1911–1932) — 91
- Kalpana Dutt (1913–1995) — 94
- Leela Roy (1900–1970) — 98
- Santi Ghose (1916–1989) and Suniti Choudhury (1917–1988) — 102
- Bhikaiji Rustom Cama (1861–1936) — 107
- Rani Gaidinliu Pamei (1915–1993) — 112
- Gulab Kaur (1890–1941) — 116
- Aruna Asaf Ali (1909–1996) — 119
- Captain Lakhsmi Sahgal (1914–2012) — 122

Chapter two: Stalwarts and Satyagrahis — 129
- Kasturbai Gandhi (1869–1944) — 131
- Manu Gandhi (1927–1969) — 139

Sushila Nayyar (1914–2001)	146
Avantika Bai Gokhale (1882–1949)	149
Renuka Ray (1904–1997)	151
Sarojini Naidu (1879–1949)	159
Dame Amrit Kaur (1887–1964)	167
Latika Bose (1902–1987)	170
Kamala Nehru (1899–1936)	173
Swarup Rani Nehru (1868–1938)	176
Krishnabai Rau Nimbkar (1906–?)	180
Lilavati Munshi (1899–1978)	182
Kamaladevi Chattopadhyay (1903-1988)	185
Jyotirmayee Gangopadhyay (1889–1945)	190
Matangini Hazra (1870–1942)	192
Ambabai (c. 1900–c. 1970)	194
Subbamma Duvvuri (1881–1964)	196
Jankidevi Bajaj (1893–1979)	198
Gammiḍidala Durgabāi Deshmukh (1909–1981)	200
Accamma Cherian (1909–1982)	203
Subhadra Kumari Chauhan (1904–1948)	205
Khurshedben Naoroji (1894-1966)	208
Satyavati Devi (1905–2010)	211
Chapter three: Partners and Politicians	**215**
Rattanbai 'Ruttie' Maryam Jinnah (1900–1929)	217
Fatima Jinnah (1893–1967)	225
Vijayalakshmi Pandit (1900–1990)	233
Begum Jahanara Shahnawaz (1896–1979)	237
Abadi Bano Begum or Bi Amma (1839–1924)	245
Amjadi Bano (1885–1947)	248
Shareefa Hamid Ali (c. 1883–1971)	251
Sucheta Kripalani (1908–1974)	254
Begum Qudsia Aijaz Rasul (1909–2001)	258
Hansa Mehta (1897–1995)	260

Conclusion	262
End Notes	268
Bibliography	274
Acknowledgements	278
Index	281

Abbreviations

AIML	All-India Muslim League
AITUC	All-India Trade Union Congress
AIWC	All-India Women's Conference
BEIC	British East India Company
BIA	British Indian Army
BJP	Bharatiya Janata Party
CPI	Communist Party of India
DSS	Desh Sevika Sangha
INA	Indian National Army
INC	Indian National Congress
IRA	Indian Republican Army
MLWSC	Muslim League Women's Sub-Committee
MNG	Muslim National Guard
TSC	Travancore State Congress
UCRW	United Council for Relief and Welfare
UN	United Nations
WIA	Women's Indian Association
WNG	Women's National Guard

Introduction

The phrases 'The British Raj' or 'Indian Independence' will typically arouse romantic notions of a British Viceroy hosting a ball in the idyllic hills of Shimla, hypermasculine Indian soldiers revolting against colonial British soldiers, or of a frail-looking Gandhi in his signature spectacles and loin cloth preaching a sermon on peace and love. Rarely will they evoke the image of a woman on horseback chasing down British soldiers with her sword raised in defiance, or hundreds of women in saris with placards and pamphlets protesting on the streets. This book will hopefully change that.

The British first came to India as traders in the early seventeenth century. Then, India was not a unified nation as we would understand it today, but rather comprised a population of two million inhabitants split across many individual kingdoms and tribes with their own rulers, religions, languages, and priorities. Most of the population followed what is today described as Hinduism (itself a contested term owing to the vast spectrum of beliefs and traditions which fall under this umbrella – therefore any reference to Hinduism in this book should be taken as a generalized concept not meant to represent all of those who would consider themselves Hindu). There were also (as there are today) significant communities of Muslims, Sikhs, and Buddhists, as well as those following a variety of other traditions such as Zoroastrianism. Independent princely states were controlled by rulers of various religious traditions, although the Islamic Mughal Empire had control over large parts of the Indian subcontinent from the sixteenth to nineteenth centuries. However, the Mughals had served as a ruling minority, and were content to let the masses follow their own religions, so long as they paid their taxes and maintained order. While many colonial powers had trading posts in India, including the French and Portuguese, it was the British East India Company (BEIC), founded around 1600, that proved most successful. The BEIC came to have its own army of British, as well as Indian, troops to protect its assets, and soon its top merchants were established as something akin to rulers in their own right.

As the BEIC's power grew, so too did local – and even British government – discontent about its influence. In 1857 the first major rebellion against the British Empire, by Indian soldiers known as *sepoys*, erupted amid a dispute about the use of animal products in bullet casings, which offended both Muslim and Hindu religious laws. This revolt was known at the time as the Indian Rebellion or Indian Mutiny of 1857 but is today remembered as the First Indian War of Independence, as it marked the start of an almost century-long fight for Indians to reclaim power over their own land. The terms 'mutiny' and 'uprising' will be used occasionally during this book to refer to this war, in keeping with how it is referred to in contemporary sources. 1857 sparked such concern among the British government that the BEIC was dissolved and forced to hand over its resources and power to the British crown. Thus, in 1858, India officially became a British colony and in 1877, Queen Victoria was declared Empress of India – despite never once setting foot in Asia. This period became known as the British Raj, *Raj* meaning rule in Hindi.

Henceforth, the British unofficially adopted a policy of 'divide and rule', making concerted attempts to classify the native population by religion, language, caste and class. Caste and class are complicated and overlapping concepts which are often used simultaneously but have very distinct meanings. Class most commonly refers to socio-economic status, and therefore lower-class families tend to be those with less financial capital, or those who work in low-skilled jobs and live a more hand-to-mouth existence. Caste, on the other hand, refers to hereditary categories according to which everyone is identified by concepts of ritual purity. The four main castes are Brahmin (the priestly elite), Kshatriya (the warriors and kings), Vaishya (the merchants and farmers) and Shudra (the labourers) – each divided into countless subgroups. Those who fall outside the caste system completely have been known as many things, most famously untouchables, or *harijans* (meaning children of God). These discriminatory and patronizing labels have been rejected by the community and today, this group is referred to as *dalits* (meaning 'broken' in Sanskrit). While many still refer to high or low castes, the preferred terms today are dominant caste (Brahmins, Kshatriyas, and Vaishyas), and caste-oppressed (referring to Shudras and Dalits), to better reflect the privileges that certain castes have experienced at the expense of the others. While the caste system originates in the Hindu tradition, South Asian communities of all religions culturally adhere to concepts of caste even where their religion formally condemns the system.

Caste and class often overlap, in part because castes are traditionally associated with certain professions which means some have historically tended to be restricted to certain, low-paying jobs. Caste discrimination (casteism) was officially outlawed in India in 1948, which has opened opportunities for social mobility across all strata of life. However, caste remains an influential force in South Asian society and casteism remains a significant challenge in India and beyond. As this book will show, there were clear trends in the nationalist movement along both caste and class lines, and this continues in the Hindu nationalist movement in India today.

Although originally reluctant to interfere in the socio-religious politics of the Indian subcontinent, British rule brought a gradual influx of missionaries who sought to critique the religious traditions of the Indian population and convert and 'civilize' them according to British Christian standards. Divisive and patronizing British policies aggravated existing tensions between Indian communities and triggered a wave of religious reform movements and nationalist groups attempting to redefine religious and national identities against the condemnation and control of the British and their religion, laws, and customs.

As with all wars, there is a tendency to simplify the battle for Indian independence into two sides, the evil British versus the good Indians. However, while this is not a completely unfounded view, given the complicity of all Brits in benefiting from the system of colonialism whatever their individual views on British imperialism, the reality is a little more complex.

Some Indians embraced what they saw as positive consequences of the Raj: improved infrastructure including railways and roads, increased access to education (especially for the poor and marginalized), unification of the country through centralizing of governments with a national language, and new employment opportunities as the British began to look to its colonies for cheap labour following its own industrial revolution. Some also saw the British as protectors against the infighting and corruption of India's princely states and hoped that belonging to an empire which spanned a quarter of the globe would open exciting opportunities for travel and trade in an increasingly globalized world. As they grew more powerful, the British emphaized these benefits as a way to allay Indian concerns and to justify Britain's assumption of power. This explains why some Indians readily joined the British police forces and military or took up posts in the British government or colonial administrative offices. These were often prosperous positions that offered generous salaries well beyond the reach of many Indians in other sectors. Many – including the majority of the most prominent nationalists – also took advantage of the new connections with Britain to travel to England for work or educational opportunities. Not all nationalists renounced the British war effort during the world wars; some asked only for dominion status within the empire rather than complete independence. Given how vastly outnumbered the British were in India, even at the peak of their power, they could not have maintained domination of the continent for centuries without some cooperation from the Indians themselves. However, this is not to belittle or justify the exploitation, manipulation, and outright brutality that the British used to seize and retain control, or to say that those who worked within the colonial system did not come to resent or reject it when faced with other options.

However, just as one should not assume that all Indians detested the British presence in India, it should not be assumed that all Brits defended the actions of their countrymen or agreed with efforts to prevent India's independence. A small, but not insignificant, number of the most prominent Indian nationalists were white, British or Irish-born women who proved just as diligent as their Indian counterparts in denouncing British imperialism and fighting to free India from foreign rule. These women were acutely aware that they would be viewed as the enemy by many Indians who had an understandable mistrust of outsiders, especially those who were born in and benefitted from the oppressing nation. However, they dedicated their lives to proving that their loyalties lay with their chosen home of India, and not with the country of their birth and that the privileges of their skin colour and nationality could aid rather than abet their contribution to the movement. Some came to India for love, some for religion, and some simply to fight for freedom which they regarded as a universal human right. Their efforts were rewarded, as they were not only accepted by Indian-born nationalists but in some cases raised by them to lead the movements. These women included Annie Besant, Freda Bedi, Margaret Cousins, Madeline Slade, Nellie Sengupta, and Sister Nivedita. Their stories are inspiring and each would be a fascinating book on their own; sadly, there is no room in the present volume to tell them. While still marginalized on account of their gender, white women have benefitted from privilege in the historical narrative, and therefore it is more important to amplify the stories and voices of the South Asian women who have been erased from their history for too long.

By the mid-nineteenth century, the disastrous consequences wrought by British imperialism on India and its people became too apparent to ignore. Indians were treated as second-class citizens in their own country, with restrictions placed on their freedom and racist discrimination rife throughout the country. Those who dared to challenge their conditions were tortured and executed for sedition. One of the most famous examples of British barbarity against Indians was the 1919 Jallianwala Bagh Massacre (also known as the Amritsar Massacre) in which anywhere between 400 and 1,000 innocent protestors (as well as civilians including women and children who were just passing by) were shot dead by British forces under the instruction of General Dyer. Thousands more were injured. This proved to be a turning point in Indian resistance to British rule and made it harder for the British to portray themselves as paternalistic protectors. Furthermore, the British obsession with classifying people into fixed boxes of religion and caste led to increased communal fighting – both political and physical – between Hindus, Sikhs, and Muslims, and caste-oppressed communities found themselves increasingly marginalized by a regime that, when it did lower itself to communicating with Indians, listened only to those of the conservative priestly (Hindu) elite.

Throughout the late nineteenth and early twentieth centuries, nationalist ideologies began to develop to resist British colonization. In 1885, the Indian National Congress (INC) was founded in Bombay (now Mumbai). Although many cities' names were changed after independence to shed their colonial legacy, throughout this work the old names for cities will be used to reflect the world in which these women lived to avoid confusion with primary sources. The INC was a political party founded by members of the educated Indian elite to promote condemnation of the British and advocate for Indian self-government. This concept was known as *Swaraj* (Indian home rule), a term which became increasingly popular after it was adopted by Mohandas Gandhi after his return to India in 1915.

Mohandas Karamchand Gandhi (1869–1948) more widely known by his honorific title Mahatma, is undoubtedly the most famous figure of the Indian independence movement, owing to his prominent role in the INC and his leadership of some of the movement's most influential campaigns. While he openly admired all faiths and professed disdain for religious nationalism, he was a devout Hindu and is often regarded as a Hindu leader, despite his eventual assassination at the hands of a Hindu extremist who saw him as too sympathetic to Islamic interests. Having fought against imperialism and tyranny in South Africa while working as a lawyer there, he used his political acumen to launch several protests against British rule and unite India as one nation. His first prominent campaign was his non-cooperation movement, begun in the 1920s, based on a concept of civil disobedience in which individuals refuse to follow the laws of a government that they believe to be unjust or immoral. By rejecting British laws, Gandhi believed that the people would force their oppressors to concede and return control to Indian hands to restore law and order. This non-cooperation movement focused on protesting Britain's economic and political monopoly over India, and thus centred around the concept of *swadeshi*, a Sanskrit word meaning 'of one's own country'. One of the primary reasons that Britain was so desperate to maintain control over India was that they were able to sell large amounts of British goods in India, which not only prevented the economic development of Indian growth but also funnelled all of India's wealth back to Britain. Therefore, Gandhi's *swadeshi* campaign exhorted all Indians to boycott foreign goods and increasingly produce their own resources, thus depriving Britain of its income while improving India's economy. He urged his followers to spin their own cloth, known as *khadi*, and adopting this became a key signifier of one's nationalist leaning.

The aspect of Gandhi's ideology for which he is most remembered, however, is *ahimsa* (non-violence). The central tenet of Gandhi's activism was that all protest and disorder must be strictly non-violent and should involve actions such as boycotts, marches, and hunger strikes, rather than violent revolt. To encompass these principles, Gandhi coined the term *satyagraha* (meaning 'holding firmly to truth' in Sanskrit) to refer to this form of peaceful resistance. Someone who practised *satyagraha* was known as a *satyagrahi*, a term which is used to refer to many women in this book. While Gandhi's non-violent campaigns were hugely popular and succeeded in mobilizing the masses to the nationalist movement, not all Indian nationalists agreed that this was the best way to rid themselves of British rule. Many took up arms against the British and risked life and limb as martyrs for the cause, either dying in battle or being executed by the British for their rebellion.

Another key figure in the battle against the Raj was Muhammad Ali Jinnah (1876–1948) a Muslim lawyer, politician, and eventual founder of Pakistan. Like Gandhi, Jinnah had begun his political career as a member of the INC, marking himself as a notable figure when he helped to negotiate the 1916 Lucknow Pact between the INC and the All-India Muslim League (AIML), the leading nationalist group among Indian Muslims. The Lucknow Pact is seen as a crucial moment in the Indian independence movement because the two rival parties agreed to allow religious minorities separate representation in provincial legislatures and it was here that the AIML formally agreed to support INC calls for Indian independence. However, Jinnah's relationship with the INC soured considerably over the coming years. In 1918, Jinnah and his wife, Ruttie, had condemned Gandhi's support of the British following protests during which the Jinnahs had been attacked by the police. They accused Gandhi of using his fasts, marches, and jail stints as publicity stunts for personal gain rather than for the good of the nation, pointing out that they led to more arrests and deaths on all sides than any legal challenge levelled by Jinnah's faction. Gandhi had also stayed silent while Jinnah challenged the Rowlatt Acts, through which the British banned public protest. Furthermore, Gandhi had urged against prosecuting the British officers responsible for the Jallianwala Bagh Massacre while the Jinnahs condemned it as evidence of British brutality.

As Gandhi's power rose, he made clear attempts to replace Jinnah in prominent positions and began to use the Jinnahs' Muslim faith to discredit them among Hindu populations. The Jinnahs and Gandhi came to a complete impasse in 1921 when Jinnah openly opposed Gandhi's non-cooperation movement which he deemed suicidal. For his disagreement, Jinnah was booed off the stage while his wife stood defiantly beside him as a pillar of political and personal support. Some of the crowd even attempted to drag her from the stage, chiding her for wearing a colourful sari and blouse rather than the white *khadi* that everyone else present was wearing. She showed no fear, and on one occasion, placed herself in the middle of a physical skirmish. Following this incident, Jinnah told a journalist: 'I will have nothing to do with this [Gandhi's] pseudo-religious approach to politics. I part company with the Congress and Gandhi. I do not believe in working up mob hysteria ... Politics is a gentleman's game'.[1] While this is an admirable statement with the hindsight of knowing the carnage that mob hysteria would inflict upon South Asia in the coming decades, it was not received well at the time and the Jinnahs were hounded the entire way home. Following this rupture, Jinnah instead proposed a comprehensive plan to protect the political rights of the Muslim minority in India. This marked a crucial moment in the Indian independence movement, as it cemented the separation between Hindus and Muslims and bolstered the motion for a separate Muslim nation, Pakistan, to be created upon liberation from British rule, a motion which was officially articulated in 1940 and would be realized seven years later when Jinnah was named the first Prime Minister of the independent Muslim state of Pakistan.

Jinnah's political counterpart was Jawaharlal Nehru (1889–1964), the first Prime Minister of independent India. Another key player of the INC, Nehru led the party for most of the crucial years of the independence struggle after Gandhi formally stepped back from party politics. It was Nehru, as INC president, who officially called for complete independence from British rule in 1929, and it was Nehru who agreed to the concept of a separate nation for Hindus and Muslims following the British departure. His political ideals helped to shape not only the freedom struggle but the very notion of what an independent India would look like. One position that he regarded as non-negotiable was that an independent India should be explicitly secular, with no preference for any religion or community. While India remains an officially secular country today, both Nehru and Gandhi advocated a nationalism that was based on Hindu principles and biases, and therefore the India over which he came to rule would prove to be a decidedly Hindu one, a legacy which has allowed far-right Hindu nationalism to flourish in India to this day.

While Gandhi, Jinnah, and Nehru negotiated what independence from British rule would mean going forward, the world further descended into chaos, only exacerbating the tensions within India. During the First World War, one million Indian troops served Britain, of whom at least 74,000 died and another 67,000 were wounded. From 1943–1945, a famine in Bengal was aggravated by the British who hoarded food for themselves, leaving thirty to thirty-five million Indians to die of starvation and disease.

The Second World War proved to be another key moment for the nationalist movement. By 1945, two-and-a-half million Indians formed part of the British army. Most of them were deployed to fight the Japanese as part of the largest British army ever formed. These campaigns cost the lives of over 87,000 Indian troops, while another 35,000 were wounded, and over 67,000 became prisoners of war. Their valour was recognized with the award of some 5,000 medals, and eighteen members of the British Indian Army (BIA) were awarded the Victoria or George Cross. Winston Churchill, who is still hailed as a hero for leading Britain to victory in the Second World War, told his Secretary of State for India, Leo Amery, that he 'hated Indians' and considered them 'a beastly people with a beastly religion'.[2] Nonetheless, even he admitted that without the aid of Indian soldiers, Britain would have been unlikely to win the war. Yet Indians were shown little gratitude for their sacrifices, and many were imprisoned or killed for speaking out against the war or the British. While most of those who died in battle were men, Indian women were equally entangled in the war, serving in auxiliary corps, medical roles, and almost every other aspect of the war effort alongside their male counterparts.

Indians were not consulted over their involvement in either world war but were rather dragged into them by the British who needed the empire's manpower to bolster its numbers against its enemies. In March 1942 Nehru supported the Cripps Mission, the British effort to secure full Indian support for the Second World War, on the condition that they would be rewarded for their support with independence following the war. However, the Cripps Mission was rejected by Gandhi, and Nehru was forced to back Gandhi's more popular Quit India Resolution. The Quit India Resolution, passed in August 1942, demanded an immediate end to British rule and was accompanied by mass protests during which almost all leaders of the INC – including Gandhi and Nehru – were imprisoned by the British. The Quit India movement divided the country further. The AIML, and sections of society loyal to the British, including several princely states, rejected the resolution, while crowds of supporters of the resolution took to the streets in protests that frequently turned violent. With INC leaders imprisoned for two years, even those in favour of this campaign struggled to stay united in their cause.

Throughout the final years of the Second World War, and immediately following it, it became clear that India had descended further and further into unrest, and that the British could no longer maintain their power over the continent. Thus, in 1946, negotiations began to finally grant India its independence from British rule and hand the power back to its people. However, this was a difficult task owing to the disputes, even among nationalists themselves, about what a free India should look like. On 18 July 1947, the British parliament passed the Indian Independence Act which formally agreed to India's independence, and partition.

The true scale of the damage that British colonialism did to India, and indeed to the entire Indian subcontinent, is still largely hidden from history. Even less well known is its specific impact on women, and the substantial role that women played in ridding their land of British rule. It is hard to generalize about the place of women in British India, as experiences differed so drastically across caste, class, religious, and ethnic lines. Perhaps the only largely homogenous group was the women of the Raj, including the wives of the viceroys and other colonial agents who were largely white, wealthy, and educated – but were still very much restricted to domestic roles other than the occasional ceremonial and hosting commitments. Many did have some interaction with Indian women, who often worked in colonial homes as nannies (known in India as *ayahs*) or other domestic roles, or through their social or missionary work which many colonial women took on to ease their boredom, but the majority remained ignorant of the struggles, customs, and desires of their Indian sisters. Indian women defied categorization even more than their male counterparts. As we will see, some of India's most powerful rulers were women, queens (known as *maharanis*, or *ranis*) who led armies of thousands – centuries before Britain even considered admitting women to their ranks. Some women were educated and respected but were hidden from public view by the restrictions of purdah (a practice by which women remain segregated from men or at least wear a veil in their company when in public) which were still adhered to by large swathes of Indian women from all communities during the late nineteenth and early twentieth centuries. Others were illiterate but were free (or forced by economic necessity) to work in the public domain as farmers or labourers among other traditional occupations. As with women across the world, all were bound to their expected roles as wives and mothers, but Indian women were gradually finding a voice for themselves in spheres which had traditionally been denied to them, and the nationalist movement proved a prime catalyst for this trend. As early as 1917, a document was presented to Secretary of State for India, Edward Montagu, on behalf of the women of India demanding self-rule for India and equal votes for women. As we will see, this momentum only continued to grow throughout the twentieth century.

Today, we are increasingly aware of the intersectionality of oppression, and the way in which women of colour are doubly oppressed through their gender and their ethnicity (and then by other identities such as religion, disabilities, and class on top of that). This is blatantly clear in the way that women were treated under the British Raj. Not only were they subject to the racial oppression of colonial subjects, but they were further victimized on account of their gender, not just by their rulers but by the men of their own communities who further policed their behaviour and ideas. As Sikata Banerjee (2005) has explored, the Indian Independence movement flourished on an ideology of toxic masculinity. British propaganda mocked Indian (especially Hindu) men as weak and effeminate, unable to protect their country, their women, or themselves from invasion. Muslim men were depicted as wild and sexually aggressive, unable to control their desires or their violent tendencies. Sikh men were objectified and dehumanized as natural warriors, a 'militant caste' who were prime fodder to bolster British military objectives. In contrast, the British depicted themselves as the ideal gentlemen, sexually potent but simultaneously restrained and chaste, embodying a tradition of Muscular Christianity which equated physical and spiritual strength. The success of the British Empire at controlling half the globe – despite impossible numerical disadvantage – was seen as evidence of the superiority of British (read: white) men. In response to these critiques, Indians began to construct an explicitly masculine nationalism which valorized the warrior ideals of Hinduism and Sikhism, and the fighting spirit of Islam (although rarely the three together) and urged Indian men to prove their masculinity by forcefully expelling the British (and later, members of rival religious communities). As is so often the case, both sides used women as a battleground. The British used practices such as widow immolation as proof that Indians were barbaric and backwards and that Indian women needed the British to protect them from their male oppressors (all the while killing, torturing, and raping women who dared to speak out against British rule). Meanwhile, in the communal fighting between religious communities, Indian men raped, kidnapped, or forcibly converted women to assert power over the men in their rival communities. Even metaphorically, women became the rallying point of Indian (especially Hindu) nationalism as India became imagined as the goddess, Mother India, a desperate maiden in need of defending by her patriotic sons. This all contributed to the enduring stereotype of South Asian women as weak, passive, victims, in need of defending by men, and whose honour is directly linked to that of their religious community and their country.

Just as women faced double oppression from both colonialism and misogyny, women from caste-oppressed communities faced further discrimination, casteism, and potentially class discrimination as well. As is so often the case with history, the most prominent voices tend to be those with the most privilege, and therefore, dominant castes and higher classes tend to control traditional narratives – even those who are already marginalized such as women. Muslims, also a numerical and often demonized minority in India, as well as other religious minorities are also harder to find in the traditional records. Therefore, amplifying the stories of female nationalists from marginalized caste, class, religious, or ethnic groups is especially important, as they are even less likely to have received recognition either from their contemporaries or later historians.

As we will see throughout this book, Indian women nationalists almost all combined their nationalist activities with activism for women's rights (causes which they saw as inseparable) and articulated their nationalist ideologies through the unique lens of universal womanhood. The reason these women remain so inspiring, even though the cause for which they fought was achieved almost a century ago, is that they were acutely aware of their self-worth and of their crucial contributions not just to their families but to society and the nation. Drawing on their religious and cultural predecessors, from the powerful Hindu goddesses such as Kali who embodied feminine power, to the educated and politically active wives of the Prophet Mohammad, and the queens of the Sikh and Mughal empires who led armies and governments alike, these women refused to be subservient to anybody on account of either their gender or their race. Even those who did not completely reject the patriarchal norms of their society redefined what it meant to be powerful. Indian ideals of womanhood focussed on concepts of purity and modesty, but women were increasingly adept at carving paths for themselves that allowed them to exercise agency without compromising their reputations or the values of their community. The non-violent ethos of the *satyagraha* movement allowed women to fight for what they believed was right without pushing the bounds of propriety by acting in a violent or unruly (read: unladylike) manner. Therefore, while we can say that the nationalist movement helped women cast off the chains of oppression, it is important to remember that those chains looked different for every woman and that the methods in which they freed themselves varied massively. However, each contribution was just as admirable and contributed in its way to the end of British rule in India. Furthermore, each disrupted the view of Indian women as nothing more than meek and subservient housewives.

Introduction

On 15 August 1947, Britain formally granted India its independence, simultaneously creating the new nation of Pakistan. The division of the Indian subcontinent along religious lines marked the end of two centuries of British control in India. This period had come at a calamitous cost for the Indian people, but the bloodshed that was to follow official independence was catastrophic. The British appointed a man who had never set foot in India to draw a dividing line across the area known as the Punjab (an area that had already seen extreme civil unrest during the latter period of British rule), calling the area to the north of the line, Pakistan, and the area to the south, India. This resulted in the biggest forced migration in human history, triggering the displacement of at least fourteen million people as Muslims stranded on the Hindu side of the border migrated to Pakistan and Hindus and Sikhs in the now-Muslim Pakistan migrated to the newly independent India. During this chaos, at least one million people died of famine, disease, and interreligious violence. We will never know the exact numbers of those who perished during Partition, but every estimate demonstrates the huge numbers affected. Behind every number is the story of a person whose life was torn apart forever. While every community suffered in the carnage surrounding Partition, women, as is so often the case in humanitarian crises, suffered disproportionately. Women were subjected to various kinds of violence from their own communities, from rival communities, from their states, and even at their own hands.

Most of the treatment toward women during Partition needs to be understood through South Asian concepts of purity and honour. Purity and pollution are hugely influential concepts in Hinduism, on which many laws of caste and ritual are centred around. The caste system is based on the idea that encountering lower castes is polluting. For example, many people from dominant castes would not eat food prepared by someone from a (supposedly) inferior caste, or even eat at the same table as them for fear that they would become impure through this interaction. Traditionally, women in general have been equated with Dalits (regardless of their actual caste) and are considered equally polluting, especially during menstruation when they are forbidden to enter certain temples or prepare food for certain people, and were often even asked to leave the home until they are ritually pure again. Islam, too, has gendered notions of purity – for example, menstruating women are not permitted to touch the Qur'an as it is seen as polluting the holy text. Sikhs, on the other hand, theoretically have no restrictions based on gender or menstruation, but in lived reality, cultural taboos often overtook religious protections, just as many Muslims in South Asia continue to observe caste distinctions despite Islam officially denouncing such divisions.

These understandings of purity are closely related to ideas of honour. In some conservative understandings of Hinduism, a woman's only religious duty is to obey and serve her husband, and therefore if a woman is seen to have done anything to dishonour her husband (such as live away from him or have intercourse – consensual or not – with another man) then she could not be considered religiously pure and would suffer the consequences in both this and the next life. While Islam does not require that brides be virgins if they are divorced or widowed, or forbid widows from re-marrying, as traditional Hinduism does, women are punished more harshly than men for adultery and are forbidden from having sex before or otherwise beyond the bounds of marriage.

Throughout place and time, the onus has been placed on women to uphold their honour, while their honour is inextricably linked with that of the family, the community, or even the nation. This was especially true during the Indian independence movement when women's bodies were increasingly portrayed as representative of the honour of India as a whole, the men being valorized as protective sons of the motherland, a land which is vulnerable to invasion and defiling at the hands of an enemy Other. In the same way that Britain had invaded and defiled India, Indian and Pakistani communities now used these same tactics against each other by invading and defiling their women.

Accordingly, much of the violence enacted upon women during Partition would today be understood as honour crimes, referring to crimes committed primarily (but not only) against women as a way of seeking revenge for transgressing sexual or moral codes and thus bringing a family or an individual into disrepute. This is especially clear in the violence women suffered at the hands of their own community's men when women were either killed outright or pressured into suicide in the name of honour. This view was propagated by Gandhi himself, who argued that suicide was 'morally preferable to submission', despite labelling women as 'the chief sufferers of 1947'.[3]

In 1946-7, thousands of women from both sides of the newly created border were abducted, raped, forced into marriage, forcibly converted, maimed, and killed. In the worst cases, women were also mutilated, their breasts cut off before they were paraded naked down the streets, while their children, friends, and relatives looked on helplessly. Many had their bodies carved with religious symbols of the community or with the nationalist slogan of the new nations, a way of branding them to signify their new ownership. They were often traded as chattel to negotiate freedom, safety, or land as their menfolk tried to forge a way for themselves in their new lands. Such incidents portray how women were reduced to their bodies, which bore the burden of the honour of the community, to be conquered, claimed, or marked to inflict harm on their community in general.

As Yasmin Khan, author of one of the most comprehensive histories of Partition explains: '[Partition] is a history of broken bodies and broken lives. Rape was used as a weapon, as a sport and as a punishment ... It sparked the deepest feelings of revenge, dishonour and shame'.[4] Women were so concerned that they would be disowned by their families that many lied or stayed silent about being raped, which added to the psychological trauma as they tried to recover their lives. Consequently, many women chose to end their lives, either out of shame of what had happened to them or because death was preferable to the trauma of sexual assault and then the stigma that came after it.

The harsh treatment of women was used by each side to point to the brutality of The Other. However, while the popular belief is that only enemy men abducted or tortured women, evidence suggests that women were equally abused by men from their own communities. For instance, older women were targeted for their property, which opportunistic men saw a chance to seize during the chaos. Similarly, many took the chance to exact revenge on those they felt had wronged them, for example by rejecting marriage proposals or committing adultery. Most commonly, however, men chose to murder their families to 'save' them from conversion, rape, or potentially more brutal murders at someone else's hands. In some homes, up to twenty-five women and children from the same family were slaughtered by their male relatives who claimed to be making martyrs of their women. But is it martyrdom if the person is not willing to embrace death? For this reason, male narratives stressed that the women decided to die, but given the lack of women's voices in these narratives, this is hard to verify. In Sikh families, women were often beheaded with a kirpan, the sword that Sikhs carry as a symbol of their religion, in an attempt to symbolize that these women were dying for their religion. Some accounts also attest to the fact that even where they did not wish to die, the women reconciled themselves to it and displayed some agency by choosing the method of execution or by choosing to commit the act themselves, ensuring that they had some power over their fate even within very restrictive circumstances. Such accounts show that contrary to the dominant narrative of women's experiences of Partition, it is important to note that they were violated for many reasons and by many forces.

The most famous example of mass suicides is that which occurred in Thoa Khalsa, Rawalpindi, where ninety women jumped into a well rather than face the trauma of rape, mutilation, and murder. Women who died – voluntarily or not – were often hailed as martyrs for their religion, family, and homeland. For example, one male survivor recalled:

'[Women] came down the stairs ... sat down and they said ... we are willing to become martyrs, and they did. Small children too ... What was there to fear? The real fear was one of dishonour. If they had been caught by the Muslims, our honour, their honour would have been sacrificed, lost'.[5]

These suicides have often been equated with murder because women were pressured into making this fatal decision through emotional blackmail that placed the onus on them to protect the honour of the family. Many were also too young or too distressed to make a rational and informed decision. Thus, we must be wary of assuming that anyone willingly chose to die during this time.

However, there is evidence that many women saw death as the best (or only) option. Many may have been influenced by the ideal of the *sati*, a widow who throws herself on her husband's funeral pyre rather than live without him, in doing so absolving both her and her late husband of their sins and guaranteeing both entry to heaven. While *sati* was only committed in certain communities and often for more socio-economic than religious reasons, this idealized Hindu concept of wifely devotion was emulated by those who preferred to die as pure and loyal wives rather than as defiled 'adulterers'. They were assured that they would be 'remembered favourably', that their family would not be judged for their perceived transgressions, and that they had a better chance at paradise in the next life (especially as they were also avoiding the prospect of a forced conversion to another faith). As one Sikh survivor, Basant Singh, recalled, converting to Islam was seen as a fate worse than death and it was this, she claims, that led her to jump into a well along with six of her children and over eighty other women. She was one of the few survivors (despite numerous thwarted attempts) because the well was already so full of corpses that there was no water left to drown her. Thus, while these women were conforming to the patriarchal notions in their society of the honour of the community resting on their purity, they took the decision consciously, albeit for the community rather than their themselves – individualism being a foreign concept to many non-Western cultures. It could also be argued that the thought of a brutal assault, rape, or death at the hands of a stranger (and the concern over how their family would react, even if they survived) was so terrifying that women preferred to take control of how they would die and choose their ending for themselves, demonstrating some agency which complicates the view of women as passive victims of male aggression – even if this decision was directly inspired by the fear of misogynistic violence. Moreover, the act of voluntarily killing yourself and encouraging others to take their own life is a type of violence too. Thus, assuming a perpetual non-violent victim position is a reductionist take on women's Partition stories.

Other ordeals inflicted upon women during Partition were perhaps less violent but equally traumatizing and dehumanizing, such as the treatment of women by the new Indian and Pakistani states. Many families had reported their loved ones – especially their women - missing or abducted. The immense scale of such reports compelled the governments on both sides to act and the United Council for Relief and Welfare (UCRW) was formed under the leadership of Edwina Mountbatten, wife of the last British Viceroy (a controversial appointment given her husband's role in creating the circumstances leading to this carnage). The UCRW compiled a list of missing persons and sent them to local police stations. In September 1947, the newly appointed Prime Ministers of India and Pakistan met at Lahore and decided to start a programme from both nations to begin the mammoth task of tracing these missing persons. On 6 December 1947, the Central Recovery Operation, comprised of women social workers and police, was launched. They faced considerable difficulty in finding women, as the local police accompanying them would often warn abductors and the women would be hidden away. Thus, authorities often had to resort to measures like disguises, false names, and force to get their way. On some occasions, the policemen sent to recover the women would rape them before reporting their discovery. This highlights the isolation and vulnerability of women who could not even rely on the supposedly righteous authorities to protect them, despite their protests that they were acting for the benefit of women.

In 1949, the Abducted Persons (Recovery and Restoration) Act was passed for the same purpose. Under this act, conversions of women and marriages solemnized after 1 March 1947 were not recognized, and these women were officially considered abducted persons. This operation went on for nine years, with around 22,000 Muslim women and 8,000 Hindu and Sikh women being 'recovered'. Almost half of those were under twelve years old, showing that the abducted women were not women at all, but girls. Of the remaining half, almost all were under thirty-five. This suggests that older women had either been killed immediately or simply left behind because they were not deemed attractive enough to be regarded as sexual assets or able-bodied enough to be put to work in their new homes. Through this act, the states of India and Pakistan decided for themselves who was to be considered an abductee and the rights and desires of the women were completely disregarded.

Thus, women who had freely chosen to embrace a new faith, or willingly entered new marriages were stripped once again of their freedom, their choices, and their agency. Many women had eventually adapted to their new circumstances, starting families with the men who had taken them (sometimes happier families than they had left behind). Aside from attachment to their new families or lives, there were other reasons why women were reluctant to go back to their hometowns. They were often told exaggerated accounts of hardships on the other side of the border by their abductors. Oral narratives from Pakistan reveal how women had initially been reluctant to return to India because abductors told them that there was no food in India, that all their relations had been killed, that those surviving would reject a 'fallen' woman, or that Indian soldiers would kill anyone that crossed the border.

Nonetheless, these women's lives were uprooted again, and they were sometimes forced to leave their children behind. Thus, in many cases, the women suffered a double trauma of abduction – once from their natal homes, and then again at the hands of the state. This highlights how the paternalistic state, as well as the patriarchal notion of a helpless woman, dictated the policies of the day and gave women no control over their families and citizenship. While, as we shall see, women had fought for their nation to be free and independent, they were not given the same courtesy. The very word 'recovered' is symbolic of their dehumanization – it suggests that they are property to be reclaimed by their rightful owners, rather than humans in (possible) need of rescue and aid. Certainly, many women were happy to be reunited with their families, but many were also forcefully taken by the officials. The relief social workers, though sympathetic to the plight of these women, were bound by law to return them to their 'real' countries, which was ultimately decided by their religion rather than their desires or national affiliation. For the authorities, women as individuals were not important. It was the idea of the goodwill of the state as a protector of its women that took priority. Both India and Pakistan used recovery efforts as a pawn in their power struggles, trying to make themselves look better and portraying the other as helpless.

Adding to the women's suffering, both the Indian and Pakistani governments refused to recognize children born to abducted women as legitimate because they were deemed to have been conceived illegitimately once marriages had been annulled by the state. Children who were able to accompany their mothers became a constant reminder of the violation perpetrated against the woman, and ergo the violation of her community. Even where the children were the product of consensual liaisons, these were often deemed illicit dalliances either with men from forbidden communities or even just affairs outside of marriage as people clung to each other in desperate times. Thus, women were forcibly separated from their children, who were left behind and considered citizens of their father's homeland. Many women were pressured into leaving their children for fear that they would not be accepted by their families back home. Accordingly, women who were pregnant were forced to either give their children up for adoption or go for a terminating 'cleansing'. Even though abortion was illegal in India, the Indian government financed mass abortions specifically for this purpose. Again, such complex and life-altering decisions were taken without empathy or consent from the people they were taken on behalf of. In the most extreme and harrowing of cases, pregnant women had their babies physically hacked from their wombs and roasted on spits in front of their families. This contributes to the increasingly accepted view that the events of Partition should be considered a genocide, as there were clear efforts on the part of the states, or at the very least of sizable communities within them, to wipe out specific religious and ethnic populations in their lands. Even where women were able to carry a baby to term, the mothers were often given the option of giving them up for adoption or being exiled from their families with no means to support their child.

However, even women without children were often terrified of returning to their families for fear of being ostracized because they would no longer be considered sexually 'pure'. Muslim women were slightly more easily accepted in Pakistan, given that Islam has more relaxed views around virginity and a more universal view of the concept of community. This is not to say that honour did not remain a hugely influential concept, and that women in Pakistan were not killed, raped, or abandoned because of notions of ruined family honour, but only that it was not articulated to such a high level as it was in India, where the issue of their 'purity' became critical. In India, pamphlets retelling the ubiquitously influential Hindu epic the *Ramayana*, highlighted the episode in which the heroine, the goddess Sita, is abducted by the demon Ravana, but stays 'pure' even when away from her husband, Ram. Unsurprisingly, these leaflets failed to include the latter half of the story in which, despite proving her innocence during a divine trial by fire, Sita is cast out by her husband because his subjects believe her purity to have been irrevocably tarnished. If even a goddess, the one who is still an archetypal dutiful wife and role model for all Hindu women, cannot be forgiven by her flawless (according to Hindu mythology) husband for her kidnap, then what chance did ordinary, mortal Indian women have? So common was the rejection of these 'rescued' women that *ashrams* (sanctuaries) were established to house them. This was supposed to be a temporary arrangement until the women could be reconciled with their families, but it rarely happened, and the women found themselves outcasts for the rest of their lives. Without the protection of a family, many faced the grim choice of a life of prostitution or virtual enslavement in government-run homes. Thus, women who had to suffer such barbarity during Partition were again subjected to humiliation and rejection because they were no longer considered pure.

Even where women were able to escape with their lives and managed to remain in their homes, their lives were impacted in many other significant ways. For example, many were left abandoned without the financial or emotional support of their husbands or family on whom they were completely dependent in an era when women were only just starting to find stable and lucrative employment in their own right. Women at this time could not inherit, and therefore if their male relatives had been killed or forced to flee, they often lost their homes and any wealth they had previously enjoyed. Partition ruptured the lives of whole families, with every person needing to work towards rebuilding that life. Women became social workers or had to find other work to support their families – a drastic change for many. This left women with little time or resources to pursue their desires or social life. Sometimes, women were simply abandoned by their families because they could no longer afford to support them, and they preferred to invest in their sons. On a more positive note, this push for women to enter the workforce created opportunities for women to enter the public sphere in an unprecedented way and built on the efforts of female nationalists and activists who had been working to improve women's social status in the century or so preceding Partition.

Finally, it should be remembered that women's experiences during Partition varied drastically. As is the case with most of history, women's recollections of their experiences are rare (although oral historians are now working harder than ever to collect their stories before Partition slips out of living memory), and therefore we already get a picture of women's experiences that is coloured to some extent through a male lens. However, this is only one of the issues that complicates generalizations of women's experiences. Some regions were generally more affected than others – with the areas around the India-Pakistan border being hardest hit with rioting and other violence. Not all families did migrate, and of those who did not all endured violence in the process. Those who had the protection of male relatives, who were higher class and had access to wealth, education, and political power, or those who already had some financial independence or income were much less vulnerable than those who had already been marginalized before Partition, and who were completely alone and destitute. Most of the women whose stories we will hear in this book, if they lived to see Partition, escaped most of the horrors outlined above and were thus free to take up the mantel of social workers and bore the brunt of relief work, largely because they were protected by power and privilege. However, this in itself must have taken a physical and mental toll on them; they must have been heartbroken at the general unrest in their beloved nations and at how all the progress they felt they had made for women's rights had apparently been for naught. Therefore, when one talks of the impact of Partition on women, it must be remembered that there was no universal experience. For every tale of barbarity and abuse of women, there is a story of women fighting back, of claiming their own power wherever they could, and rising from the ashes of Partition to carve new lives for themselves in their newly free nations.

While the British used the carnage they left in their wake as vindication that India had indeed needed their interference to maintain peace, it was abundantly clear to most that the horrors of Partition were a direct consequence of British policy which consistently pitted religious communities against one another, sharpening polarized identities and exacerbating any existing tensions between communities who had lived relatively harmoniously for centuries. That both nations had also been stripped of resources by centuries of colonialism also contributed to the starvation and disease which killed so many refugees, and led to an inevitable fighting over resources, not only between the new nations but their people too. Furthermore, the dividing line had been drawn with no consultation with Indians who knew the complex social and political landscape of the area. The British left India so quickly after the decision was made that they made very little attempt to ensure that systems were in place to help the new nations ease into the transition. While there is little excuse for the atrocities committed on all sides during the bloody summer of 1947, they cannot be understood without their context: two centuries of colonial oppression that left the Indian subcontinent a boiling pressure cooker and the horrors of Partition can be seen as the result of that finally exploding.

※

Despite the chaos that independence brought, Mohandas Gandhi, Jawaharlal Nehru and M.A. Jinnah are today hailed as nationalist heroes. Famous male freedom fighters, such as Bhagat Singh, who fought and died to free India from British oppression are the subjects of many a book and Bollywood movie. While the accomplishments and legacies (both good and bad) of these brave and astute men should not be forgotten, there is a huge group of freedom fighters who have been left out of the glorified nationalist histories of India and Pakistan: the women. Gandhi, Nehru, and Jinnah were always aided by their female relatives and supporters, who are now remembered merely as footnotes in the story of their lives – if they are remembered at all. With as much bravery and vigour as their male counterparts, women across the Indian subcontinent exposed and resisted the cruelty and injustice of the British Raj and shared their vision of a free nation. While some, especially those of dominant castes or British education, were celebrated in their day, the majority have been lost to time, subsumed in a narrative of successful men who have become the poster boys of Indian independence ever since.

Partition overall is too often forgotten and overlooked in history, especially in Britain where the curriculum completely ignores any semblance of guilt over its colonial past. It is entirely absent from school curriculums and ignored in popular culture. Even if Britain hadn't been directly involved in the carnage, it is incomprehensible that the biggest mass movement of people in history and one of the worst incidences of interreligious violence could ever slip under the radar. Add Britain's culpability for making such irresponsible (at best) and immoral decisions, and that just cements an extra layer to the shame that Britain as a nation should feel for its shocking ignorance of the events surrounding Partition – an act which continues to affect the political and social landscape of South Asia and South Asian diasporas to the present day.

However, even within the little-known story of Partition, the complex lives of the female victims and survivors get lost. It is virtually impossible to comprehend the unimaginable pain they suffered, not only at the hands of outsiders but at the hands of their own communities as well. Their experiences are an extreme and harrowing example of the danger that placing concepts of purity and honour onto women's bodies brings, and of the unique ways that women suffer in times of unthinkable tragedy and inhumanity. The stories of these women scream with loss and waste – all the bodies that were destroyed, families torn apart, and lives that were ruined or ended in the name of meaningless, unquantifiable concepts of honour and purity that patriarchal societies hold so dear.

In many ways, this book is a celebration of the casting out of British oppression and the massive victory of India and Pakistan in creating new and free nations. Inside are stories of women who fought and died for that future. However, many independence activists foresaw the danger of the plans for Partition, and most were devastated that they were left with two divided, hate-filled countries, instead of one strong, united India. Thus, among the celebration and perseverance of those who fought for freedom, it is important to remember the millions who suffered during Partition and in particular the women whose stories have slipped through the cracks of history.

However, in part, focussing on the horrific plight of women during and after Partition plays into the narrative of women, especially South Asian women, as passive and oppressed victims of male brutality and subjugation. In truth, many resisted and endured. One such example is recalled by Khurshid Begum who was born into a Muslim-majority village, Langeri, and was twelve years old during the turbulent Partition days. She recalled overhearing her male relatives discussing whether the girls of her family should be rounded up and killed for their 'protection': 'There was no question' of the girls having a say in whether they lived or died.⁶ She was saved from this fate by her formidable grandmother:

'It's their life and they also have the right to take a decision'. She spoke to the two male elders of the family saying '[she] talked sense to them … Grandmother literally ordered the men to leave, and they had to listen … She was a brave woman … like a man, strong'.⁷

This story is just one of the many that prove that women were not just feeble victims of Partition and that they did not just willingly submit to the depravity of men. They had not lost the independence and the fire that they had exhibited during the nationalist movement and long before. Rather, many refused to stand by and let themselves and their sisters, daughters, and mothers, be destroyed for male honour. They survived to tell the tales of Partition, to pass down the stories that made them who they are, as women always have, and they helped to raise a new generation of Indians and Pakistanis who would never have to know the trauma they suffered so that they could live freely.

Thus, while the horrors that they endured during Partition must be remembered, honoured, and understood, the rest of this book hopes to show the other side of women's independence story. Because, far from being mere victims of political decisions made purely by men, from the earliest days of colonialism in India, women had played an active part in rising against the British and campaigning for their nations' independence. They also played a crucial part in building (and re-building) these new nations. Modern-day India and Pakistan are shaped by the blood and sweat of these female freedom fighters as much as by the blood of the female victims of Partition, and it is these women that this book hopes to write back into history.

This is an attempt to further illuminate the fallacy of submissive stereotypes of South Asian women and rewrite the narrative of the Indian independence movement by showing that everything men were doing, women were doing too – often more successfully despite much harsher odds. In an attempt to avoid the colonial folly of classifying Indians by religion or caste, and owing to the difficulties that changing borders and national identities presents to a geographical classification, I have chosen to structure the stories of these women in the way that I hope they would want to be remembered – by their actions. In each section, you will find short biographies of a myriad of women who should be just as famous and instantly recognizable as Gandhi, and who I hope reveal something of the true spirit of South Asian women – determination, empowerment, and bravery in the face of oppression.

Chapter one
Ranis and Revolutionaries

From the earliest days of British colonialism in India, women led the revolution against it. These women came from all backgrounds – from the Ranis who ruled over kingdoms, to the Dalits who were all but invisible in the social hierarchies of India. Yet, despite their drastically different circumstances, these women found themselves united against a common enemy, and fighting the British proved the perfect opportunity to show their friends and foes alike what they were truly made of. These women were trailblazers in several ways, not only in shattering the stereotypes of Indians (and Indian women especially) as meek and peaceful people who spurned violence of any kind and woefully submitted to their fate, but also in shaping the very nature of the Indian nationalist movement by inspiring future generations of women to do their part – whether by the sword or by more peaceful means – to drive out the British and reclaim their beloved land. This section tells the stories of some of these Ranis and revolutionaries, some of whom paid the ultimate price for freedom which would be centuries in the making.

Ahilya Bai Holkar (1725–1795)

While many women raised their voices against the British from the start, the first recorded voice was Ahilya Bai Holkar, the hereditary queen of the Maratha Empire. Ahilya was born into a respected Marathi Hindu family in Chaundi, Maharashtra. Girls generally did not go to school then, but Ahilya's father taught her to read and write. Legend says that as a child she caught the eye of Malhar Rao Holkar, a commander in the army of Maratha Peshwa Baji Rao I and ruler of Malwa, during a temple service. Struck by her pious character, Malhar married Ahilya to his son, Khande Rao, in 1733 when Ahilya was just eight (child marriage being common across all communities at the time). While accompanying her husband on his campaigns, she was raised and guided by her mother-in-law, Gautama Bai, who is praised for the principles instilled in Ahilya and for training her in administration, accountancy, and politics. Ahilya gave birth to a son, Male Rao in 1745, and a daughter, Muktabai, in 1748.

In 1754, Khande Rao was killed while fighting for the Mughal emperor, Ahmad Shah Bahadur. On learning of his death, Ahilya was allegedly so distraught that she had to be stopped from committing *sati*. To bolster her spirit, her father-in-law decided to train her in military affairs, and sent her on a military expedition to Gwalior in 1765. In the same year, she proved her military might when she succeeded in defending her land from an invading army in her father-in-law's absence.

Malhar Rao Holkar died in 1766, twelve years after his son. Ahilya's sixteen-year-old son, Rao Holkar, inherited the throne and became the ruler of Indore, with Ahilya acting as regent. However, her son passed away within a few months of acceding to the throne. Thus, Ahilya became outright ruler in December 1767, despite objections by some factions of the court. In 1780, Ahilya's daughter committed *sati* and Ahilya was alone except for her adoptive brother-in-law, Tukoji Rao Holkar, who became head of her military. Ahilya immediately demonstrated fairness and mercy by reinstating a priest who had previously opposed her, as well as regularly visiting her subjects and making herself available to their needs.

When Ahilya came to the throne, other princely rulers found themselves drawn into trade with a new global powerhouse, the BEIC. Yet Ahilya warned against association with the British, writing in 1772: 'Other beasts, like tigers, can be killed by might or contrivance, but to kill a bear is very difficult. It will die only if you kill it straight in the face, or else, once caught in its powerful hold, the bear will kill its prey by tickling. Such is the way of the English'.[8]

This proved to be an insightful premonition, given the power that Britain would grow to hold over the Indian subcontinent. However, despite her words, the British displayed an unusual reverence for Ahilya that they showed to few other native rulers. In the 1820s, Sir John Malcolm, the British official most directly concerned with the 'settlement' of central India, collected oral memories regarding Ahilya and described how: 'Ahilyabai's extraordinary ability won her the regard of her subjects and of the other Maratha confederates ... With the natives of Malwa ... her name is sainted and she [is viewed as] Incarnation of the Divinity. In the soberest view that can be taken of her character, she certainly appears ... to have been one of the purest and most exemplary rulers that ever existed'.[9]

While Ahilya never directly fought the British and ruled centuries before the total control of the British Raj, she inspired some of the most prominent figures of the independence movement. Jawaharlal Nehru upheld her reign as evidence of the capability of Indians to rule their own country prosperously: '[Ahilya's reign] has become almost legendary as a period during which perfect order and good government prevailed and the people prospered. She was a very able ruler and organizer, highly respected during her lifetime, and considered as a saint by a grateful people after her death'.[10]

Similarly, British-born INC president, Annie Besant, idealized Ahilya's reign as one in which Indians of all ethnicities and religions lived harmoniously. Many sources attest to her demonstrating care for her subjects; she is still celebrated as a ruler who left her land in a considerably better position than she inherited it.

Rani Velu Nachiyar (1730–1796)

While Ahilya took up the pen against the British, the very first woman (that we know of) to take up the sword against them was Rani Velu Nachiya, known in Tamil as Veeramangai (Brave Woman). Velu was born on 3 January 1730, in Ramanathapuram, Tamil Nadu. She was the only child of the king and queen of the Ramnad kingdom. Lacking a male heir, the royal couple raised Velu as a prince, training her in traditional martial arts, archery, and horse riding. She was also an able student and could speak several languages fluently including Urdu, French, and English. At sixteen she was married to Muthuvaduganathur Udaiyathevar, son of the King of Sivagangai. He acceded to the throne in 1750 and became its longest-reigning monarch, ruling for over twenty years. Together, he and Velu had one daughter named Vellachi.

In 1772, Sivagangai was invaded by BEIC troops in league with the son of the Nawab of Arcot. King Muthuvaduganathur was killed in the subsequent battle during which women and children were slaughtered, making it one of the bloodiest battles of the colonial era. However, some of the most prominent figures in the kingdom escaped, including Velu and her daughter, who fled and sought refuge in Virupachi, near Dindigul, where they stayed for eight years. While in hiding, Velu slowly built her powerful army, earning important support from Sultan Hyder Ali of the Kingdom of Mysore in southern India. Although initially reluctant to intervene, Hyder Ali was extremely impressed with Velu's determination and bravery, as well as her ability to converse with him in Urdu. The Sultan gave his word to support the queen in her crusade to retrieve her kingdom. He also gave her the use of a royal fort and provided a monthly stipend of 181kg of gold. He gave her weapons, 5,000 infantry, and 5,000 cavalry troops to fight the British. Velu constantly changed her base to confuse British spies while she concocted her revenge plan.

In 1780, Velu came face-to-face with the British and officially became the first queen to fight for freedom against them. When she discovered the

Brits' ammunition store, she decided that a suicide bomber was the best way to destroy it. An army commander and a loyal follower of the queen, a Dalit woman named Kuyili, came forward to carry out the mission. Kuyili took oil and ghee from festival lamps and doused herself in them before setting herself alight. She then jumped into the British armoury, blowing everything up in flames with her. We know little else about Kuyili, but in this act, she is considered the first (recorded) female suicide bomber. Her story serves as a reminder of the many Dalit women who contributed to the nationalist movement despite belonging to one of the most marginalized groups in history, and whose contributions have largely been forgotten in the shadows of those from dominant castes or classes, just as her story is completely overlooked by her queen's. Velu's adopted daughter, Udaiyaal, also gave her life fighting the British. In her memory, the queen built up a woman's army and named it after her. Kuyili got no such honour.

Thanks to the sacrifices of Kuyili, Udaiyaal, and the rest of her troops, Velu was able to defeat the British and expel them from her land. After recapturing the Sivaganga estate, she ruled for the next decade, naming her daughter, Vellacci, heir to the throne. After her victory, Velu expressed her deep gratitude for the support given by Sultan Hyder Ali by constructing a mosque and a church at Saragani, in response to his having built a temple inside his palace for her. Velu also maintained good relations with the notorious freedom fighter Tipu Sultan, the son of Hyder Ali, whom she considered a brother.

Rani Velu Nachiyar Velu died of heart failure aged sixty-six on 25 December 1796. Today, she has rightly become a folk hero in India, a symbol of successful resistance against the British. She was undoubtedly a heroic leader, but her victory would not have been possible without the backing of the brave women who helped make up her army and died so that their queen might live. Velu may have been the first woman to take up arms against the British, but as we shall see, she was by no means the last.

Rani Kittur Chennamma (1778–1829)

Two years before Velu's historic victory over the British, Kittur Chennamma was born on 23 October 1778, in Kakati. As a member of a Hindu royal family, she was educated in traditionally masculine pursuits like horse riding, sword fighting, and archery – all of which she excelled at. When she was fifteen, she was married to Raja Mallasaraja of the Desai family. He had been married before, to a woman named Rudramma who herself was a renowned writer. Mallasaraja clearly had a type, as his second wife, Chennamma proved just as eloquent. She was known to be politically wise and an excellent warrior and despite her youth instilled both fear and reverence in all who saw her. Renamma soon retired from public life, and it was Chennamma who became Mallasaraja's famous consort.

By 1818, the British had conquered much of the surrounding area and now set their sights on the most prosperous city of all: Kittur. Mallasaraja had passed away in 1816, leaving his son, Shivalingarudra Sarja, on the throne. However, he was a weak and incompetent ruler and thus became a figurehead behind whom his mother, Chennamma, effectively ruled the kingdom. Even during her husband's reign, Chennamma had been an active political advisor and had fought alongside the army in several wars. Thus, she was well respected as a military strategist, warrior, and politician. When Shivalingarudra died in 1824, Chennamma was officially crowned Queen of Kittur.

Before his death, Shivalingarudra had decided to adopt a boy, Shivalingappa, as his son and successor. After his death, the Queen adopted Shivalingappa herself. In 1848, British Governor-General Lord Dalhousie introduced the controversial Doctrine of the Lapse, which decreed that any Indian state whose leader died without an heir would automatically lapse into BEIC control. They viewed Chenamma's assumption of the throne as a direct violation of this doctrine and ordered that Shivalingappa be exiled because – as an adopted son – he was not recognized as a legitimate male heir.

The British had long waited for an excuse to invade prosperous Kittur, and this was the perfect one. When Chennamma received written instructions to submit to British rule, she refused and instead wrote to the Lieutenant-Governor begging for a reprieve. He refused to intervene, and the Rani declared war. The British demanded she surrender her kingdom's treasure – worth over one and a half million rupees. In October 1824, John Thackery of the BEIC led a force of over 20,000 men into Kittur. The overconfident Thackery expected this to be a triumphant victory, but he could not have been more wrong. Chennamma led her men into battle, defeated the BEIC, killed Thackeray, and took British hostages. The British were humiliated – not only had they lost to a vastly numerically inferior army of supposedly inferior Indians, but it was also an army led by a woman. Meanwhile, Chennamma's prestige and status were now unsurpassed.

In her mercy, she agreed to return the British hostages if they agreed never to invade her kingdom again. The British accepted, and she returned the hostages. However, in an unsurprising twist, the British betrayed her and returned with greater force. Chennamma once again faced them valiantly and held them off with severe British casualties. Eventually, however, the numerical advantage proved too great, and she was captured and imprisoned in Nailhongal Fort. She died there, a British prisoner of war, on 21 February 1829. Her lieutenant and adopted son were both also arrested and killed, and Kittur finally fell into British hands.

Despite her eventual capture, Rani Chennamma's initial victory over the British invasion was another monumental moment in Indian history, demonstrating that Indians could successfully fight for their land, despite the numerically superior force of the British army, and that a woman was the most effective leader in organizing these triumphs. Although Chennamma, like many others, made the fatal mistake of trusting the British, she fought the injustices she witnessed and fearlessly gave her life trying to ensure that future generations would not suffer as she had at their hands.

Maharani Jindan Kaur (c. 1817–1863)

While for most Indian nationalists, Queen Victoria was a distant figurehead of the institution they detested, for Maharani Jindan Kaur, her battle against 'Queen and Country' was much more personal.

Jindan Kaur Aulakh is believed to have been born around 1817 in Chachar, Gujranwala in the Punjab. Her father was the overseer of the royal kennels of the Sikh Maharajah, Ranjit Singh, 'Lion of the Punjab'. Ranjit was the first king to unite the Sikh states and his rule is regarded as a golden period in Sikh history. Having heard of Jindan's exquisite beauty and intellect, Ranjit demanded that she be brought before him and was so impressed that he immediately proposed to marry her, which he did in 1835 when Jindan was in her late teens. Three years later, she gave birth to their only child, a son named Duleep Singh. Ranjit had up to twenty wives, but it was clear to everyone that Jindan was his favourite and he doted on her until he died in 1839.

As the last wife and latest heir, Jindan and her son had little influence in the immediate aftermath of Ranjit's death and lived a rather quiet life. However, the Sikh empire was rife with internal division as Ranjit's heirs fought among themselves for power. Eventually, Jindan's five-year-old son was proclaimed king by those hoping to use him as a puppet ruler. However, they had not counted on one thing: his mother. Jindan was fiercely protective of her son's rights and publicly condemned the new vizier, Hira Singh, for presuming to act like a sovereign. Surprisingly, the court supported her, and she gradually began to assert control as regent for her young son. Duleep had been very low in the line of succession at the time of his father's death and unlike many of her sister-wives, Jindan had not come from a royal background so was not trained in the arts of statecraft. Therefore, in the initial days of her reign, she relied heavily on male advisors and was said to have made many mistakes owing to inexperience.

Despite these initial teething pains, Jindan gradually grew in confidence and when the army professed their loyalty to her, she officially assumed control of the kingdom. Her priority was to restore balance between the military and the civil administration – a feat which no one had achieved since Ranjit's death. As regent, she headed court business and publicly addressed her troops as their commander. She is said to be the only person that her unruly soldiers would listen to. She was known to emasculate and debase her men until they obeyed. Her troops were especially delighted when the young queen showed her beautiful face, throwing off the conventions of purdah, and she caused delight (and outrage from the more conservative among her advisors) when she addressed 2,000 soldiers with her face exposed. Another of her great achievements was the foundation of a new town, Duleepgurh, which she established and is said to have left in the control of a slave girl, a remarkable example of female rule in an age when men were carving up India for themselves.

However, one should not assume that the young queen had an easy transition to power. Other heirs remained to challenge her son's claim, most notably his half-brother, Pashaura Singh Kanvar. Her clan chiefs demanded reduced taxes, her soldiers demanded a pay rise and local nobles wanted the lands that had been seized by previous rulers restored. Furthermore, her increased militarization to restore peace had used up significant funds from the royal coffers, which were already depleted after misuse by her predecessors and unruly viziers, including Hira Singh. Many parties were still wrestling for power, and she came to learn that some were not-so-secretly liaising with the BEIC who, learning of the unrest within, had begun to gather troops at her empire's border. The Maharani gathered a council of her most respected statesmen and army leaders and betrothed her son to the daughter of the Governor of Hazara, a powerful member of the Sikh elite. She managed to find extra wages for the troops and successfully replaced her treacherous vizier with her brother, Jawahar Singh.

However, when Jawahar was murdered in 1845, the British decided that this was enough unrest to justify intervention, and invaded the Punjab on 13 December 1845, marking the start of the First Anglo-Sikh War. Again, due largely to internal divisions within the Sikh forces, the Sikhs lost this year-long war and in March 1846, the Treaty of Lahore was signed. While the terms of this treaty were extremely harsh on the Sikh kingdom, the British 'allowed' the now seven-year-old Duleep Singh to maintain his title of Maharaja and permitted his mother to call herself his regent. However, the British took issue with Jindan trying to retain this role in anything more than name. As one interaction between the British Resident and Jindan attests, they became unhappy with her 'interference' in the running of her own kingdom, but she remained defiant that it was her right as true ruler. The Resident chastised her for acting in a disreputable and undignified manner, claiming that he only cared that she should tarnish her honour with her behaviour. He suggested that she stick to traditionally feminine duties such as almsgiving. Unimpressed, she responded by sarcastically thanking him for his concern for her reputation but reminding him that, as the rightful king's mother, she was as good as sovereign herself.

Jindan did her best to restore stability while keeping under the terms of the Treaty, but it soon became clear that her kingdom was too divided and that she and her son were at risk of assassination from rival claimants. This was reason enough for the British to abandon their support for Jindan and replace her with a Council of Regency, headed by a British Resident. To prevent further rebellion, the British heavily rewarded the Sikh leaders who had switched allegiance during the war, including Lal Singh and Tej Singh. Jindan and her son regarded these men as traitors for their role in the defeat of the Sikhs and for accepting the honours bestowed on them by the colonial administration. Thus, in August 1847, the young Maharaja refused to bestow Tej Singh the title of Raja of Sailkot. To punish the boy for his intransigence, the British Resident, Henry Lawrence, threw Jindan in jail. She was dragged from court by her hair and taken first to Lahore Fort and then moved to a fortress. Distraught at being separated from her young son without so much as a chance to say goodbye, Jindan wrote desperate letters to her captors imploring them to let her return to him. Little did she know that she would not see her son again for over thirteen years. Without the protection of his mother and advisor, the ten-year-old Maharajah was forced to sign a treaty handing over his empire to the 'protection' of the British. When a new Resident, Sir Frederick Currie, took over the following year, he refused to release Jindan, whom he believed was too great a threat as a figurehead for further rebellion and a 'serious obstacle' to British domination.[11] She was exiled from the Punjab and imprisoned in the Chunar Fort, having been stripped of all her jewels and treasure.

While this understandably caused outrage among the Sikhs, it also drew disappointment from neighbouring Muslim rulers such as Dost Mohammad Khan of Afghanistan who openly condemned the British for treating an Indian queen so deplorably. The British countered this by creating a narrative portraying Jindan as a dangerous seductress who had paid her generals with sexual favours, and whose unrestrained recklessness posed a serious threat to the stability of the Punjab because she cared more for her lusts than for her country. The most damning indictment came from BEIC agent Major George Broadfoot, who compared her licentiousness to that of Messalina and Catherine the Great and claimed: 'The cause is the Ranee's mind having been seriously affected by her excesses ... She has become stupid instead of clever and lively, is sometimes for days in a state bordering on fatuity ... She takes but little concern in the public business compared with what she used to do and then is chiefly guided by her low paramours and servants'.[12]

The dismissal of powerful women as having slept their way to the top is a tale as old as time, so there is likely little truth in these accusations beyond internal rumours that she may have been involved in a sexual relationship with one of her close advisors. Indeed, other British sources openly debunked this reviling of her character. The truth did not matter though, as the British succeeded in besmirching her reputation enough to stem some of the outcry at her arrest.

However, they underestimated Jindan by assuming she would quietly accept her treatment. In 1849, it was revealed that she was behind an earlier plot that was a major contributing factor in the Second Anglo-Sikh War.

While imprisoned, she also acquired the services of a British lawyer to fight the defamation of her name in the English press – causing the British to introduce new laws cracking down on challenges to the media. A year after her transfer to Chunar Fort, Jindan surprised everyone by escaping dressed as a servant. Remarkably, she travelled on foot across 800 miles of forest until April 1849 when she arrived in Kathmandu hoping to seek sanctuary. This was a risky move, as the Nepalese had refused to help the Sikhs during the war, despite having previously allied with Ranjit against the British. Luckily the risk paid off and she was eventually granted sanctuary by Nepal's Prime Minister who built her a palace and helped restore her to some of her former dignity, much to the chagrin of the British.

In the decade since his mother's incarceration, Duleep had been raised by a Scottish couple, under Queen Victoria's strict instruction. Eventually, the boy was permitted to visit London on what turned out to be a permanent visit. The queen immediately adored Duleep, gifting him an estate and allowance. He grew up alongside the Royal Family living a life of extravagance and decadence, protected by his close friendship with the Prince of Wales. Prince Albert even designed him a crest and a motto: 'Do Good Rather Than Be Conspicuous' – which proved easier said than done as one of the few people of colour at court. Queen Victoria instructed that he be found a suitable bride, and he was soon married and started a family of his own.

Despite their long estrangement and the fact that he had been so young at their last meeting, Duleep never forgot his mother. In November 1856, the Nepali prime minister intercepted a letter from Duleep to his mother, asking that she visit him in England – a naive request that suggests the young Maharajah did not yet fully comprehend the circumstances under which he had lost his kingdom. When a representative of Duleep's was denied access to see Jindan, Duleep became suspicious and decided that he would visit her himself. The British were initially reluctant to agree to this request (showing that despite his gilded cage he was essentially still a prisoner). In 1860, a more sympathetic British Resident reported to Duleep that his mother was almost blind and a shadow of her former self. It was only on being assured of her weakness that the British regime consented to let mother and son reunite in Calcutta (now Kolkata) on 16 January 1861.

One can only imagine Jindan's joy at finally embracing her son after thirteen long years of exile, although it is said that – blind as she was – she wept when she felt that he had cut off his long hair which is a mandatory symbol of faith for Sikh men. This, she felt, was a mark of his complete alienation from his true identity. Their reunion coincided with the return of several Sikh regiments from the war in China, and these troops were visibly overjoyed to witness the return of their rulers to India. Thousands of armed Sikhs surrounded the hotel where Jindan and Duleep were staying, causing panic among the British that their nightmares of a revolution were coming true. Thus, they implored Duleep to return to England as soon as possible, taking Jindan with him. At this point, Duleep was loyal to the British, having spent more of his life at the English court than at his own, and he happily obliged, booking himself and his mother onto the next boat home.

Everyone had heard stories about this beautiful and courageous Maharani, and eagerly awaited the opportunity to meet her in the flesh. However, they were sorely disappointed to find a broken woman, almost blind and hardened from a life of suffering. However, it was noted that 'the moment she grew interested and excited in a subject, unexpected gleams and glimpses and the torpor of advancing age revealed the shrewd and plotting brain of her, who had once been known as the 'Messalina of the Punjab'.[13] Much to her surprise, she discovered that her son had managed to negotiate the return of her confiscated jewellery, which he returned to her on her arrival in England. She was ecstatic, and was ostentatiously bejewelled for the rest of her life. The only jewel that the British refused to return was the infamous Koh-I-Noor diamond, which Duleep had surrendered to Queen Victoria years before. The British crown's refusal to return the world's biggest diamond to India is a controversy which continues to this day.

While Duleep had succeeded in finding a castle for his mother, she refused to leave his side again and remained living in his house. She used this time to fill him in on the true circumstances of his family's downfall, her years in exile, and the injustices that they had both suffered at British hands. This opened his eyes to the propaganda his British guardians had fed him since childhood. She also re-educated him about the Sikh faith, of which he knew little, having been raised Christian by his guardians. He soon reconverted, stating that he had been indoctrinated into accepting Christianity. The efforts Jindan made to remind her son of his birth rights would later lead to his catastrophic falling out with Queen Victoria and the British establishment as he began to fight for what they had taken from him. Alas, he never succeeded, although his legacy lived on in his daughters who later also became Indian nationalists and well-known suffragettes.

On 1 August 1863, Maharani Jindan Kaur died peacefully in her sleep. Her son requested that he be allowed to return her body to India to be cremated according to Sikh custom, as cremation was at that time illegal in Britain. His request was denied, and her body lay in the Dissenters' Chapel in Kensal Green Cemetery for almost a year until Duleep was finally granted permission to return her to India for cremation. However, they still would not honour her final wish of allowing the cremation to take place in her hometown of Lahore. Thus, even in death, Jindan was deprived of her rights. Her granddaughter, Bamba, would later move her remains to Lahore where a small memorial was erected in her memory, in the hope that her soul would finally be at peace now that her final wishes had been fulfilled.

Jindan has often been hailed the 'Lioness of the Punjab' in reference not only to the epithet of her late husband but also to her motherly instinct to protect her cub from the predatory British at all costs. However, beyond her role as wife and mother, she proved herself a lioness in other senses too. She was an independent and astute stateswoman, not only succeeding in uniting a kingdom of warring factions where many male predecessors had failed to do so, but in standing against the world's biggest empire to defend the rights of her son and their kingdom. Furthermore, she managed to escape the clutches of her oppressors and remain resilient during decades of isolation from everything she knew and loved. While she could never replace the years that had been stolen from her, she must have taken some comfort in finally being reunited with her son and she took the opportunity to use her last years to remind him of the injustice perpetrated by the British Empire, and to instil in him and his children the fighting spirit and self-assurance which had powered her all her life and which led them to fight for Indian independence long after her death.

Rani Avantibai Lodhi (1831–1858)

With previous generations showing that women could succeed in defeating the British where countless men had failed, it is no surprise that women came to play a crucial part in the first organized and widespread revolution against the BEIC in 1857. One such woman was Rani Avantibai Lodhi. Because of a lack of written sources concerning her, most information that we know about this warrior queen comes from oral history and folklore. Despite this, her story has been used as an inspiration for female politicians, especially those from caste-oppressed backgrounds.

Avantibai was born on 16 August 1831. Her family belonged to the Lodhi caste, which is today categorized as an 'Other Backward Class' (an umbrella term used by the Indian government to classify castes which are considered to have an educational or social disadvantage). However, they claimed descent from warrior Rajput blood. Avantibai's royal connection was solidified when she married a Rajput prince, Vikramaditya Singh Lodhi, heir to the kingdom of Ramgarh (present-day Dindori). The pair had two sons, Aman and Sher. When her father-in-law died in 1851, Avantibai effectively assisted her husband in state affairs and was hugely popular with the people.

Keen to claim the wealth of Ramgarh for themselves, the British soon declared Vikramaditya insane (whether he was or not we will probably never know). Refusing to appoint his young sons as successors, the British declared the state as 'Court of Wards', a legal system created by the BEIC claiming to 'protect' heirs and their estates during their minorities. The British would rule on the heir's behalf, while the young boy was educated with the necessary skills to manage his inheritance independently (in accordance with British customs and laws). Rani Avantibai, who would normally have acted as regent during her son's minority, was unsurprisingly outraged by the British claiming control. She immediately ejected the British administrator and declared war.

Avantibai sent messengers (with gifts of bangles) to neighbouring states with a provocative call to arms: 'If you think you have a duty towards our enslaved Mother India, raise your swords and jump into war against the British, otherwise wear these bangles and hide yourself in your houses'.[14] This was one of the first times we hear India referred to as 'Mother India', a concept which would become increasingly important in the nationalist movement. Bangles and purdah are both traditional symbols of womanhood and femininity in Indian culture, and thus Avantibai challenged the very masculinity of her neighbours. Reluctant to be seen as less ferocious than a woman, many of the nearby princes immediately joined her cause. It is estimated that around 4,000 soldiers joined her army, aided not just by the princes who had pledged their support but also by the Indian soldiers in the British army who revolted and deserted to join the queen in battle. Led by Avantibai herself, it is said that the entire north of India rallied together against the British.

Avantibai set up her front near the village of Kheri, intending to invade Mandla. However, the British confronted her before she had a chance to act. Despite the ambush, the supposedly superior British army proved useless against Avantibai's might. When the British Commander, Waddington, confronted Avantibai (probably thinking her an easy target) she raised her sword and decapitated his horse. Horrified by the queen's strength and ferocity, Waddington jumped from the lifeless body of his steed and hurriedly retreated into the anonymity of the fighting forces. Avantibai personally slaughtered many British soldiers and soon the whole British army retreated in defeat.

The humiliated Waddington vowed revenged for his distressing loss, and soon returned to besiege Avantibai and her forces in her capital, Ramgarh. On hearing of the size of his forces, the Rani vacated Ramgarh and headed for the hills of Devhargarh. As he advanced, Waddington seized control of many key towns and cities enroute. However, when he finally reached Ramgarh to find that the Rani had already left, he burnt the city to the ground in rage and set off in pursuit. Avantibai opted for a tactic of guerrilla warfare and scattered the British army during an attack on their camp.

However, it became clear that the odds were against her; the British were soon joined by Indian forces from some northern provinces. Undeterred by the opposition's swelling numbers, Avantibai valiantly continued to fight, despite her own dwindling forces. When the enemy surrounded her on Devhargarh hill, she turned to her most trusted aide, Umrao Singh, and told him that she would rather die than be captured alive by the enemy.

Soon realizing that her forces had been decimated and that she would be unable to evade capture, she followed through on her intent and struck herself through the stomach with her own sword. Legend has it that she did not die immediately but was brought back to consciousness by Waddington who demanded that she name her key supporters. She reportedly replied that she bore all responsibility for the war and shouted 'Hari Om' (a common Sanskrit mantra believed to ease all suffering) before passing away. Thus, on 20 March 1858, she became one of the first female martyrs in the fight against the British.

Her story has been remembered primarily through folklore and oral tradition. One such folk song, preserved by the Gond people, a forest-dwelling tribe of the region, recalls: 'The Rani who is our mother, strikes repeatedly at the British. She is the chief of the jungles. She sent letters and bangles to others (rulers, chieftains) and aligned them to the cause. She vanquished and pushed the Britishers out, in every street she made them panic so that they ran away wherever they could find their way. Whenever she entered the battleground on horseback, she fought bravely, and swords and spears ruled the day. O, she was our Rani mother'.[15]

Since 2012, following pressure from nationalist parties, she has been included in the national Indian curriculum, which will hopefully help her story be more widely remembered.

Rani Lakhsmibai of Jhansi (c. 1828–1858)

Perhaps the most famous woman revolutionary from this period, and certainly the one who has endured most in Indian memory as a symbol of the nationalist movement is Rani Lakshmibai, also known as the Rani of Jhansi. Her story has become so tangled up with legend that it is often hard to separate fact from fiction. Even the date of Lakshmibai's birth is debated, with estimates varying from between 1828 to 1835. We do know that she was born Manikarnika Tambe (nicknamed Manu), and that she grew up in the holy Hindu city of Benares (now Varanasi) in a Marathi Brahmin family. Her mother is said to have been a very intelligent woman, but she died when Manu was four. Her father's boss, the Peshwa Baji Rao II of Bithoor district, doted on Manu whom he nicknamed Chhabili meaning 'beautiful and cheerful'. Following her mother's death, she was raised among her father's troops and thus was educated more in keeping with boys of her age. While she was taught to read and write (unlike most women of her status), her studies also included shooting, horse riding, and fencing. Even as a young girl, she was known to reject purdah and speak up for herself among men much her senior in age and rank – including British diplomats. Compared to most dominant-caste women, she enjoyed a greater degree of independence and was often seen riding between the palace and the temple on horseback.

In May 1842, the teenage Manu was married to the middle-aged Maharajah of Jhansi, Gangadhar Rao Newalkar, whose first wife had died childless. She was renamed Lakshmibai as per the Maharashtrian tradition that women take a new name after marriage. Her husband was said to be a temperamental man who was quick to punish anyone who angered him. There were rumours that the king enjoyed cross-dressing, which the British were quick to highlight as a sign of his debauchery and deviancy. In September 1851, Lakshmibai delivered a son, Damodar Rao, but he died just four months later.

On his deathbed in 1853, the childless Maharajah adopted his cousin's son, whom he also renamed Damodar Rao. The adoption was completed in the presence of two British officers; the Maharajah asked that they promise to recognize his adopted son as heir and protect him and Lakshmibai, swearing to ensure that she would be treated fairly. Unsurprisingly, the British failed to keep this promise, despite the British officer noting that Lakshmibai was a high-esteemed and capable woman who could effectively assume control.

Lakshmibai rejected the restrictions which traditional Hinduism placed on young widows. She conceded to wearing only white as was expected, but she refused to shave her head, to surrender her precious jewels, or live a life of seclusion. She observed purdah only in the presence of British men, and she continued to live an active life – supposedly partaking in a spot of weightlifting, wrestling, and horseracing before she even had her breakfast. She was also known to wear men's clothes, although this may have been more of a practical consideration given the unsuitability of traditional women's attire for such physical activities. Lakshmibai would have been aware that her country could not afford for her to hide away in isolated grief – rather she needed to secure her adopted son's legitimacy and fend off the British who were already grasping for control of her kingdom. When Gangadhar Rao died, the British refused to acknowledge his adopted son as a legitimate heir and used Governor-General Dalhousie's Doctrine of the Lapse to claim Jhansi - and the four million pounds a year revenue that came with it – as their own.

Later legends state that when Lakshmibai was informed, she screamed and refused to cooperate. However, it seems that she was initially keen to keep positive relations with the British. She first reasoned that Jhansi was not without an heir, given her husband's adoption of a son which she pointed out was an ancient and accepted practice in Hindu kingship. The British Resident was sympathetic (in fact, the British deemed him *too* sympathetic, and he was transferred under disciplinary proceedings for his leniency in dealing with Lakshmibai). Having lost her early ally, she now appealed to Dalhousie himself to reverse his decision. Predictably, he was unrelenting and made Lakshmi surrender her palace and fort to the British. Thus insulted, she recruited the services of a British lawyer, Mr John Lang, who had successfully claimed back Indian land from British hands. She received him in opulence, making a clear show of her queenship. Notably, Lang recorded that Lakshmibai was attended only by her women and had no male advisors – disputing claims that the Rani was just a figurehead for men of lesser status, accusations by those who would not accept that a woman could prove as remarkable and effective a ruler as Lakshmibai without a man's direction.

In June 1854, Lang and Lakhsmibai presented a comprehensive appeal based on the grounds of previous treaties with the British and which proved the validity of Damodar Rao's adoption. When these were dismissed, she called the robbery of Jhansi a clear transgression of British honour and bemoaned her damnation to a life of subjugation and deprivation following the British seizure of her riches and authority. These pleas fell on deaf ears, but Dalhousie did concede to offer her a pension to ease her financial hardship. This was a bad deal, as the British also demanded that she be personally responsible for any state debts that Jhansi as a kingdom had accrued, and these far negated any pension he was proposing. Understandably insulted, she rejected this offer and prepared to return to Benares. However, the British needed her to remain to legitimize their rule, and thus she was convinced to stay by Dalhousie's employee, Robert Hamilton, who seemed to have a begrudging respect for her refusal to cower under British pressure. However, while she may have conceded to stay in Jhansi, she continued to issue appeals for the British to restore her lands and revenue, and she publicly condemned the British for allowing cow slaughter – a grievous insult to Hindus – and for appropriating revenue that was intended for temple donations. Such actions were viewed as a direct attack on the Hindu religion, fanning the flames of the looming conflict.

Such displays of religious insensitivity across India proved the catalyst of the 1857 uprising, and Jhansi found itself at a strategic junction between four major cities of the rebellion – Kanpur, Lucknow, Agra, and Delhi.

When the unrest finally reached Jhansi, Lakshmibai asked the local British captain for permission to establish a bodyguard for her own protection, to which he agreed. Originally, it seemed that Jhansi had escaped the worst of the turmoil, but that was soon to change. On 5 June 1857, Indian rebels invaded a British garrison at the Star Fort outside Jhansi. The British sent to the Rani for aid, but she was scared to intervene given her equally vulnerable position isolated with only 150 bodyguards for protection. Within just three days, the Indian rebels had slaughtered all the British prisoners – including women and children – having previously promised them safe passage.

Some reports asserted that Lakshmibai had been complicit in this assault. For example, a British army medic, Thomas Lowe, wrote a scathing attack dubbing her a traitor and blaming her for all the bloodshed. This suspicion came from the fact that before the rebels left Jhansi, they were given a large sum of money from the queen. However, evidence suggests that Lakshmibai was just as fearful of the unruly rebels and that her only concern at this time was maintaining peace in her kingdom. Reports show that the rebels had threatened to destroy the Rani's palace had she not agreed to give them funds, and therefore, this should be seen as a sign of exhortation rather than complicity. It seems that the British at first agreed that Lakshmibai was not involved, for when she explained her version of events and condemned the merciless brutality of the rebels, the British general wrote back asking her to manage the region until they could join her. This shows that not only did they see her as loyal, but they also judged that she had both the means and authority to uphold order. They were right, and her army successfully routed an attempt by the rebels to replace Lakshmibai on the throne with one of her late husband's nephews – again negating claims that she had been working with the mutineers all along.

For the first time, Lakshmibai found herself in sole control. She was able to move back into the palace and resume authorization over state affairs. Anxious to protect herself from future violence, she ordered the manufacture of weapons as peace was slowly restored. She began wearing diamond bangles and a silk blouse with a bodice alongside a traditionally male turban and sword, combining her feminine beauty with her masculine authority. She ensured that food and clothing were distributed to the poor, for which even the British commended her, praising her courage, intelligence, and determination, as well as her generosity to her subjects. In 1858, Jhansi was besieged for two months by a neighbouring queen. This unprovoked and unexpected attack scared Rani into fortifying her defences, which swelled to over 15,000 troops.

Throughout this period, the British were enacting revenge on Indians across the land through indiscriminate torture and murder. In Lakskhmibai's homeland thousands were killed, their corpses either publicly displayed as warnings or blasted from British cannons for their dismembered parts to rain down in an apocalyptic show of vengeance. While later nationalists prefer to pretend that Lakshmibai had been a stalwart of the rebellion from the very beginning, in reality, she was understandably more desperate than ever to stay in the good favours of the British. Lakshmibai wrote to Hamilton in January 1858 offering her full support in return for the protection of her people who were on the edge of complete collapse.

Sadly, however, something seemed to have changed in the minds of the British and they soon decided that she was in fact an enemy – even though she had followed all their instructions thus far. When Jhansi was again invaded by troops from Orchha and Datia (both allies of the BEIC) Lakshmibai appealed to the British to intervene. They ignored her calls for help; it was clear to the Rani that she was now on her own. Yet the ever-resourceful Lakshmibai was not one to surrender into melancholy and immediately ordered that the city walls be re-enforced, that weapons manufacturing be stepped up, and that food supplies be hoarded in case of another siege. She also savvily ordered all the trees outside the walls to be cut down so that any approaching enemy would be left to the mercy of the unrelenting summer sun. When some of her citizens began to flee, she endeavoured to reassure her people by organizing a huge *Haldi* ceremony (a Hindu ritual usually reserved for weddings) for every woman in the town.

Soon, however, the danger became too close to ignore.

The British recruited fresh troops under the leadership of seasoned soldier General Sir Hugh Rose to quash Lakshmibai's defences. Rose established cavalry camps around the city, digging in trenches which would prevent any escape. The city walls were bombarded with huge cannon as Rose vowed to starve Lakshmibai and her people out. Yet it soon became apparent that they had underestimated the Rani. Her reinforced walls easily repelled the British artillery, and she defiantly made herself seen riding her horse along the fort inspecting and heartening her troops. The British could not help but admire Lakshmibai for her bravery, comparing her to the mythological Amazonians.

When her childhood friend and fellow mutineer, Tatya Tope, was defeated attempting to rescue her, Lakhsmibai realized that she must face the British alone. Facing frightening odds, her troops engaged the British with whatever weapons they could find. Lakshmibai led her soldiers from the front, dressed in male clothing. However, it soon became apparent that the British were faring better, and her contemporaries described the Rani's agony at the treatment of her people and how she threatened to blow herself up rather than be captured by the British.

It is here that the facts and fiction of Lakshmibai's story begin to dramatically blur. Fantastical accounts depict her escaping by leaping from the walls of her fort on horseback with her son strapped to her back. While this is an evocative image, it is a highly unfeasible one. Firstly, the walls of the fort were so high that Rani and her horse would certainly have been killed – or at least badly injured – in the fall. Secondly, her son was probably around ten years old by the time of this battle, and therefore would not have been carried by his mother like a babe. In fact, Damador Rao himself later wrote that no such incident occurred. Rather, it is likely that Lakshmibai escaped in the middle of the night of 3 April 1858, accompanied by her son and a few hundred soldiers.

Lakshmibai spent the next few weeks travelling through a hundred miles of scorching hot desert until they reached Kalpi to join the remaining rebels including Tatya Tope. The British were hot on their heels and soon confronted the Rani and her comrades who were forced to battle in temperatures of up to forty degrees Celsius. It was a ferocious fight, but one from which the British ultimately emerged victorious. One of the last confirmed sightings of Lakshmibai comes from one of the Indian rebels who fought alongside her and described how, dressed as a man, she looked tired and miserable.

Lakshmibai's final battle is steeped in myth. The most popular story is that Rose finally caught up with the Rani, clad in her priceless pearl necklace atop her armour. Her last recorded statement was that the outcome of the battle would either be to enter heaven or rule the world, and she seemed content with either fate. This is hard to authenticate but fits well with the heroic narrative of her final hours. Some accounts claim that she was fatally wounded by a British soldier during hand-to-hand combat. Others claim that she was already injured before this battle but was finally dispatched, while she lay bleeding, by a soldier she had earlier shot at. The most likely version of events is that given by a British eyewitness who reported: 'There was no pretence of resistance any longer except from a slight, fully armed figure that was helplessly whirled along in this cataract of men and horses. Again and again this one leader, gesticulating and vociferating, attempted to stem the torrent of routed rebels, but all in vain ... A moment later, the swaying figure was overtaken, and one stroke from a [British] sabre ended the whole matter ... It was discovered that it was the Rani of Jhansi herself who had thus ended her meteoric career'.[16]

As a British officer, he had no reason to exaggerate the bravery of his opponent or her determination to fight until the very end, so the fact that he felt the need to document it as such is a testament to the enduring regard with which everyone held Lakshmibai regardless of their allegiance.

Her death may have been befitting of a queen and warrior, but at the end of the day, she was still a woman – a fact which necessitated her troops burning her body immediately after her demise for fear that the British would rape or otherwise defile her corpse, a tragic fate which many women, from peasants to queens, have endured after death throughout history. Although she had ridden ahead, her troops turned on each other for failing to protect their beloved Rani. With Lakshmibai gone, the rest of her army quickly surrendered. Her son escaped for another two years by living in the jungle, but later surrendered to the British and was given a healthy pension and eventually returned to Jhansi under the guardianship of British governors.

Rani Lakshmibai of Jhansi remains one of the most enduring symbols of the Indian independence movement. Even the British could not help but honour her legacy. Colonel Malleson recorded in 1878: 'Whatever her faults in British eyes may have been, her countrymen will ever remember that she was driven by ill-treatment into rebellion, and that she lived and died for her country, we cannot forget her contribution for India'.[17] Lakshmibai's story has often been manipulated for political ends, which makes it even harder to discern the real woman behind the legend. However, while parts of her story may have been embellished for dramatic effect, the truth is just as inspiring. Her refusal to bow to patriarchal restrictions put upon widows, her defiance in the face of British colonial agendas, and her bravery in facing death at the hands of the enemy rather than submit herself or her land to subjugation under a foreign ruler make her a worthy role model for the generations who continue to be inspired by her story centuries after her death.

Jhalkaribai (1830–1858)

While Lakshmibai was undoubtedly a remarkable leader, she also relied on the help of class-oppressed women to secure her victories, women who have not been remembered with the same enthusiasm as their Rani. One such woman was Jhalkaribai, a warrior who fought alongside Lakshmibai during the 1857 uprising, acting as her advisor and body double during the Siege of Jhansi.

Jhalkaribai, daughter of Sadova and Jamunadevi Singh, was born on 22 November 1830 in Bhojla. She was a member of the Dalit Koli caste who were later criminalized for their 'anti-social' activities against the British. As a child, Jhalkaribai supposedly killed a tiger with an axe when it tried to attack her, and she also apparently once killed a leopard with a stick meant for herding cattle. She was a fearless spirit all her life. Tragically, her mother died when Jhalkaribai was very young, so she was raised by her father. Although she received no formal education, as was usual for a girl in her village, she was trained in horse riding and combat – skills that would serve her well in her future battles.

When she married Puran Kori, a soldier in the army of Raja Gangadhar Rao, her husband taught her archery, wrestling, and shooting, completing her military training. The story goes that Jhalkaribai often accompanied her husband to the palace, where she was hired as a maid. It is here that her martial prowess was noted, as was her remarkable resemblance to the Raja's wife, Rani Lakshmibai. This, combined with her martial skills, made her a perfect recruit for Lakshmibai's all-female army, and the queen soon recruited her.

Jhalkaribai quickly rose through the ranks and, as Lakshmibai's most trusted advisor, was soon placed in control of the women's army when the Rani's attentions were taken up with leading the male soldiers during the 1857 war. In 1858, their armies became besieged by General Rose and his British forces. Jhalkaribai took the opportunity to use her resemblance to the queen to their advantage. She approached the British camp and declared herself to be Rani Lakshmibai of Jhansi, at great personal risk to herself. The resulting confusion provided the real queen with time to escape to safety with her son, while Jhalkaribai fought in her royal disguise alongside her husband. When her husband was delivered a fatal blow, Jhalkaribai was described as a 'wounded tigress' who channelled her grief into aggression against the British who felt the full wrath of her sword.[18]

Sources disagree about how Jhalkaribai met her end. Some state that she was killed during the battle, and it was only after her death that it was discovered she was not Rani Lakshmibai. Others say that she escaped to fight another day.

However she eventually met her end, she immediately became an icon both in her homeland of Bundelkhand and across India. Many local Dalit communities view her as a divine incarnation and celebrate the likely day of her death as Martyr Day. The movement to establish Bundelkhand as a separate state drew on the story of Jhalkaribai to celebrate and construct the Bundeli identity. There are plans to set up a five-storey museum in her honour at the Jhansi Fort. Today, many are rightly calling on Jhalkaribai to be remembered with equal fervour as her Rani. The reason she has not thus far is probably to do with her caste, as not only is history written by the victors, but by the elites. However, her people have remembered her and continue to hold her as a perfect example of Koli womanhood.

Begum Hazrat Mahal (c. 1820–1879)

Rani Lakshmibai may be the most famous woman revolutionary of the 1857 war, but the leader of the biggest army raised against the British in 1857, and the only rebel leader never to submit to the British was Begum Hazrat Mahal, also known as the Begum of Awadh. However, her story has been completely downplayed, even in the narrative that hails the Rani of Jhansi as a national heroine, probably because, as a Muslim, she does not fit the Hindu nationalist propaganda which has worked so hard to promote Lakshmibai as a symbol of fighting spirit.

Born Mohammadi Khanum around 1820, she was the daughter of Umber, an African slave of Ghulam Ali Khan, and his mistress, Maher Afza. As a teenager, her parents sold her as a courtesan in Lucknow. While this sounds harsh to modern audiences, this was a prestigious prospect for a girl born into illegitimate obscurity. Courtesans were highly trained dancers and musicians who brushed shoulders with the elite and wielded influence over the men enchanted by their beauty and talent. They held important ritual roles at the royal court, and they often enjoyed wealth and prosperity that most could only dream of. Thus, while there were undoubtedly sexual components to the role, becoming a courtesan was an aspirational role for a young girl.

From 1847, Awadh was ruled by Nawab Wajid Ali Shah, a king who – although beloved by his people – was regarded by the British as a lazy and debauched king who made little attempt to develop his kingdom. He had wives from all caste, class, religious, and ethnic backgrounds and kept many mistresses alongside his legal wives. This womanizing ruler had a particular penchant for darker-skinned women and thus was immediately captivated by the half-African, half-Asian Mohammadi when he saw her performing at court. He ordered that she be brought into his Institution of the Pari (fairies), a group of young courtesans who were trained in theatrics. If they entertained the king enough, they were made his temporary wives (a Shi'a Muslim tradition allowing men to engage in casual sex without shame). At this point, Mohammadi was renamed Mahak Pari.

In 1845, having become the favoured courtesan of the king, Mahak Pari fell pregnant and bore a son. She was thus allowed to veil her face and was given two new titles: Iftikhar-un-nissa (the Dignified Among Women) and Begum Hazrat Mahal (the Honoured Lady), the title she used forevermore. She was lavished with jewels and money and was given slaves of her own to command. However, just five years later, the king divorced her, most likely at the instigation of his mother who had always looked down on Hazrat Mahal's humble beginnings. However, divorce was probably for the best given that their politics were soon to take a drastic divergence.

In the 1830s, famous British travel writer Fanny Parkes commented that regardless of their rulers' indifference, the people of Awadh had no interest in succumbing to British rule, being perfectly content with the riches they already enjoyed. However, in February 1856, law and order broke down as people rebelled against the BEIC's greed. This gave the British a perfect excuse to annexe Awadh in the name of restoring peace from troublemaking locals. Wajid Ali Shah was exiled to Calcutta, from where he urged people to follow his example and submit to British rule. His ex-wife, remaining in Lucknow with their son, took the opposite stance and vowed to resist the colonization of her land. One of her co-wives, Begum Sayda, recalled that Hazrat Mahal's bravery sent the enemy fleeing in fear.

By July 1857, the Indian Mutiny was in full swing, and the British were retaliating with brutal force. It was amid this chaos that Hazrat Mahal's son, Birjis Qadr, was crowned the new King of Awadh. However, being a minor, the Begum became the de facto leader. The coronation was a rallying point for troops across Awadh, and 7,000 rebel sepoys gathered in Lucknow, in addition to thousands of peasants and various other soldiers from across the region who came to join the Begum's army.

From July to March 1857, Hazrat headed resistance in Lucknow, commanding the siege of the British Residency where 3,000 British men, women, and children were held hostage. Half of these hostages fled or were killed during the four-and-a-half-month siege, and British reinforcements frequently retreated rather than facing the mob's wrath. The British often commented on Hazrat's influence and political acumen. She issued frequent proclamations to her army, calling on them to stand with her against the British, whom she wanted not only to drive from her lands but to annihilate completely. Riding astride an elephant, Hazrat personally led a charge against a small band of British men as they hid inside Alambagh palace.

As the British began to regain control across India, Awadh became the last stand of rebellion. In December 1857, Hazrat began to realize that the British were rallying, and the courage of her troops was waning as stories flooded in of the horrific retribution the British had enacted on rebels elsewhere. For example, in Benares, Colonel James Neill had hosted 'hanging parties' where people were lynched in the street, and Allahabad had been razed to the ground with its residents inside. At a meeting of her war council, Hazrat lamented the listlessness of her forces and threatened that she would bargain with the British for her own life if they did not step up. This was an idle threat, for she was always scathing against the Indian rulers who had submitted to British bribes and surrender. She herself had refused a 100,000-rupee yearly pension in return for her surrender, an offer that she would reject countless times throughout her life.

However, as British fortunes continued to turn, the Begum faced increasing internal threats too. A self-proclaimed holy man, Maulvi Ahmadulah Shah, had publicly claimed that he had been sent by God to wage a holy war on the British, and by January 1858 the Begum's forces became divided between those who remained loyal to her and those who preferred to throw in their lot with this man who supposedly had God on his side. This played right into the hands of the British whose divide and conquer policy had long proved effective.

Not one to concede defeat to internal or external adversaries, Hazrat launched a plan to build a defensive wall around her fort. She gave her generals 500,000 rupees – bolstered by the sale of her personal fortune – towards the building of the wall. The British were taken aback by the scale of the operation, and one British commentator recorded how much power and influence the queens and consorts of India wielded. That they were once again being outsmarted by not just an Indian, but an Indian woman, must have been a crushing humiliation for the British, but they were soon to outsmart her themselves.

The British had enlisted the help of the Gurkha fighters of Jung Bahadur, from neutral Nepal. The Gurkhas were notoriously fearsome fighters, and thus the Begum sought to intercept them and better the British's offer. However, the British caught wind of this plan and murdered her messengers before they could reach Jung Bahadur. Soon after, the Begum's general, Man Singh, abandoned her. Although she retaliated by selling off all his land, she was left to face almost 60,000 British troops alone. Although she and her forces fought valiantly, they simply did not have the numbers to fight such a large force and were driven to retreat on 15 March 1858. The British remained surprisingly admiring of the Begum, reluctantly praising her persistence, and comparing her to the mythical Amazonian heroines. They noted that when all her men were throwing in the towel, only the Begum remained unphased and undeterred.

The British tracked her down to a country house where she was again forced to engage with their forces on 21 March, alongside her past rival Maulvi Ahmadullah Shah. Their newfound unity was not to last, however, as they were forced to scatter in retreat. For over a year, they continued to be hunted in small groups as the Begum made her way to the Nepali border. Refusing again to surrender, she established a fort at Baundi and managed to gather some 15,000 troops to her service. She held this position for over a year, remarkably still managing to pay her army and establish a court where she ruled over internally divided factions and restless troops.

In November 1858, Queen Victoria herself issued a proclamation promising to preserve religious freedom so long as the Indians remained loyal to the British. Hazrat Mahal responded with a scathing rebuttal, listing the numerous occasions in which the British had desecrated Hindu and Muslim holy sites, forced their Indian subjects to act contrary to their faiths, and attributing the 1857 Uprising purely to the interference of the

British with the religion of people who would rather die than surrender their faith. Her calling out of the British pretence of religious tolerance was reinforced by the knowledge that even while the proclamation was being meted out across India, mosques and temples were being turned into British barracks. She also listed the many princes who had been forced to surrender their kingdoms to the British without their consent and condemned the laundering of Indian riches by the BEIC.

Even after having sought refuge in Nepal, British sources attest to the constant armed resistance of Hazrat Mahal and her followers. Eventually, however, almost all of her followers submitted to the British and she was forced to admit defeat and cease her attacks. Her heroism was not repaid by the men in her life. Aside from her treacherous generals, her ex-husband publicly disowned her, claiming that he had no knowledge of her actions and that he despised them. Even her son, in whose name the Begum had acted all along, submitted to Queen Victoria after his mother's death and returned home. Hazrat Mahal lived in Nepal for the rest of her life until she died in 1879, buried in an unmarked grave. Thus, she was condemned to die as she had been born – in poverty and obscurity. She was the only rebel leader not to submit to the British.

Following her defeat, the British had boasted of their 'indescribable' plunder of the Begum's goods and their desecration of her palace. They also destroyed all evidence of her leadership, burning any paper trails which pointed to her command or her successes. It is not surprising that they wanted to erase all traces of a mixed-race, low-class, Muslim sex worker who proved to be Britain's unbeatable enemy. They almost succeeded in erasing her memory, as it was not until the 1960s that the Indian government acknowledged Hazrat Mahal's contribution to the nationalist movement with a marble memorial erected in Hazratganj. Her tomb is now marked and cared for by the Jama Masjid in Kathmandu.

While her counterpart, the Rani of Jhansi, later became a model of Indian nationalism and women's political acumen, Hazrat Mahal was never evoked as a national hero. Her nefarious (at least according to the prudish standards of the Victorian era) background as a courtesan, her association with men who had come to vocally support the British, her mixed-race heritage, and her status as a woman and a Muslim all meant that she did not fit into the Indian nationalist narrative that was constructed in the coming century – a narrative that was built by and focussed on upper-class, ethnically Indian, primarily Hindu, and avowedly celibate women. Hopefully, in the coming generations, this can be remedied, and she can claim her well-deserved place at the centre of Indian history.

Uda Devi Pasi (1830–1857)

While Hazrat Mahal may have been downplayed in history on account of her religion, her soldier, Uda Devi Pasi, was erased because of her caste. Uda's husband, Makka Pasi, was a Dalit soldier in the army of Hazrat Mahal. Uda and Makka, like many in their community, were increasingly outraged by the injustices enacted upon them by the British, and Uda took her grievances straight to the top by reaching out to Hazrat herself and asking to enlist in the war against the British. The Begum was impressed by her fortitude and helped Uda to form a women's regiment under her authority. When the British invaded Awadh, both Uda Devi and her husband took up arms and joined the battle. Her husband was killed, fuelling Uda's hatred of the British.

In November 1857, Uda Devi took part in the Battle of Sikandar Bagh. After issuing instructions to her battalion, she climbed up a tree from which she shot at advancing British soldiers. William Forbes-Mitchell, who fought against Hazrat's army, recalled what happened next:

'[Captain Dawson] called to Quaker Wallace to look up if he could see any one in the top of the tree, because all the dead under it had apparently been shot from above ... He almost immediately called out, "I see him, sir!" and cocking his rifle ... He fired, and down fell a body dressed in a tight-fitting red jacket and tight-fitting rose-coloured silk trousers; and the breast of the jacket bursting open with the fall, showed that the wearer was a woman. She was armed with a pair of heavy old-pattern cavalry pistols, one of which was in her belt still loaded, and her pouch was still about half full of ammunition, while from her perch in the tree, which had been carefully prepared before the attack, she had killed more than half-a-dozen men. When Wallace saw that the person whom he shot was a woman, he burst into tears, exclaiming: 'If I had known it was a woman, I would rather have died a thousand deaths than have harmed her".[19]

Forbes-Mitchell does not name the fallen woman, and her identity is still debated, but she is now widely believed to have been Uda Devi Pasi, who was known to have been killed by the British at the battle. That a British source would admit to having suffered losses at the hands of a woman is remarkable and suggests that this discovery was so unusual that it warranted special attention among the hundreds of casualties. However, the professed grief the soldier felt for having killed her should be taken with a pinch of salt given that the supposed defence of Indian women was one of the key themes of British pro-imperial propaganda. Thus, being known to happily kill a woman would somewhat have damaged their civilizing guise (although in reality – as we have seen and will continue to see throughout this book – the British were not above harming women who dared to speak or act against them).

Every year, 16 November is commemorated as the day of Uda Devi Pasi's martyrdom. Her story is especially treasured by Dalit women as a symbol of resistance and heroism against injustice and oppression. Uda Devi Pasi's name should be remembered, because while she was not a queen of high and noble birth like other heroines of 1857, she was a Dalit who rose above colonial and caste barriers to contribute to the fight against the British and gave her life in doing so.

Mahabiri Devi (died 1857)

Another Dalit woman who fought not only to overcome caste, gender, and colonial oppression but died as a martyr for her country in the 1857 war was Mahabiri Devi. As is so often the case with Dalit heroines, the historical record of her life is sparse and what has survived has been passed on through local folklore and plays which are still performed in the Muzaffarnagar region of western Uttar Pradesh. Mahabiri is usually referred to as *Viranagna*, a Sanskrit word meaning 'she who is brave', often used in Dalit oral narratives to describe inspirational women from their community.

Records do not show when Mahabiri was born, only that she came from the village of Mundbhar. We also know that her family belonged to the Bhangi caste, whose traditional jobs included scavenging. Like most of her caste, she grew up in abject poverty and received no education. However, from a young age, she was noted for her intelligence and bravery. Her experiences of casteism endowed in her a deep sense of justice and a desire to fight against oppression in all its forms. Thus, when she was still very young, she formed a group of women intending to protect women and children from doing 'dirty work' and attempting to bestow upon them a sense of dignity that they were denied by their society.[20]

As Mahabiri grew, she turned her disgust for oppression to the British and vowed to fight their subjugation of her people. In 1857, as Indians across the land began to rise against the British, she saw her chance to join the noble battle when British troops laid siege to Muzaffarnagar. Having already proven her ability to mobilize the women of her village, she gathered a group of twenty-two women who armed themselves with iron weapons and attacked the British troops. Caught off guard by the ferocity of these women, many British troops succumbed to Mahabiri and her comrades. Eventually, however, the British forces were able to rally, and the entire group of women were killed.

The names of Mahabiri's sisters-in-arms have been lost to history.

Remarkably, Mahabiri's survived. However, their story remains a testament to the ferocity, ability, courage, and integrity of these, and the many other Dalit women who, despite being the most overlooked of Indian citizens, played just as crucial a part in the fight for India's freedom as their more privileged compatriots.

Asghari Begum (died 1857)

While the lives of queens have been recorded in relatively good detail, other women fought for only their names and deaths to be recorded, as is the case with Asghari Begum. 'Begum' is an honorific title primarily given to Muslim women, so we might accurately guess at her religious identity. According to one source, she was around forty-five years old in 1857, and played an important role in the mutiny in Uttar Pradesh, but we have no details of exactly what part she played. It is reported that she was captured by the British and burnt alive. It may be that the British burnt her body precisely so that we would know so little about her, in the hopes that she would gradually be forgotten so no one could look to her for inspiration. Fortunately, they failed, and her horrific death now serves as a tragic reminder of the sheer brutality of the British in silencing anyone who dared oppose them.

Nanibala Bandyopadhyay (1888–1967)

Even once the 1857 rebellion had finally been crushed and India had been formally colonized under the British crown, women continued to take a leading role in revolutionary activities rejecting British rule. One such woman, who used stereotypical views of Indian women to trick the British, was Nanibala Bandyopadhyay, the first and only woman taken as a State Prisoner of British Bengal.

Nanibala was born in the Howrah district of modern-day West Bengal to a strict Brahmin family. She received a few years of education from Christian missionaries, before being married at the age of eleven. Her husband died a few years later and she was returned a widow to her father's house. As she aged, she sought shelter in the home of her nephew, Amarendranath Chattopadhyay who was the leader of the revolutionary Jugantar (sometimes spelt Yugantar) group. She was immediately adopted by the revolutionaries who were all too eager to put her to work for the cause. As the group increasingly became monitored by the police, Nanibala moved with them into hiding in French Chandannagore.

A young widow attracted no attention as she went about her daily business and was thus the perfect choice to act as smuggler and informant for the group. She used her traditional domestic roles as cover for her revolutionary activities, while also acting as a genuine homemaker and caretaker of the men in the group. In 1915, one of these men, Ramchandra Majumdar, was arrested and imprisoned for his role in an arms-looting case. Nanibala donned the trappings of a married woman and entered the jail pretending to be his wife so that she could find out where his hidden revolvers were kept. When the police discovered her subterfuge, she fled to Peshawar but was arrested and sent to jail in Benares.

Suffering from cholera by the time she reached the prison, Nanibala was tortured by the British. On one occasion, they inserted chilli powder into her vagina in an attempt to extract information about Jugantar members. Despite being severely weakened by disease and torture, Nanibala refused to tell her captors anything. Eventually, they gave up and transferred her to the Presidency Jail in Calcutta. Here too, she was tortured and went on hunger strike in protest at her treatment. After twenty-one days without food – for the duration of which she was still being tortured daily – she was declared a state prisoner and the torture was ceased.

Nanibala's life had all the potential to be a tragic tale: a child bride, condemned to a life of restrictive widowhood, uneducated, and discarded by her family now that she was no longer a marriage prospect. Then, captured and brutalized by the British, her young body ravaged by disease and torture, and her freedom stolen from her. However, Nanibala wrote her own destiny. She refused to let widowhood be the end of her story and used her delegation to the domestic shadows as a guise under which she could aid the fight for her nation's freedom – and in doing so secure a new freedom for herself too. Furthermore, she amazed the British (and no doubt her male compatriots) by withstanding unimaginable physical cruelty, never hesitating for a moment to sacrifice herself for her country's freedom. She not only endured pain which would have broken many men but even deepened it by choosing to starve her already weakened body rather than bow down before the British and their demands. She succeeded in receiving recognition as a genuine freedom fighter, alongside her male counterparts, and showed the British that women were anything but an easy target.

Bhogeshwari Phukanani (1885–1942)

One of the oldest martyrs of the independence movement was 'the 60-year-old martyr' as she is remembered today, Bhogeshwari Phukanani. Bhogeshwari was born in Assam in 1885. She had eight children with her husband, Bhogeswar Phukan. Despite having her hands full with such a large family, she was also highly active in the Quit India Movement. She made it her mission to make sure her children were also involved, and often took her sons with her on protests. She helped the INC establish offices in Berhampur, Babajia, and Barpujia, where she worked to support the cause, often participating in peaceful protest marches. In 1930, she was arrested by the British for picketing, a key tactic of the non-cooperation movement.

In September 1942, the INC office in Berhampur was shut down by the British, amid a climate of increasing British brutality in the Nagoan region. Now almost sixty years old, Bhogeshwari and her sons joined a protest march that resulted in the office being reopened, to a rapturous celebration from the demonstrators. Refusing to be humiliated and disobeyed, the British sent a large troop to close, and potentially destroy, the office once and for all.

At least two accounts exist of what happened next. In the first and most told account, Bhogeshwari and another woman named Ratnamala, led a large mob carrying Indian flags and shouting nationalist slogans. When the police tried to restrain the procession with force, Bhogeshwari – who was carrying the flag – was struck to the ground by a British captain named Finch. The other version claims that she was not present when the British first arrived, but that she joined the fray when she saw Captain Finch aiming a gun at her sons.

However, both accounts agree on what then happened. Either in defence of her sons, or the flag, Bhogeshwari rushed forward and struck the British officer over the head with a flagpole. Humiliated by being struck not only by an Indian but an old woman, he retaliated by shooting her in the head. She died of her injuries a short time later. Thus, at the age of sixty, she became a martyr in the fight for India's freedom.

Today, her name is relatively unknown outside of Assam, where various public institutions are named in her honour. While we cannot be sure whether her actions came from a dedication to die for her country's flag, or out of a motherly need to protect her sons, we do know that Bhogeshwari was one of many women who threw themselves wholeheartedly into the struggle for India's independence and who lost their lives at the hands of British brutality.

Bina Das (1911–1986)

Another revolutionary happy to risk her life for independence was Bina Das. Bina was born in West Bengal in August 1911. In her autobiography, she credits her family with inspiring her revolutionary spirit. Her father, a famous leader of the Brahmo Samaj (a monotheistic Hindu reform movement), was a teacher to the famous Indian nationalist Subhas Chandra Bose, and both Bina and her sister credited him with opening their eyes to the plight of India and drawing them into the nationalist cause. Bina received her education at Bethune College in Calcutta, where she wrote a paper on Saratchandra Chatterjee's novel, *Pather Dabi* (1926), despite it having been banned by the British as seditious material.

While at university, Bina, her sister Kalyani, and two of their friends, Surama Mitra and Kamala Das Gupta, organized a student group where women could discuss politics. They formed the Chattri Sangha (Association for Female Students) and through it organized study groups, athletic and swimming groups, cooperative stores, libraries, and a youth hostel. This impressive mobilization and success at uniting and organizing women led the INC to turn to the Chattri Sangha for help recruiting more women to the cause. Bina threw herself into the chaos that the Chattri Sangha caused and waited eagerly for her chance to prove her dedication.

Two years later, the opportunity she had been waiting for presented itself when, on 6 February 1932, she attempted to shoot the Governor of Bengal at the Calcutta University Convocation ceremonies. Having been recruited by a secret society in 1928, she made her radical decision to become an assassin after several of her comrades were arrested, beaten, and murdered. They had frequently condemned the colonial policy which allowed the police to detain alleged terrorists and restrict their freedoms. In the run-up to the assassination attempt, Bina had been tutoring a woman whose husband was incarcerated without charge by the British and later wrote how seeing his family wasting away not knowing when or if they would see him again, without even knowing of what he was accused, had a deep effect on her. As she grew increasingly despairing of the situation, she concluded that dying for her country was her only option as she could no longer bear to live under such circumstances.

Thus inspired, the twenty-year-old Bina confronted her target at the library. She fired a revolver between three and five times, but her victim managed to dodge the bullets and Bina was swiftly arrested for possession of arms and attempted murder. Despite confessing to the crime, the government undertook a drawn-out investigation into how such a respectable young woman, who had no known (at least to the British authorities) ties to any revolutionary organizations, could have come to commit such a crime given that she had never been known to handle a gun before (perhaps explaining her difficulty in hitting her target). They painted a picture of a young woman who was lonely and depressed, but respectable and sensible. Both her father and brother spoke highly of her as a sensitive and studious young woman who worked as a tutor to help supplement the family's income. Her father swore to the police that he knew nothing of her plans, but Bina later admitted that he had edited her confession and that her family were instrumental in formulating and encouraging her plans. Her accomplice, Kamala Das Gupta, who had supplied her with the revolver was arrested but released for insufficient evidence.

Far from regretting her failed attempt at murder and martyrdom, Bina penned (in English so that her adversaries could understand every word) a five-page confession, which was leaked despite strict censorship from the British. In this statement, she gave further insight into her motivations behind the attack. She listed many crimes of the colonial regime, including the riots at Midnapore, Hilki and Chittagong, each of which was instigated by the shooting of prisoners in detention camps. As well as showing her passionate disdain for the government, the document is also important as it displays a self-awareness of its own place in history and shows that Bina saw herself as situated in the wider history of national struggle. The confession stated:

'My object was to die, and if to die, to die nobly fighting against this despotic system of Government, which has kept my country in perpetual subjection to its infinite shame and endless suffering – and fighting in a way which cannot but tell ... I have been thinking – is life worth living in an India so subjected to wrong, and continually groaning under the tyranny of a foreign Government, or is it not better to make one's supreme protest against it by offering one's life away? Would not the immolation of a daughter of India and of a son of England awaken India to the sin of its acquiescence to its continued state of subjection and England to the iniquities of its proceedings? All the ordinances, all measures to put down the noble aspiration for freedom in my countrymen, came as a challenge to our national manhood and as indignities hurled at it. This hardened even the tender feminine nature like mine into one of heroic mould'.[21]

Aside from the stirring patriotic sentiment, Bina's confession is interesting for also alluding to the gendered aspects of Indian nationalism. As Durba Ghosh has noted, Bina frequently used gendered imagery to justify her actions which she realized radically diverged from expectations of Indian women. Bina directly blamed the British for forcing women to cast off their womanhood and explicitly equates India's right to freedom with its masculinity. To defend the nation's masculinity, women must themselves become masculine to fight for its protection. This is an inversion of male nationalist rhetoric which more commonly talked of 'Mother India', feminizing India as a land in need of the protection of virile menfolk. Rather, Bina envisions India as a man whose virility has been threatened and who requires stereotypically weak and passive women to shed their humility and save their land. She acknowledges that her actions will be judged harshly by those trying to uphold the ideals of Indian womanhood, which at the time were that a dominant-caste woman should be chaste, dutiful, educated, religious, and restrained. However, Bina demonstrated her desire to shed these stereotypes, arguing that the British have already made it impossible to adhere to the old customs of womanly virtue anyway.

While Bina's rousing confession and attempted martyrdom made her a hero among revolutionaries, it further angered the British who charged her with attempted murder and sentenced her to nine years' incarceration. Bina's sister, Kalyani (whose own trial had partially inspired Bina's attempt on the governor) wrote a scathing account of the British's treatment of Bina. She said that they had only imprisoned her because they lacked the courage to fulfil Bina's wish of martyrdom. Fortunately, Bina managed to secure an early release during a prisoner amnesty and was freed in 1939.

Upon her release, Bina immediately joined the INC, and in 1942 joined the Quit India Movement for which she was again jailed for a further three years until the end of the Second World War. Despite her previous revolutionary proclivities, she now adhered to Gandhi's more peaceful form of protest. She joined him in helping to reconstruct villages destroyed by communal violence in 1946 and was working on this project when she heard that her dream of Indian independence was coming true. The same year, she married Jatish Chandra Bhaumik, a fellow independence activist.

From 1946 to 1947, she was a member of the Bengal Provincial Legislative Assembly and, from 1947 to 1951, of the West Bengal Legislative Assembly. In 1960, she won an award for her social work, and her sister dedicated a book called *Bengal Speaks* in her honour. Bina herself wrote two autobiographies in Bengali. She later admitted to having been involved with the group behind the Dalhousie bombing of August 1930, a failed attempt on the life of the British police commissioner.

In the 1980s, Bina was interviewed about her revolutionary days and admitted that she was drawn into the nationalist movement when all the local boys claimed that women could not participate in the movement alongside them and she did not understand why. Historians have noted that this interview displays a different type of feminist confidence than her earlier written confession. Here, rather than highlighting how her womanhood was compromised by her violent activities, she instead emphasises the wider role of women in the freedom movement and more explicitly criticizes the narrow gender stereotypes which portray men as the sole heroes of the Indian independence campaign. It is interesting, and empowering, to see how Bina matures from denying her womanhood (by stating that she had to shed it to commit to her revolutionary activities) to embracing it and situating it in the forgotten narratives of the many women whose womanhood was a key factor in their heroic efforts.

Unfortunately, Bina's heroic life has a contested, but certainly sad, ending. Following her husband's death, she never remarried and lived a life of solitude. The circumstances surrounding her death are debated. Some sources say that her decomposing body was discovered on a roadside on 26 December 1986 and that police took over a month to determine her identity. Another report says that she was only found unconscious by the roadside and was taken to hospital but died the following day. Whatever the truth, it seems that she died a lonely and anonymous death – a tragic end for such a spirited fighter.

In 2012, Calcutta University posthumously conferred Bina with the graduation certificate which the British had denied her, but this goes little way towards showing her the remembrance and celebration that she deserves for her willingness to die free rather than live in oppression.

Pritilata Waddedar (1911–1932)

Another Bethune College graduate who joined the revolution was Pritilata Waddedar, known today as Bengal's first female martyr. She was one of six siblings born to a Brahmin family on 5 May 1911 in the Chittagong District of the Bengal Province of British India (today in Bangladesh). Pritilata was a conscientious and high-achieving student, with a particular aptitude for arts and literature. One of her favourite teachers, Usha Di, inspired the girls with stories of Rani Lakshmibai of Jhansi, and in doing so instilled her students with a sense of both nationalist and feminist spirit. Pritilata graduated from school in 1928 and a year later was admitted to Eden College in Dhaka, where she came top of her class as well as getting her first taste of activism through social initiatives she joined there. She then attended the famous nationalist hub of Bethune College from which she graduated with distinction in Philosophy. However, her degree certificate was withheld by the British in retaliation for her nationalist proclivities, and it was only posthumously bestowed upon her in 2012. Having graduated, she returned to Chittagong where she worked as headmistress of an English-speaking high school.

Her nationalist leanings brought her to the attention of Surya Sen who established a revolutionary group known as the Indian Republican Army (IRA). They met with her on 13 June 1932, and Sen and his friends asked her to join their mission. However, a fellow revolutionary named Binod Bihari Chowdhury objected to the idea of allowing a woman to join their group. Chowdhury was overruled – not because his comrades were ardent believers in female equality but rather because it was decided that a woman would be a much less conspicuous smuggler of weapons and thus could serve the organization well. Chowdhury later accepted that she was a worthy addition to the group, stating: 'Pritilata was young and courageous. She would work with a lot of zeal and was determined to drive the British away'.[22]

Her male comrades might also have realized they needed all the help they could get. When it was decided that they would assassinate Mr Craig, Inspector General of Chittagong, the two assassins, Ramakrishna Biswas and Kalipada Chakravarty, mistakenly killed two Indians instead. The assassins were arrested on 2 December 1930. Chakravarty was exiled, but Biswas was sentenced to death by hanging. Biwas' loved ones could not afford to travel to Chittagong to visit him. Given that Pritilata was already there, she was asked to visit Alipore Jail and meet him under the guise of being his sister. Many came to speculate that the two were lovers, fuelled by the fact that upon her death, she was found to be carrying a photo of him close to her heart. Some British reports stated that Pritilata was the wife of another revolutionary, Nirmal Sen, who had also been killed by the British, but there is little evidence to support this, although it is possible given her prominent place at the heart of the revolutionary movement.

Pritilata also participated in some of their more successful missions, including attacks on telephone and telegraph lines and police offices. She was given the responsibility of supplying explosives to the revolutionaries during the Jalalabad Hills battle on 22 April 1930 when a British force of over 22,000 was defeated by a mere fifty Indian revolutionaries. While these numbers may have been exaggerated by Indian narratives, it was undoubtedly one of the greatest revolutionary victories in India's struggle for independence, and Pritilata played a crucial role in it.

Inspired by their 1930 victory, in 1932, Surya Sen planned to attack the Pahartali European Club. This club had become a focal point of Indian fury when it erected a sign reading 'Dogs and Indians not allowed'. Sen decided that a woman should lead this attack and appointed Kalpana Dutt. However, when she was arrested a week before the planned attack, he assigned Pritilata instead. She was sent for arms training at Kotowali and a plan of attack was formulated. The date was set for 24 September 1932, and all the assailants were given a cyanide capsule with instructions to swallow it should they be captured by the British.

Pritilata, dressed in Punjabi male attire, launched her attack at 10.45 pm. Around forty British people were inside the club at the time. The fifteen or so revolutionaries, in three separate groups, began shooting into the club and then set the building alight. One elderly woman was killed, and several others were injured. A few colonial police officers who had been in the club at the time of the attack returned fire, and Pritilata was shot – luckily it was just a superficial injury. However, she was soon trapped by the British police and, as per her instructions, she swallowed the cyanide before she could be placed under arrest. She was twenty-one years old at the time of her death.

Her body was found a hundred yards from the club the following day. On her body, they found the photo of Ramkrishna Biswas, bullets, whistles, and a plan of attack. She also left a suicide note, detailing that she had planned to end her life all along and become a martyr for her country. It included her famous statement which opened this book:[23]

'I wonder why there should be any distinction between males and females in a fight for the cause of the country's freedom? If our brothers can join a fight for the cause of the motherland why can't the sisters? Instances are not rare that the Rajput ladies of hallowed memory fought bravely in the battlefields and did not hesitate to kill their country's enemies. The pages of history are replete with high admiration for the historic exploits of these distinguished ladies. Then why should we, the modern Indian women, be deprived of joining this noble fight to redeem our country from foreign domination?'

While Pritilata may have been inspired by the warrior women who came before her, she herself has become an emblem of empowerment for not only her contemporary women nationalists but for countless generations of women since.

Kalpana Dutt (1913–1995)

Kalpana Dutt (sometimes spelled Datta), the woman in whose place Pritilata Waddedar had led the European Club mission, had quite the revolutionary career herself. She was born on 27 July 1913 to a dominant-caste family in Sripur, Chittagong. While many female nationalists were initiated into their activism by nationalist relatives, Kalpana later recalled how her family had embodied the opposite of the ideals she would later risk her life for. Her father was a government employee and her family refused to adopt *khadi* as most other prominent families were doing, opting instead to continue to use foreign goods. Of her early education, Kalpana later wrote that it was hearing about the Rani of Jhansi that gave her the courage and spirit to begin to see herself as a freedom fighter.

After finishing school, she went to Calcutta to study science at Bethune College where she soon joined the Chhatri Sangha. She was especially close with Pritilata, whom she called Preeti, and the two bonded over their inner conflict between pursuing their careers as scientists or dedicating themselves wholeheartedly to the fight for Indian independence. The latter urge won. In 1931, at the age of seventeen, Kalpana joined the Chittagong branch of the IRA having been impressed by Surya Sen. She was trained in guerrilla warfare and how to make gun cotton. Her status as a woman in the armed revolutionary movement attracted attention everywhere she went, attesting to the fact that this was still considered an unusual sight during this period of the freedom struggle. One leader, Anant Singh, later admitted that Kalpana's determination showed him that he 'had a wrong idea about the worth of women in revolutionary work'.[24] Thus, even as a teenager, Kalpana was destroying stereotypes and proving that women could do anything the freedom struggle required of them just as ably as their male counterparts.

On 18 April 1930, Kalpana participated in the Chittagong Armoury Raid, an IRA plan to raid the armoury of British police and auxiliary forces. The plan was to capture the armouries, destroy communications channels, take British hostages to ransom for prisoner exchanges, and raid imperial banks to provide funds for the revolution. They succeeded in destroying communication and railway lines, and Sen hoisted the Indian flag outside the police armoury, declaring a revolutionary government and saluting the rebels. However, the eighty-plus raiders failed to locate the armouries and were forced to flee. Despite the interference with communications, the few captured British were able to alert their troops, who sent thousands of reinforcements to surround the revolutionaries' hideouts, arresting a significant number of them. A few days later, there was a major battle in which up to ninety people were killed.

Having managed to escape, Kalpana was chosen to lead the second assault on the European Club in Chittagong in September 1931. However, she was arrested while scouting the area. Although she was released on bail, she remained under heavy surveillance from British police, who had visited Kalpana's parents to scold them for 'allowing' their daughter to get involved with a terrorist organization. Instead, it was decided that her best friend, Preeti, should lead the attack as she could slip under the radar. When Preeti was tragically martyred during this attempt, Kalpana was deeply affected with guilt that her friend had died in her place.

Kalpana was forced into hiding in Gairola, but on 16 February 1933, the British finally discovered the hiding place and surrounded the village. They arrested Surya Sen, but Kalpana once again managed to escape by hiding in a body of water, almost drowning as British troops continued to fire on her while she hid below the surface, only occasionally raising her nose to breathe. She then crawled through the forest until she was out of the firing line. Despite managing to get to safety, she returned to the village with explosives in an attempt to free Sen, but she failed and was once more forced to flee. The women of the village who had harboured the revolutionaries were brutally beaten and dragged to prison, to be sentenced later to four years hard labour.

Kalpana was eventually 'overpowered and arrested' on 18 May 1933, in a raid in which two of her fellow revolutionaries were killed by British forces.²⁵ She was taken to the Hijli Jail which had been designated for the incarceration of female political prisoners. Here, she met Bina Das who was serving her sentence for the attempted murder of the governor of Bengal. She also received a visit from Mohandas Gandhi, who gave her his support, despite disagreeing with violent resistance. At the end of the trial, she was sentenced to transportation for life, but given her gender and that she was just on the cusp of adulthood her sentence was reduced to imprisonment. She was finally released in 1939.

During her imprisonment, she was introduced to the ideology of communism through her comprehensive readings of Marx and Lenin, and she began to subscribe to communism as the only solution to India's problems. She strongly believed that India's most oppressed communities, including women, must be mobilized. British imperialism was, she argued, part of a wider problem of capitalist greed in which she saw the Indian elite as equally complicit. Despite being from a middle-class background, she was especially critical of this social stratum as being complicit in capitalist oppression. Thus, she framed her anticolonial activities within a wider system of caste and class struggle in South Asian society. Her objectives therefore changed slightly from merely the expulsion of the British from India to a complete overhaul of society.

Kalpana became disillusioned with her prior revolutionary activities as she believed that terrorism could achieve at most small-scale individual emancipation. Only communism, she argued, could bring about the full regeneration of Indian society even after the departure of the British. She formally joined the Communist Party of India (CPI) in 1940, the same year she graduated from Calcutta University having finally been able to return to her studies following her internment.

In 1943, Kalpana acted as a relief worker during the Bengal Famine. This same year, she married the CPI's General Secretary, Puran Chand Joshi. Together they had two sons. She was thirty when she married, and thus would have been considered something of a spinster given that the average age of marriage for an Indian girl at this time was fourteen. This shows her dedication to the cause – like her education, her personal life took a back seat to her commitment to the revolution against British rule. She had little regret about this, however, having been able to choose a husband for herself whose ideals so closely aligned with her own. In 1946, she stood as a CPI candidate in the Bengal Legislative Assembly but was defeated. She worked instead as part of the Indian Statistical Institute until her retirement, fulfilling her childhood dreams of being both a scientist and a revolutionary. She eventually passed away in Calcutta on 8 February 1995 at the age of eighty-one.

In October 1945, Kalpana published an autobiographical book in Bengali, with her husband providing a preface. It was also translated into English. This was a hugely important account of the role that women played in the revolutionary movement at a time when their contributions were acknowledged as a footnote to male glory, if they were mentioned at all. Her account stressed the involvement of the many anonymous figures who had sacrificed their lives and received no acknowledgement for their part in the nation's history. We owe it to her to remember her own place in this revolutionary history, a woman who proved to everyone that women were strong enough, brave enough, and smart enough to stand up against the might of the British Empire and live to tell the tale.

Leela Roy (1900–1970)

Another of Bethune College's revolutionary graduates was Leela Roy, a woman who combined her patriotic activism with social work. Leela Nag was born into an upper-middle-class family in Goalpara, Assam on 2 October 1900. Her father, Girischandra Nag, tutored nationalist S.C. Bose, who would become Leela's lifelong friend and comrade. The family moved from Assam when she was young and she grew up in Sylhet, Bengal (now in Bangladesh). This placed her in the middle of one of the key centres of the nationalist movements, especially when she joined Bethune College to study English and proved herself an able and award-winning student. In 1921, she reached out to Bose to ask if she could be of assistance to him in his relief efforts following the Bengal floods. She raised donations and gathered goods for the disaster fund by establishing the Dhaka Women's Committee. Demonstrating a feminist zeal from her student years, she fought to become the first female student to graduate from the University of Dhaka in 1923, receiving special permission from the Vice Chancellor to undertake an MA in Bengali and Sanskrit.

Immediately upon graduating, she threw herself wholly into social work, particularly taking an interest in women's education (having had to fight so bitterly for her own). She founded an organization known as the Dipali Sangha in 1923. Through this organization, she founded numerous free primary schools for girls. Leela was a strong believer in the futility of gender roles, especially when it came to economic participation, and was strongly critical of what she saw as the subservient role that women were playing, not just in the economy but also in the independence movement. She encouraged girls' educational skills, but she also encouraged them to receive vocational training so that they were not bound to rely on traditional woman's skills and homemaking (which girls' education focussed around). Thus, the girls were taught leadership skills alongside their general education. Controversially, she also trained her students in martial arts so that they would not be so vulnerable in their dangerously patriarchal society. Pritilata Waddedar was one of the students who benefitted from Leela's training.

In 1926, Leela joined the revolutionary organization named the Shree Sangha, whose founder, Anil Roy, she would later marry. She made history as the first female member of this group and joined other groups which thus far had been restricted to male revolutionaries. Initially women were reluctant to follow Leela's example, and when they did, they were restricted to more secondary positions. However, Leela soon paved the way for women recruits to be taught to handle weapons and make bombs, as well as being given the opportunity to circulate seditious materials. While women were not forced to take risks they did not feel comfortable with, Leela helped find them positions in educational establishments or other roles which indirectly benefited the movement, thus ensuring that women were still playing a key part in the founding of a new India.

In 1927–1928, women activists began to be targeted by physical attacks when out campaigning. Rather than second-guessing the place of women in the movement, Leela established a fund she called the Mahila Atmaraksa Fund (Fund for Women's Self-defence). This was a women's-only self-defence group and was the first of its kind in the region. In 1928, she also stepped up her educational efforts, founding three new schools which could host large numbers of girls. Notably, she also established a school for Muslim girls – showing that unlike some of her comrades who were extremely Hindu-centric in their vision for independence, Leela wanted to create an India where all women were educated and independent. Given the dangerous climate, she made sure to build a women's hostel in Calcutta where her students could safely stay while pursuing their education. She was frequently arrested for her activities but was never deterred.

In 1931, Leela released *Jayasree Patrika*, the first nationalist magazine edited, managed, and written solely by women. She launched the magazine as a response to the crackdown on press freedom following the Chittagong Armoury Raid in an attempt to keep the patriotic zeal alive and provide a path for Bengali women to channel their nationalist spirit. The magazine struggled during Leela's frequent spells in prison (showing the integral part she played in the project), but when she was finally released in 1938 it was successfully relaunched and continued to encourage women's contributions to every aspect of society.

Following her release, she was assigned to the National Planning Committee of the INC by Bose, who at the time was INC president. A year later, she married Anil Chandra Roy and the pair became more united than ever in their activism. When Bose resigned as president to establish his own party, the Forward Bloc, the newlyweds followed him and became founding members. In 1941, Leela and Bose founded the Unity Board and the National Service Brigade in response to a serious bout of communal rioting in Dhaka. Leela was arrested alongside her husband for their participation in the Quit India Movement in 1942 and was not released until 1946. Throughout the early 1940s, Bose entrusted her with increasing responsibility in the daily running of the Forward Bloc, which led her to be a key proponent of the conspiracy theory that Bose did not actually die in a plane crash in 1945, but rather had gone into hiding, safe in the knowledge that his party was in Leela's capable hands.

In October–November 1946, the Noakhali riots unfolded in the districts of Noakhali in the Chittagong Division of Bengal (now in Bangladesh), a year before India gained independence from British rule. These were marked by semi-organized massacres, rapes, abductions, looting, and arson. Following her release from prison, Leela, a key figure in these events, embarked on a challenging ninety-mile journey on foot. Her objective was to rescue 400 women and establish a relief centre in the affected region. Gandhi himself acknowledged and commended her humanitarian efforts during his visit to the camp.

As India officially attained freedom and communal violence escalated, Leela continued her impactful initiatives. She founded homes for destitute and abandoned women and additional refugee relief centres for those escaping East Bengal. From 1946–1947, she set up seventeen relief camps in Noakhali, one of the worst-hit areas.

On 9 December 1946, Leela was sworn in as the only woman from Bengal to be elected to the Constituent Assembly, the government body that was assigned to design the Constitution of independent India. However, after only a few months, she stood down from her post in protest at Partition and the violence surrounding it.

In her dedication to social welfare, Leela also played a role in establishing the Jatiya Mahila Sanghati, a women's organization in West Bengal. Her active political career spanned until 1962, after which she retired. Leela Roy passed away eight years later in June 1970, following an extended illness.

Leela left behind a legacy of female empowerment from which numerous generations of girls and women benefitted. She ardently rejected traditional gender roles and established her own brand of Indian womanhood which was based on courage, determination, and utility. Most importantly, in stepping down from a record-breaking political position to get her hands dirty on the frontline of the most traumatic events in South Asia's history, Leela Roy proved that her life of political activism had not been motivated by personal ambition for power (a charge which was levelled at many of the male nationalist leaders who seemed to sacrifice their country's peace for the promise of political prestige).

Santi Ghose (1916–1989) and Suniti Choudhury (1917–1988)

The first and only women nationalists to successfully assassinate a British officer were scarcely women at all, but two sixteen-year-old girls, Santi Ghose and Suniti Choudhury.

Santi was born in Calcutta on 22 November 1916. Her father was a prominent nationalist and philosopher, so she was raised with a strong pride in and dedication to her country. In 1931, she became a founding member and secretary of the Chhatri Sangha. Inspired by nationalists in her circle, she joined the Jugantar Party, and began to train herself in the art of self-defence, using weapons traditionally reserved for men including swords, lathis, and guns.

Suniti was born on 22 May 1917 in the Comilla District of Bengal (present-day Bangladesh). She grew up alongside many of the founding members of the Jugantar Party, and joined the Chhatri Sangha. In May 1931, Choudhury was elected captain of the Women's Volunteer Corps in the Annual Conference of Tripura Zilla Chhatri Sangha, where she used the alias Meera Devi. She was chosen as the 'custodian of firearms' and oversaw the training of female members of the Chhatri Sangha in effective weapons' use.

Choudhury's daughter later explained how the Brits' indiscriminate slaughter during the 1930s inspired her mother to take drastic action. On 14 December 1931, Ghose and Choudhury, who were both just sixteen at the time, entered the office of the district magistrate of Comilla, Charles Geoffrey Buckland Stephens. They asked if they could present him with a petition to host a swimming competition at their school. When Stephens bent to examine the document, the girls revealed automatic pistols which they had hidden under their shawls and fired at the magistrate and his Indian orderly. Stephens was killed immediately. Choudhury's daughter explains that this assassination had not been undertaken on a childish whim, but rather that it had been an extensively thought-out plan, hatched over the course of almost a year.

Although the orderly had been injured, he managed to detain the girls until the police arrived – largely because they offered no resistance. When the police arrived, they were badly beaten and immediately incarcerated. Never had such young women attempted such radical action, and the police had no idea how to deal with them. Contemporary sources disagree about the motives behind their crime. Western sources claimed that they were reacting to Indian outrage against the suppression of free speech and other Indian civil rights as instigated by the Earl of Willingdon. Indian sources, however, state that they were seeking revenge for British magistrates' rape and assault of Indian women under the protection of diplomatic immunity. It is likely to have been a combination that drove these girls to murder. The fact that Ghose and Choudhury themselves were beaten by their arresting officers proves that women were not exempt from the violence of the British – so there is little reason to question why they would have retaliated with similar force.

Almost two months after their arrest, Ghose and Choudhury were finally given a court trial. They were sentenced to life in prison, but this was remitted to ten years on account of their age. *TIME* magazine recounted the trial as such:

'In Calcutta Miss Santi Ghose and Miss Sunity Chowdhuri [sic], convicted of fatally filling District Magistrate Charles Geoffrey Buckland Stevens full of bullets, appeared in court for their sentences. In bright coloured saris, with flowers in their hair, they listened unmoved as they were sentenced to transportation for life from Bengal Presidency. Said they lightly: "It is better to die than live in a horse's stable"'.[26]

Both girls were visibly disappointed that they were not to be executed, as they dreamed of becoming national martyrs. When the girls' convictions were made public, the British intelligence services discovered a flyer which had been circulating. This flyer praised Ghose and Choudhury as nationalist heroes. It also displayed their photographs beneath lines from Robert Burns' poem *Scots Wha Hae* (written about the movement for Scottish independence from England): 'Tyrants fall in every foe! Liberty's in every blow!"[27]

Despite their age and the esteem in which they were held by their fellow nationalists, the girls had an extremely difficult time in prison. Ghose was frequently beaten and humiliated by the officers and other prisoners. They were not kept in relative comfort as political prisoners often were, nor were they placed among their contemporaries from the educated upper classes, but rather with the lowest class of prisoners. This did not seem to faze Choudhury, as she dedicated her time to learning the local crafts from different prisoners and teaching their children (who were allowed to stay with their mothers until they turned five).

After seven years in jail, the girls were finally released in 1939 as part of an amnesty deal between Gandhi and the British. While both women went on to live full lives, they took very different paths – although they remained firm friends. Ghose decided to stay in politics and after graduating from the Bengali Women's College she joined the Communist movement where she helped organize unions in cigarette factories, and later joined the INC. In May 1941 she wrote to women asking them to elect ten delegates, and involved herself in organizing meetings, electing delegates, and working towards social reform. After marrying Professor Chittaranjan Das in 1942, Ghose served on the West Bengal Legislative Council and in the West Bengal Legislative Assembly throughout the 1950s and 1960s. She also published her own book, *Arun Bahni*. She died in 1989.

Choudhury's daughter wrote of the difficulties that her mother faced upon her release from prison. While she was incarcerated, two of her brothers had been similarly imprisoned without charge, her grandfather had lost his government pension, and her uncle had died of tuberculosis, which was aggravated by the family having starved without proper income since Choudhury's arrest. Destitute and homeless, Choudhury sought shelter in Kalyani Das' home for destitute women in Tiljala. She had long dreamed of becoming a doctor but had missed her exams given that she was imprisoned during what should have been her final years at school. However, she studied extremely hard and was able to sit and pass a special exam (designed for those who had to flee Calcutta during the Second World

War) and passed with distinction. She was then able to gain admittance to Asutosh College where she had to walk miles every day to attend her courses. Studying for a medical degree in a homeless shelter was no easy task, and thus Choudhury was taken in by the family of a trade union leader who would later become her husband. He helped tutor her in maths and science while his sister taught her English. She passed her exams but was initially rejected on account of not being able to pay her fees. However, she begged for her circumstances to be taken into consideration and was eventually able to complete a diploma and then a Bachelor's which allowed her to live her dream of becoming a doctor. Some questioned the hypocrisy of a convicted killer becoming a doctor. Her reply was that she viewed her assassination as a political necessity and not as murder and therefore saw no contradiction.

Following independence, both the INC and CPI had tried to entice Choudhury to join, but, unlike Ghose, she refused. She also refused the pension offered to freedom fighters and preferred to earn her own money. When she was transferred from her hospital after Chandannagar changed from a French colony to part of West Bengal, she believed she was being punished for helping to voice the grievances of nurses, and so she quit the hospital and established her own nursing home. Her daughter noted that her mother, along with Ghose and their fellow nationalist friends, used to question whether the turbulent times India endured after independence lived up to the hopes they had risked their lives for. She spoke of her mother's disillusionment with the power grabs made by the emerging politicians of the new Indian republic. Choudhury died on 12 January 1988, just one year before her life-long friend Ghose.

Undoubtedly, both women overcame the drama of their youth to work for a fairer India for the people – one through politics and one through her medical career. If they had achieved their goal of martyrdom, many would have lost out on the benefits of their later lives. Humbly, the women never regarded themselves as heroines or trailblazers. According to Choudhury's daughter:

'These women never thought about their "contribution". It was a job that needed to be done. They didn't think it was a huge thing. Much later, when the head of the department of political science had asked my mother a similar question about her "contribution", she had said: "I am grateful that I have had the opportunity to serve my country ...'".[28]

When one thinks of an Indian freedom fighter in a blaze of bullets, very few would picture two teenage girls. And yet, it was two sixteen-year-old girls who took on not only a grown man, but the might of the world's largest empire, and won.

Bhikaiji Rustom Cama (1861–1936)

Even those who were exiled from Indian soil, such as Bhikaiji Rustom Cama, sometimes known as Madam Cama, took part in the revolution against the British in the early-twentieth century. Madam Cama was born Bhikaiji Patel in Bombay to a large Parsi family. Parsis are descendants of Zoroastrianism who fled from Persia to India during the seventh and eight centuries after persecution by Muslim rulers. Parsis came to be a wealthy and influential community in colonial India, and Bhikaiji's family were no exception. Her father was an extremely wealthy and influential lawyer and merchant, who drew his daughter into politics from an early age by having her observe his business, educational, and philanthropic pursuits. She attended the Alexandra Girls' English Institution where she was known as a conscientious student with a gift for languages.

On 3 August 1885, she married Rustomji Cama, a prominent lawyer with a passion for politics. However, their politics clashed – Rustomji being pro-British, admiring the British way of life and their policies, and Bhikaiji being a staunch nationalist who argued that the British had done unsurmountable damage to India. Thus, their marriage was an unhappy one and the couple avoided spending time together wherever possible, with Bhikaiji devoting herself to philanthropic pursuits instead. A year after her marriage, Bombay was hit by famine and an outbreak of the bubonic plague. Bhikaiji joined the Grant Medical College, caring for the sick and later vaccinating the healthy. However, Bhikaiji soon contracted the disease herself. While thousands succumbed to the plague, she happily survived, albeit brutally weakened.

In 1902, still suffering from ill health (exacerbated by her marital strife) Bhikaiji was forced to leave India to receive medical treatment in London. Two years later, while preparing to return to her homeland, she met Shyamji Krishna Varma, an Indian nationalist living in London. Varma introduced Bhikaiji to Dadabhai Naoroji, then president of the British Committee of the INC, for whom she came to work as a private secretary. Together with

Naoroji and another activist, Singh Rewabhai Rana, Bhikaiji supported the founding of Varma's Indian Home Rule Society in February 1905.

Bhikaiji made no secret of her involvement with the nationalist cause, herself often addressing crowds in Hyde Park criticizing the British. Subsequently, the British warned her that she would not be allowed to return to India unless she promised in writing not to participate in nationalist activities upon her return. She refused to do so. Instead, she relocated to Paris, where she helped found the Paris Indian Society. Together with other exiled Indian nationalists, Bhikaiji authored, published, and distributed revolutionary literature for the movement, including *Bande Mataram* (founded in response to the British banning the nationalist poem *Vande Mataram*) and later *Madan's Talwar* (in response to the execution of nationalist Madan Lal Dhingra). These publications were banned in both Britain and India but were smuggled in via the French colony of Pondicherry; French India consisted of five geographically separated enclaves on the Indian subcontinent that had initially been factories of the French East India Company. They were de facto incorporated into the Republic of India in 1950 and 1954.

In addition to this seditious material, she volunteered to aid the revolution in any way possible, donating time, money, and ideas to the cause, all the while evading British capture.

In August 1907, Bhikaiji attended the second Socialist Congress at Stuttgart, Germany, which was attended by thousands of delegates from across the globe. She gave a rousing speech detailing the devastating effects of a famine on India, and appealing for human rights protections, equality, and independence from British rule. During her speech, she unfurled what she called the Flag of Indian Independence. She is said to have declared: 'Behold, the flag of independent India is born! It has been made sacred by the blood of young Indians who sacrificed their lives in its honour. In the name of this flag, I appeal to lovers of freedom all over the world to support this struggle'.[29] In response, most of the audience stood and saluted the first flag of an independent India, and Bhikaiji was satisfied that she had brought global awareness not only to the deprivation of her people, but also to their desire for independence. This was an act of huge bravery, given that the cause was not as popular then as it would later become, and when doing so could have resulted in her imprisonment in horrific conditions. Her dedication to providing a voice and a focal point for her people's plight also cemented her place in history as the first person to raise the Indian flag on foreign soil.

The tricolour flag Bhikaiji unveiled, which she co-designed based on the flag of Calcutta, became a template for the design of the current Indian flag. On her flag, the top green stripe had eight blooming lotuses representing colonial India's eight provinces. *Bande Mataram* (meaning: Mother, I vow to thee, and sometimes spelt 'Vande'), the slogan of Indian nationalists, was written across the central saffron stripe in Hindi. On the bottom red stripe, to the right was a half-moon (representing Islam), and the rising sun (representing Hinduism) was on the left. The original flag was later smuggled into British India by socialist Indulal Yagnik and is now on display at the Maratha and Kesari Library in Pune. In 2004, politicians of far-right Hindu nationalist party, the Bharatiya Janata Party (BJP), attempted to identify a later design from the 1920s which does not bear the Islamic crescent moon, as the flag that Cama raised in Stuttgart does.

After the 1907 conference in Stuttgart, Bhikaiji toured Europe and the United States, attempting to mobilize public support for Indian independence. In 1909, following Madan Lal Dhingra's assassination of William Hutt Curzon Wyllie, aide to the Secretary of State for India, Scotland Yard arrested several key activists living in Britain at the time. They requested that Bhikaiji be extradited from Paris, but the French government refused. Instead, the British seized her sizeable inheritance. However, she cared more for her cause than for riches. It is said that Lenin invited her to reside in the Soviet Union, but she declined.

Influenced by the British Suffragette movement, Cama was fervent in her advocation for gender equality. Speaking in Cairo in 1910, she asked where all the women were, and reminded the crowds that people, and the nations they built, were nothing without their mothers. Bhikaiji frequently promised that an independent India would guarantee women's freedom. In 1920, during a conversation with Herabai and Mithan Tata, two other Parsi women, about women's suffrage, she is said to have observed that working for India's independence would inevitably lead to women's complete emancipation too. This demonstrates how for Bhikaiji, feminism and nationalism were inextricably intertwined.

While France had initially protected Bhikaiji from British persecution, this changed with the outbreak of the First World War when Britain and France became allies. She was advised to leave France and travel to Spain, but she chose to remain in France, one of only two members of the Paris India Society to do so. She was briefly imprisoned in October 1914 for trying to disrupt Punjabi troops passing through Marseilles on the way to the front, shaming them for fighting for the very people who had enslaved their land. While her comrade was deported to Martinique, Bhikaiji was interned in Vichy. However, owing to her ill health, she was released from prison and allowed to return to a friend's house in Bordeaux, providing she report to the police twice a week.

Bhikaiji took great risks by continuing to correspond with Indian, Irish, and Egyptian revolutionaries, as well as French and Russian socialists. In 1917, she was allowed to return to Paris where she stayed for almost two decades. In 1935, aged seventy-four and having been paralyzed by a stroke, she wrote to the British governor asking to be allowed to return to India. The request was granted on the condition that she renounce her revolutionary activities, a condition which she finally accepted. Accompanied by the governor, she arrived in Bombay and died in hospital nine months later, on 13 August 1936. Testament to her dedication to gender equality, Bhikaiji bequeathed most of her personal assets to a girl's orphanage and to her family's temple.

Bhikaiji should be remembered for her commitment to advancing women's rights and calling out the colonialism and patriarchal governance that can only ever damage a nation. Her original flag shows her celebration of the religious diversity in pre-independence India. The attempts to erase this earlier template are also symptomatic of modern Hindu nationalists' relentless Islamophobia. Thus, Bhikaiji is not only a great example of the key role of women in the Indian independence movement, but also of the way that Indian nationalists since then have rescripted and rewritten the history of the country. Forty years before India finally achieved independence, Madam Bhikaiji Cama's dedication and bravery highlighted India's bondage and suffering to the world, providing a template (literally and figuratively) for those who would follow in her footsteps.

Rani Gaidinliu Pamei (1915–1993)

Another teenager who was regarded as a revolutionary queen, despite her non-violent means and humble beginnings is Gaidinliu Pamei who, as a Naga spiritual leader who ventured into politics to lead a revolt against the British, earned the title Rani Gaidinliu. Gaidinliu was born on 26 January 1915 in Nungkao, a village in present day Manipur. Unlike most of the women we have seen so far, Gaidinliu was from a tribal family, specifically the Rongmei Naga tribe (also known as Kabui). She was the fifth of eight children, only one of which was a boy, so it is fair to assume that she grew up surrounded by many strong women. Hers was the ruling clan of the village, but despite her status, she did not receive a formal education as there were no schools in her area. She was always keen to preserve the identity and culture of her community, the Zeme, Liangmai, Rongmei, and Inpui, a mix of blood-related tribes that are also referred to as Zeliangrong and are spread across Assam, Manipur, and Nagaland.

When she was just thirteen, Gaidinliu joined her cousin, Haipou Jadonang, in the Heraka movement, a socio-religious movement seeking to revive their monotheistic tribal religion while also resisting the British incursions in the area. Jadonang had founded the movement in the 1920s, and Gaidinliu became his lieutenant in his efforts to resist the infiltration of Christian missionaries, and the reforms imposed by the British government, including forcing the tribes into harsh labour and imposing high yearly revenue tax on every household.

The movement garnered support from many of the Zeliangrong tribes. By the age of sixteen, Gaidinliu, along with her family, fell under suspicion of stirring up communal tensions. In 1931, Jadonang was hanged by the British for killing some British merchants. Having already been inspired by Jadonang's mission and values, Gaidinliu emerged as his spiritual and political successor, more determined than ever to resist the regime which had executed her beloved relative and guru. She declared war on the British and called upon the Zeliangrong people to refuse to pay their taxes. She linked her spiritual role as a leader of the Herka movement to her role as a nationalist, and constantly evoked Gandhi's national non-cooperation efforts to rouse her people against the British. Her own non-cooperation movement made it difficult for the British administration to function in the region.

Gaidinliu received donations from the local tribes who also rushed to volunteer in her fight. The British organized a (wo)manhunt for her, but she evaded them by constantly crossing borders between Assam, Nagaland and Manipur, never staying in one village long enough to be traced. Humiliated by their failure to locate her, the British Governor of Assam sent the 3rd and 4th battalions of the Assam Rifles, under the watch of the Naga Hills Deputy Commissioner J.P. Mills, to retrieve her. They offered financial rewards to anyone who gave her up and promised that any village who provided information would be given a decade-long tax break. No one took them up on this tempting offer, showing not only distrust and resentment towards the British, but also their devotion to Gaidinliu. Her men often engaged in armed conflict with the British and were victorious every time given their home advantage.

However, Gaidinliu's luck ran out when her followers decided to erect a wooden fortress in Pulomi village. This construction blew their cover, and the Assam Rifles launched a surprise attack on 17 October 1932. Gaidinliu was peacefully arrested in a nearby village, but protested her innocence, denying that she had sent her men to engage the British or that she had any knowledge of the construction of the fort. In December 1932, some of her followers murdered a Kuki watchman from the Naga Hills, accusing him of betraying Gaidinliu's position. Gaidinliu was taken to Imphal, where she endured a ten-month trial, at the end of which she was convicted of murder and abetment of murder and sentenced to life in prison. All those arrested with her were either executed or jailed. She was just sixteen years old at the time of her internment. For fourteen years, she was moved between various jails. Initially, many rebels continued to refuse their taxes in Gaidinliu's name, but when the last of her followers were arrested in 1933 her movement lost momentum.

In 1937, Jawaharlal Nehru visited her at Shillong Jail, and promised that he would have her released. He released a statement in the *Hindustan Times* declaring her a daughter of the hills and queen of the people, hence her being regarded as Rani ever since. He wrote to the British MP Lady Astor, asking her to secure Gaidinliu's release, but the Secretary of State for India intervened and refused to release her out of fear that her movement would be revived, and trouble would follow. However, Nehru was true to his promise and when the Interim Government of India was established in 1946, one of his first requests was that Gaidinliu be released. She lived with her brother until 1952, when she was finally permitted to return to her home village. In 1953, Nehru visited Imphal where Gaidinliu personally thanked him for securing her release. She promised him the goodwill of the tribes, and later met him in Delhi to petition for the welfare of the Zeliangrong people and the development of the tribes of the newly independent India.

Despite having the respect of the prime minister, Gaidinliu was not universally popular. She opposed the establishment of an independent Naga state, and the Christian Naga leaders detested her attempts to reinvigorate the animistic native religion. Their threats forced her into hiding in the jungle in her old age. After six difficult years underground, Gaidinliu emerged from hiding on the condition of protection from the government. She went straight back to dedicating her life to advocating for the betterment of the tribal people through decidedly peaceful and democratic means. However, on 24 September, 320 of her followers officially disbanded. She received several awards throughout her life for her role as a freedom fighter.

In 1991, Gaidinliu returned to her home village to finally enjoy some peaceful years before her death on 17 February 1993, aged seventy-eight. The widespread reaction to her death was testament to her popularity and the close ties she had shared with the Indian government. However, because of her supposed hatred of Christianity, her feats were not widely celebrated among the Nagas, the majority of whom had converted to Christianity by the middle of the twentieth century. The prominent Naga nationalists also refused to acknowledge her, believing her relationship with the Indian government to be a betrayal of her roots. Thus, in 2015, when a memorial hall for Gaidinliu was announced, several Naga officials protested. In 2021, a Rani Gaidinliu Museum was opened in Manipur, serving to preserve and exhibit the history of tribal freedom fighters who participated in several anti-colonial revolts, including the Anglo-Manipuri War, Kuki-Rebellion, Naga-Raj movements, and others, including Gaidinliu's.

Gaidinliu's story is extraordinary in the already overlooked narrative of female freedom fighters. As a tribal girl, she did not benefit from the education or the dominant-caste privilege which many of her contemporaries shared. Tribal communities, with their unique culture, religion, and languages have long been marginalized and regarded as impoverished and backward groups regardless of their actual status or religion. Hence, they became popular targets both of Christian missionaries and Hindu nationalists who saw them as vulnerable to conversion and bribery. Gaidinliu's movement is a testament that everyone was wrong to underestimate her and her people. They would not easily surrender to incursions from the British or anyone else who sought to erode their religion and culture. While she may have favoured strictly non-violent means which aligned her more closely with Gandhian nationalists than with her fellow revolutionaries and being more sympathetic to the Indian establishment following independence than many of her fellow tribal leaders, she never compromised her values or her identity. She channelled the pain the British had caused her family into a cause which she ultimately used to fight for the rights of her people, and for that, Nehru was right to dub her a queen.

Gulab Kaur (1890–1941)

As the independence struggle loomed on into the 1940s, women continued to reject traditional gender roles in favour of contributing to the revolution. One such woman was Gulab Kaur, whose story also shows that the Indian independence movement reached well beyond the borders of British India.

Gulab was born around 1890 in a small village in the Punjab to a family of poor Sikh farmers and was married to Mann Singh at a young age. The couple knew that their prospects were dim if they chose to remain in their village, as several peasants had lost their livelihoods under British policies. They felt that their only future lay in America but decided to first head to the Philippines and settle in Manila. In Manila, Gulab attended lectures of an organization by Sikh Punjabis called the Ghadar Party (*ghadar* meaning revolt or revolution in Punjabi). The party aimed to drive the British out of India, using revolutionary tactics if needed, and to improve the conditions of Indian immigrants in the diaspora across Asia and the Americas. Greatly inspired, Gulab vowed to do whatever she could to support the party.

She began by dressing in disguise and acting as lookout for the party printing press. She then progressed to posing as a journalist to smuggle arms and ammunition to party members. Gulab followed other party members across the country distributing party propaganda and motivational lectures to Indian travellers, who she also provided with arms and ammunition. It is also said that when party members tried to back out of the movement, she would dramatically remove her bangles, a traditional symbol of femininity, and shout: 'If anyone retreats from this rare opportunity to fight for the cause of motherland, he should wear these bangles and sit aside ... we women will fight in their place'.[30] In this she was emulating another Sikh woman warrior, Mai Bhago, who famously humiliated a group of male deserters in a battle against the Mughal army by offering them her bracelets to shame them for their cowardice before leading her army to battle herself. Again, this shows the power of historical heroines in inspiring the women of the freedom movement, proving that theirs was not a new-found strength but rather one inherited from generations of strong and spirited women.

As the Second World War approached, Gulab and around fifty of her comrades decided to return to India to continue the fight on home soil. However, it was at this point that her husband decided that he no longer wished to fight but rather to return to their original plan of starting a new life in America. Gulab, however, stuck to her convictions, and asserted that she would rather die for the freedom of her nation than comfortably abandon it to tyranny. Having reached an impasse, they decided to divorce, and her husband left for America. Gulab began to use the surname 'Kaur', meaning either lioness or princess, a name designated by one of the Sikh gurus so that women could use a name linked solely to their faith rather than their ties to their husband or their father.

Gulab Kaur set sail for India via Singapore along with revolutionaries from Korea. Once in India, she travelled around Kapurthala, Hoshiarpur and Jallandhar attempting to incite the masses to armed rebellion against the British. Eventually, however, the British caught up with her, and she was arrested and imprisoned for sedition, sentenced to two years in the Shahi Qila fort at Lahore. Once imprisoned, she refused to cooperate with her gaolers, and was subsequently tortured throughout her sentence. All that is known of the end of her life is that she passed away in 1941 aged fifty-one, from a short illness. Whether this illness was in any way related to the torture she endured at the hands of the British we will likely never know.

Gulab Kaur's story is heroic in more ways than one. Obviously, her revolutionary activities and her bravery in never submitting to British rule, even under torture, puts her in line with more famous and well-celebrated male Sikh revolutionaries like Bhagat Singh. However, Gulab should also be admired for rebelling against the patriarchal norms of her time, by leaving first her home in search of a better life, and then in rejecting marriage and motherhood in favour of the revolution. At a time when women were expected to obey their fathers and husbands above all else, and were raised to believe that their only duty was to their family, it was no mean feat for a young woman to reject the safety and protection of male relatives, the promise of a comfortable and prosperous life abroad, and the patriarchal norms of her society in order to risk her life for her country. In part, this is a testament to the legacy of her forerunners who paved a different model of what it meant to be an Indian woman, and to the Sikh faith which (in theory) grants spiritual and social equality to both genders. Mostly, however, it is a testament to Gulab's free spirit and her belief that she and her countrymen (and women) were worth more than a life of subjugation and oppression.

Aruna Asaf Ali (1909–1996)

A woman who found herself torn between Gandhi's non-violent methods and more radical measures to rid India of the British was Aruna Asaf Ali. Aruna Ganguly was born on 16 July 1909 in Kalka, Punjab. Her father was a Bengali Brahmin and her mother's family were active Brahmos, related by marriage to Nobel Prize winner, Rabindranath Tagore. Her sister, Purnima, was also a freedom fighter. Aruna refused to consider an arranged marriage and instead pursued her education and later career as a teacher. However, while on holiday in Allahabad, she met a Muslim barrister from Delhi, Asif Ali. Her family were outraged at the prospect of her marriage to a man twenty years her senior, and a Muslim man at that. However, she defied their objections, and the pair were married in 1927.

Following her marriage, Aruna joined her husband in the INC and was arrested for participating in the Salt Satyagraha aged just twenty-one. This march (also known as the Salt March), was an act of nonviolent civil disobedience in protest at the British monopoly of the salt market. The twenty-four-day march lasted from 12 March to 6 April 1930. Gandhi embarked on this march with seventy-eight of his most trusted confidants. Tens of thousands of people joined the march along the 239-mile route, and the march sparked acts of disobedience across India. While held prisoner at the Tihar Jail, she protested the poor treatment of political prisoners by launching a hunger strike. She was successful in improving conditions in this jail, but as a consequence was transferred to another and placed in solitary confinement. She was recorded by the British as being a vagrant, and thus was not released in 1931 under the Gandhi–Irwin Pact which stipulated the release of all political prisoners. In solidarity, other female prisoners refused to leave until she was also freed, and eventually, her release was secured with the intervention of Gandhi and public agitation.

In 1941, Aruna was briefly imprisoned again, this time after offering individual *satyagraha* (the term used for satyagrahis who offered themselves up for arrest as a protest). When the INC announced the Quit India resolution and its highest leaders – including Aruna's husband – were arrested, Aruna presided over the remainder of the session. She also unfurled the INC flag while denouncing the arrests, amid a fog of teargas thrown by police in an attempt to dispel the crowds.

Following the flag-raising unrest, a warrant was again issued for her arrest, but she met with other INC delegates and decided to return to Delhi and go underground. She and her conspirators believed they needed to turn the mob's righteous anger into organized resistance. They also sought to bring as much disruption to the British war effort as possible, and to continue to inspire the people to reject British rule. While in hiding, she edited *Inquilab*, the INC's monthly magazine. In 1944, she wrote in the paper that the youth must act and join the revolution rather than wasting time by debating the virtues of violence versus non-violence. The British offered a reward of 5,000 rupees for her capture, and Gandhi tried to compel her to surrender and donate the fee to the cause. However, while she treasured his correspondence, she refused to surrender and preferred to work underground and continue with more drastic means.

Gandhi was critical of her support for the Royal Indian Navy Mutiny, which she saw as a key opportunity to unite Hindus and Muslims. Gandhi, however, argued that she would rather unite them through war than democracy. He was not the only one who questioned her revolutionary tactics as even her female comrades criticized her disruption of the war efforts. However, Aruna argued that her actions were not violent but rather necessary collateral:

'Dislocation is a common and effective method used by enslaved and oppressed peoples against their rulers … Thus, if telegraph wires are cut, fishplates on railway lines are removed, bridges are dynamited, industrial plants put out of order, petrol tanks are set on fire, police stations are burnt down, official records destroyed – they are all acts of dislocation. But a bomb thrown at a market place or a school or a *dharmashala* [a shelter for pilgrims] is not dislocation. It is either the work of agent provocateurs or misdirected energy'.[31]

Following the release of INC leaders in 1945, the Working Committee met and condemned the violence that the underground revolutionaries had enacted. However, Aruna and her associates refused to apologize for their actions, claiming that they had noble intentions and had acted on the authority of the All-India Congress Committee. Despite publicly condemning her tactics, key INC leaders maintained their support for Aruna – Gandhi praised her bravery and met her while she was in hiding, and on his release from prison, Nehru singled Aruna out as a hero of the nation.

Following India's independence, Aruna became disillusioned with the INC's attitudes to women, and joined the socialist party in 1948. Ten years later, she was elected the first Mayor of Delhi, and enjoyed the patronage and friendship of Nehru and other key congressmen throughout her life. She died in New Delhi on 29 July 1996, aged eighty-seven. Before her death, she was awarded the Lenin Peace Prize (1964), the Jawaharlal Nehru Award for International Understanding (1991) and India's second-highest civilian honour in 1992. A year after her death, she was posthumously awarded the Bharat Ratna, the highest civilian honour.

Both in her lifetime and since her passing, Aruna has been hailed for her bravery and commitment. *Roshni*, the All-India Women's Conference (AIWC) journal equated her with a fictional character, Devi Chaudharani, a bandit queen who robbed from the rich and gave to the poor. She was also compared to Rani of Jhansi. Aruna was dubbed the Heroine of the 1942 movement for her bravery in the face of danger and became known in her later years as the Grand Old Lady of the Independence Movement.

Captain Lakhsmi Sahgal (1914–2012)

Another woman who took the fight against the British beyond Indian shores was Captain Lakshmi Sahgal, a revolutionary who fought against the British during the Second World War. Lakshmi Swaminathan was born into a dominant-caste family in Madras on 24 October 1914. Her father, S. Swaminathan, was a criminal lawyer, and her mother, A.V. Ammukutty (also known as Ammu Swaminathan) was a social worker and independence activist who inspired similar leanings in her daughter. Young Lakshmi was horrified when her mother walked into her room and confiscated all her young daughter's dresses to throw on a bonfire made of foreign goods. Lakshmi's family raised her to hold and express political opinions and gave her the freedom to enjoy activities which were highly unusual for a girl of her status at the time, such as horseracing and cycling. Lakshmi demonstrated her activist nature as a young girl when she protested the strict caste rules of Keralan society. Her grandmother would often pass judgement on the local tribal people. One day, much to her grandmother's horror, Lakshmi walked up to a young tribal girl and led her by the hand to play. Regardless of the wrath she experienced from her grandmother, Lakshmi won the battle in a quest for justice which would prove lifelong. She later recalled how in Southern India, the freedom fight was inseparable from other social justice campaigns around caste and gender issues such as restrictions of Dalits into temples, child marriage, and dowry.

Despite her interest in the nationalist movement, Lakshmi prioritized her education and enrolled in university to train as a doctor, eventually specializing in gynaecology and obstetrics, bringing her into closer contact with women of all backgrounds. After qualifying, she worked at the Government Kasturba Gandhi Hospital in Chennai. Some sources state that during this time she had a failed marriage to P.K.N. Roa, a pilot. However, it is a pleasant surprise to find a narrative of a historical woman whose romantic life is restricted to a footnote in a wider narrative of heroic feats, rather than the other way around.

By the time she graduated in 1939, the Second World War had begun, and the British were attempting to enlist all Indian doctors to assist the BIA. Lakshmi was not keen to assist the British in any way, so in 1940, aged just twenty-six, she left India to live with relatives in Singapore where she established a successful medical practice. When the Japanese attacked Singapore in 1941, Rashbehari Bose, a renowned freedom fighter founded the India Independence League which all Indians in Singapore were expected to join. Lakshmi later recalled that although not forcefully enlisted, it was to her benefit to join because they were given ration cards and were allowed to keep their property (which was otherwise deemed belonging to the enemy given that India was under British control). However, she was disappointed to learn that as a woman her involvement was limited to welfare work and underground broadcasts.

In February 1942, Captain Mohan Singh founded the Indian National Army (INA) for Indians who wished to fight against the British and not for them. The INA leaders asked the Japanese government for assurance that they would be treated as an ally. They did not receive adequate reassurance and thus proposed to disband the army. However, over eighty per cent of its 60,000 troops refused to go back on their oath of allegiance and refused to desert. In 1942, the British surrendered Singapore to the Japanese, and Lakshmi found work treating the wounded prisoners of war. When S.C. Bose arrived in Singapore from Germany to take control of the INA, Lakshmi requested a meeting with him, keen to encourage his inclination to include women in his army. She had a five-hour meeting with him during which she convinced him to set up a woman's regiment, named after the famous Rani of Jhansi. Lakshmi admitted that she did not have high hopes of women taking interest as the middle classes, who traditionally made up the forefront of the Indian nationalist movement, had mostly returned to India. Bose responded that on the contrary it is always the working people who uphold revolutions. He was proved right when Lakshmi began her recruitment on 8 July 1943 and quickly amassed a regiment of 1,500 women willing to train as soldiers. To her surprise, it was women whose families had not lived in India for generations who proved the most passionate recruits. In reward for her efforts, Bose named Lakshmi Minister of Women's Affairs and appointed her to the rank of captain, a title and name which she would proudly use for the rest of her life.

For three months, the women of the Rani of Jhansi regiment were put through the same gruelling regime as their male counterparts and were subjected to forty-mile marches, rock-climbing, and mountain hikes. They wore the same uniforms as their male comrades, and while the women were not forced to cut their hair, over ninety per cent opted to, including Lakshmi who had always hated being forced by her mother to wear her hair long. The women were trained to use military weapons including rifles and grenades, as well as other military tactics such as navigation. Because most of the women were from the South and did not speak Hindi but rather Tamil or other local languages, they were also given Hindi lessons. Their nationalist fervour was stoked by political lectures from Bose himself. These brave and infrangible women were undeterred even when British aircraft destroyed their camp. They scripted their own war cry asserting that while women were not the ones who caused war, and were not supposed to fight, they were the ones brave and smart enough to lift their swords and defend India.

A story of one of Lakshmi's recruits has survived. Seventeen-year-old Janaki Davar heard of the new women's regiment in the local newspaper and attended one of Bose's speeches. She offered him her earrings in return for being allowed to join his army. In an age when women generally did not work and were largely excluded from inheriting their father's lands and business, a South Asian's woman's main, if not only, financial asset was her gold jewellery, passed through the women in a family. Thus, women offering their jewellery for the cause is a theme which we will see throughout this book. When her parents forbade her to enlist, Janaki invited Captain Lakshmi for dinner. Janaki recalled how after one conversation with Captain Lakshmi, her father was persuaded to allow his daughter to enlist, demonstrating the personal role Lakshmi played in building up this army.

In December 1944, the INA marched into Burma alongside the Japanese forces. Lakshmi wrote:

'Moving into action, the regiment took part mostly in guerrilla attacks ... The Japanese soldiers proved to be the biggest male chauvinists. They initially objected to the women's regiment and did not give us land or campsites. But when they saw us functioning, were sufficiently impressed to change their minds'.[32]

However, the INA was overpowered by the might of the British, and within a few months it became clear that they were on the losing side. Thus, the INA leaders made the difficult decision to withdraw their malnourished and ill-equipped forces before it was too late. While many women were escorted back to safety, every single member of the women's regiment signed, in blood, a petition demanding to stay in the field and promising to die there if necessary. They kept their spirits up by putting on plays re-enacting the story of their namesake, proving the enduring legacy of the original Rani of Jhansi and her revolutionary spirit. Despite their extreme dedication, there were soon no battles for them to join and thus Lakshmi began working in a hospital for mortally wounded INA soldiers. The hospital was buried deep in the jungle, but spies discovered it when they followed Bose and almost all the patients were killed under heavy bombardment. Lakshmi was captured while trying to evacuate survivors in May 1945.

Following her arrest, she was interrogated and then detained under house arrest in the Burmese jungle until March 1946 when she was returned to India for trial. The INA trials in Delhi proved a huge rallying point for the nationalist movement and became a target of propaganda against the British government in India. Many soldiers fighting in the BIA began to rebel against their superiors, and the Royal Indian Navy fell into outright mutiny for over a fortnight. The unrest caused by the INA trials has been cited by some historians as a significant factor in Britain's decision to relinquish control of India, as it proved that they could no longer rely on Indian troops to uphold their authority in the subcontinent. Therefore, one could argue that Captain Lakshmi and her women's regiment was a critical part of the decision to free their country with their open rebellion as their namesake had done in her own mutiny almost a century before.

A few months before India finally won her independence, Lakshmi married Colonel Prem Kumar Sahgal, a fellow soldier in the INA. Together they had two daughters and after Partition, the family settled in Kanpur, where she established her own medical practice dedicated to treating refugees wounded in the violence of Partition, and later those fleeing the floods in Pakistan. She regarded herself as an atheist and was loved and trusted by members of all religious communities, making her a central figure of peace in times of extreme interreligious turmoil.

Lakshmi remained involved in social justice campaigns for the rest of her life through social work, as a politician, and as a doctor. At the age of ninety-two, she was still seeing patients every day in her practice. When interviewed about why she was still working at such an old age, she answered 'the fight will go on'.[33] In 1998, Sahgal was awarded the Padma Vibhushan (the second-highest civilian honour) by the Indian president. On 19 July 2012, Sahgal died of a heart attack at the age of ninety-seven. At her request, her body was bequeathed to a medical college for research, proving useful to her country even after death. Politicians and public figures paid tribute, and revolutionary slogans rang out across India in her honour. Although part of the wider INA, the Rani of Jhansi regiment has long endured in popular memory as an example of women's bravery and dedication which was equal to, if not surpassing, that of men. They fought not only external enemies, but also internal bias and scorn.

It may be hard for many readers to sympathize with a figure who fought against the British during a war which remains a pivotal and largely proud moment in British history. In popular imagination, fighting against the British meant fighting for the Nazis, a view bred by history curriculums that simplify the Second World War as Britain/America vs Nazi Germany and Good Allies vs Bad Enemies – ignoring the involvement of the rest of the world completely. It is thus understandably difficult to see those who refused to assist the British during this war, which was fought in part to end the oppression of the Jewish and other marginalized peoples, as in anyway motivated by social justice. Rather, one would expect that Indians, who knew what it was to be oppressed and called themselves 'freedom fighters', would fight tooth and nail to defend the freedom of others too. It should be noted that millions of Indians did indeed support the war effort in a myriad of ways. Bose certainly had sympathy for Nazi ideologies, and in fact came to Singapore directly from Germany before raising his INA. However, we can never know for sure to what extent the other soldiers of the INA knew about Nazi atrocities, or what their thoughts were on the wider motivations behind the war. From the insights we do have into the minds of Lakshmi and her comrades, it is clear that they were deeply critical of a British government who claimed to fight for freedom from oppression and would wage war to prevent countries being invaded by foreign powers, when the British state, more than any other, had invaded countless foreign lands and oppressed their people. Indian freedom fighters had witnessed the brutality of British colonialism first hand, and now felt that they were being dragged into a British war without consultation to fight an enemy who, in the minds of many Indians, were no worse than the British. Given the close connections between India and certain African countries during this period, many Indians would have been aware of the concentration camps established by the British during the Boer War and the squalid conditions within them as exposed by Emily Hobhouse. In British India, Indians found themselves imprisoned for peacefully protesting the establishment, subjected to laws that suppressed some of their dearly held customs, and beaten and killed for disobeying orders. Thus, we must be careful not to equate a reluctance to support the British war effort with sympathy for the Nazis or their crimes; but rather to view it as a refusal to support the hypocrisy of the British government who only objected to the oppression of certain groups and turned a blind eye – or directly conducted – the oppression of others.

Captain Lakshmi's life testifies to her compassion and all those who knew her spoke of the joy and hope that she aroused in them. In every battle, Lakshmi took the side of the marginalized and downtrodden. Many have noted her ability to always prioritize women's rights alongside the wider political studies of the nation. In an interview given shortly before her death, she wisely concluded: 'Freedom comes in three forms. The first is political emancipation from the conqueror, the second is economic [emancipation] and the third is social ... India has only achieved the first'.[34]

Portrait of Ahilyabai Holkar (date unknown). (Picryl)

A statue of Kittur Chennamma. (Flickr)

A portrait of Rani Lakshmibai of Jhansi, 1947. (Picryl)

Drawing of Hazrat Mahal. (Picryl)

Statues portraying Rani Lakshmibai of Jhansi and Jhalkari Bai in battle. (Jhansi Museum)

Bengali Hindu women in jail c.1856. (Zeno)

The male-dominated first Indian National Congress Meeting, 1885. (The British Library).

Two women with charkha (spinning) wheel, a symbol of the Indian independence movement, c. 1875–1940. (The University of Edinburgh).

Muslim woman in purdah, c.1900–1915. (Library of Congress)

Portrait of Jindan Kaur painted by George Richmond in 1863. (Picryl)

Sarojini Naidu, 1912. (Picryl)

Kasturbai and Mohandas Gandhi on their return to India from South Africa, in 1915. (Picryl)

Above: Fatima Jinnah, date unknown. (Wikimedia)

Left: Rattanbai (Ruttie) Jinnah, date unknown. (Wikimedia)

The Nehru Family: Standing (left to right) Jawaharlal Nehru, Vijaya Lakshmi Pandit, Krishna Hutheesingh, Indira Gandhi, and Ranjit Pandit; Seated: Swarup Rani, Motilal Nehru and Kamala Nehru, 1920. (Picryl)

Two Devadasis in Tamil Nadu, 1920s. (Picryl)

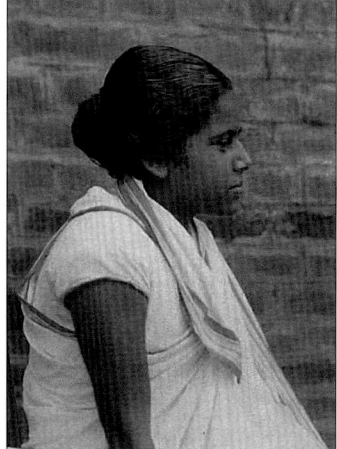

Above left: Women preparing a meal during the 1930 Salt March. (Wikimedia)

Above right: Santi Ghose, date unknown. (Wikimedia)

Right: Pritilata Waddedar, 1932. (Picryl)

Below: Delegates of the All-India Convention of the Indian National Congress in New Delhi, 1937. (Picryl)

Above left: Rajkumari Amrit Kaur, 1933. (The Modern Review)

Above right: Vijayalakshmi Pandit, 1938. (National Portrait Gallery)

Below left: Kamala Nehru, 1936. (Picryl)

Below right: Begum Aziz Rasul, 1938. (The Indian Listener)

Above: Captain Lakshmi Sahgal and members of the Azad Hind Fauj, 1940. (Picryl)

Left: Begum Amjadi Bano and the rest of the All-India Muslim League Working Committee, Lahore, 1940. (Picryl)

Leela Roy (wearing the garland) and other members of the Samaj Sebi Sangha, 1946. (Picryl)

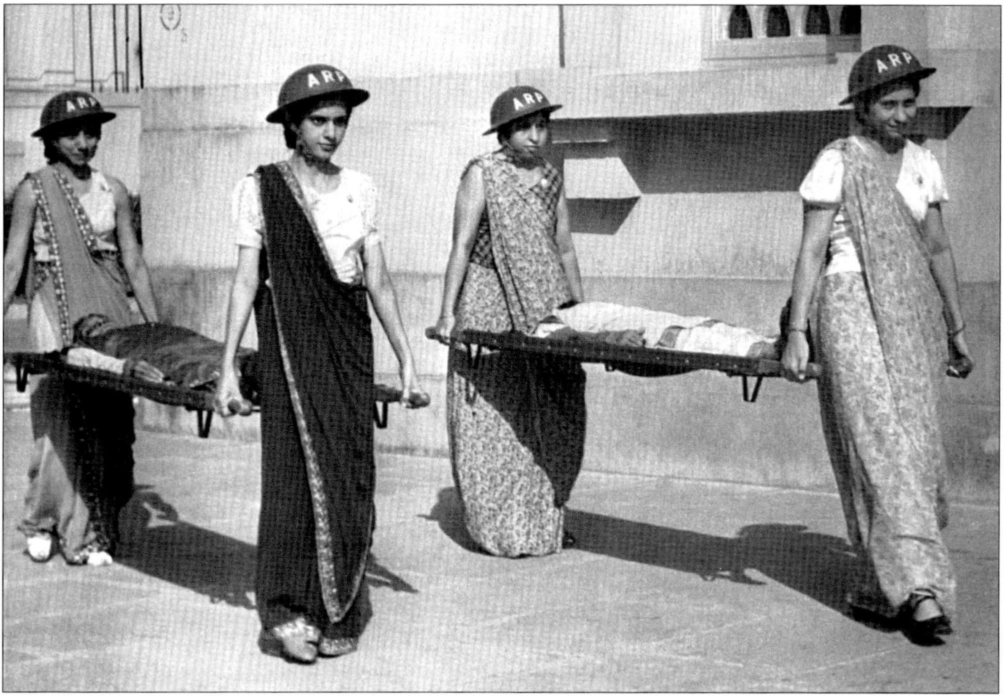

Indian women training for air raid precaution duties in Bombay, 1942. (Imperial War Museum)

Bina Das, 1942. (Sukhi Grihakon)

Matangini Hazra, also known as Gandhi Buri, date unknown. (Calcutta Mahajata Sadan)

A woman caring for her starving husband during the Bengal Famine, 1943. (Picryl)

Kamaladevi Chattopadhyay, date unknown. (Indian Express)

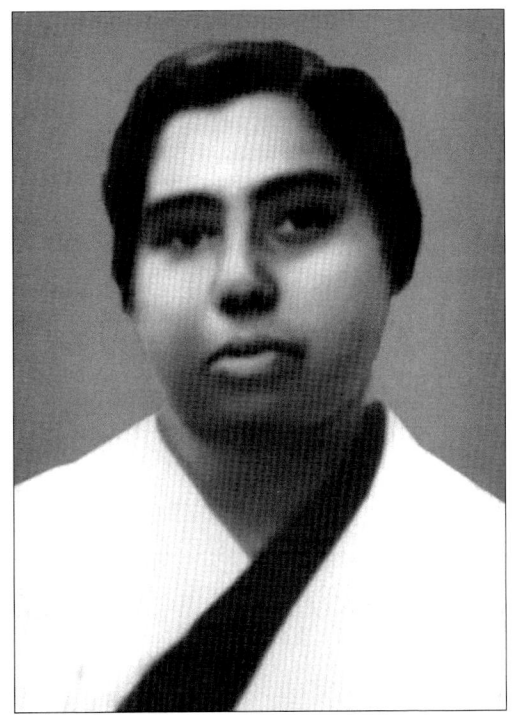
Accamma Cherian, date unknown. (Wikimedia)

Ammu Swaminathan, 1945. (Indian Express)

Gandhi meeting followers at Calcutta Maidan, 1947. (Wikimedia)

Above: M.K. Gandhi with his great-nieces, Abha (far right) and Manu (far left) and Amrit Kaur (middle) at the All-India Radio, New Delhi, where Gandhi gave a radio message to refugees, in 1947. (Picryl).

Left: M.K. Gandhi with his grandniece Abha and his physician Dr Sushila Nayyar, 1947. (Picryl)

Constituent Assembly of India, date unknown. (Wikimedia)

Emergency trains crowded with refugees during the Partition of India, 1947. (Picryl)

Violence in Calcutta during the Partition of India. (Flickr)

Gandhi and his female followers at a prayer meeting, on 29 January 1948. (Picryl)

Prayer meeting at Birla House with Gandhi 1948. (Picryl)

Usha Mehta, 1996. (Government of India).

British police use tear gas during a communal riot in Calcutta, 1948. (Picryl)

Indira Gandhi. (Ritva Bäckman).

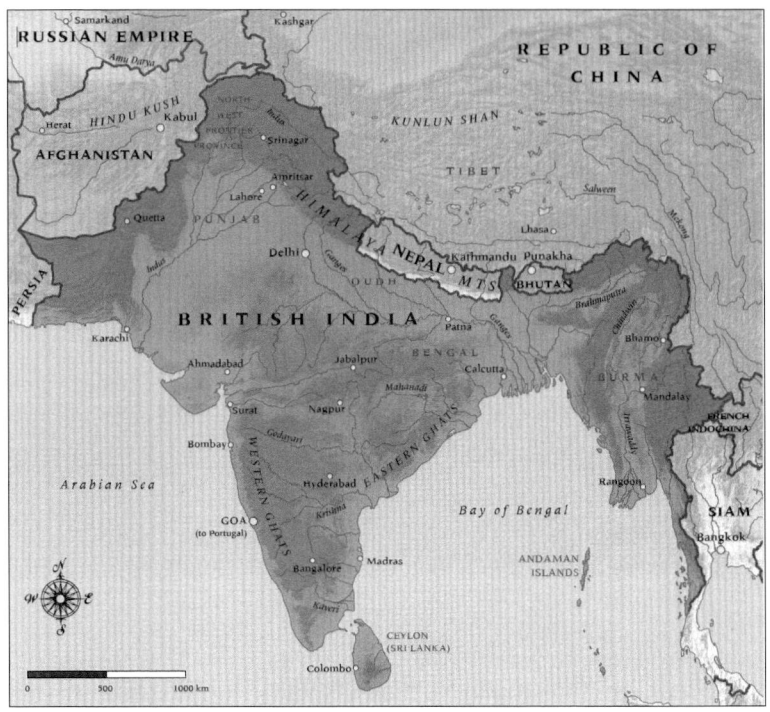

Map of British India, pre-1947.

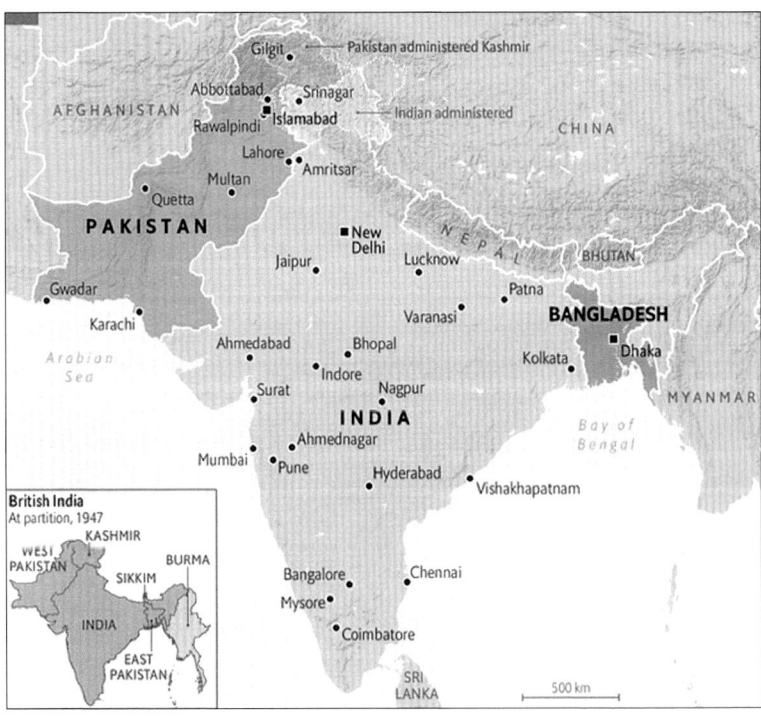

Indian subcontinent post-Partition, after 1947.

Chapter two
Stalwarts and Satyagrahis

While many women took up arms against the British, especially in the first century of the Indian nationalist movement, the movement took on an increasingly non-violent tone, due in large part to Mohandas Gandhi's *satyagraha* campaign. As discussed in the introduction, *satyagraha* was an ideology based on non-violent opposition to the British government and was seen as a method of civil disobedience which would drive the colonial regime out without bloodshed. This soon became the predominant strand of nationalism as opposed to the more revolutionary tactics of previous decades. Those who adhered to this movement, *satyagrahis*, were bound by strict rules and expected to ascribe to several key principles. All were expected to hold to the ideals of non-violence, truth, control of desire or celibacy, religious equality, a sincere belief in God, and the benefits of hard labour. The daily life of a *satyagrahi* was not easy. They were urged to give up all but essential possessions and were expected to only wear *khadi* (which they were urged to spin themselves). Alcohol and certain foods were forbidden, and they were expected to face every struggle with serenity and bravery. Gandhi established a series of rules which all *satyagrahis* were obligated to follow when in prison or during protests, mainly restricting them from retaliating against the British, but also forbidding *satyagrahis* to show the British any undue respect.

Although women were initially dissuaded from participating in this movement, it was soon realized that the *satyagraha* ideals closely aligned with the traditional Indian womanly virtues of peace and spirituality, and that this movement offered them a way to participate in the nationalist struggle without engaging in violent (and therefore what men perceived as unladylike) behaviour. As Gandhi and his ideologies garnered respect among Indian men, they began to slowly grant their approval for women to join this movement, and soon women were engaging with politics on an unprecedented scale. Many of the women who found their fame as revolutionaries or politicians were involved with the *satyagraha* movement at some point in their careers. This section will tell the stories of some of these women *satyagrahis* and how they contributed to the movement for which Gandhi is often given all the credit.

Kasturbai Gandhi (1869–1944)

Gandhi is without a doubt the most well-known figure of the Indian independence movement, in fact, maybe one of the most well-known names in the world. But upon hearing the name, almost everyone will first think of Mohandas Karamchand Gandhi, rather than his wife, Kasturbai (also known as Kasturba). This is a great tragedy and does Kasturbai a great disservice. Not only was she an ardent activist in her own right, but – by his own admission – she made Mohandas the man he was.

Kasturbai Gokuldas Kapadia was born in Gujarat on 11 April 1869. Her family were traders and relatively progressive, but she received no formal education. Sadly, little else is known of her childhood. In May 1883, when she was just fourteen, she was married to thirteen-year-old Mohandas Gandhi. Mohandas later recalled that they did not fully understand what getting married meant, other than that they were given delicious sweets and fancy clothes, which highlights how young and innocent they were upon their marriage. However, Mohandas soon came to view his wife as a possession, there to satisfy his sexual and other demands. He later recalled his guilt for the mental and physical abuse he inflicted on her in the early years of their marriage, demanding complete subservience. He confessed to being jealous and controlling and admitted that he made life unbearable for her, especially when she rebelled against him. This paints a somewhat darker picture of a man who is world-renowned for his peace-making, but also shows the fiery spirit of Kasturbai even as a child bride, never one to meekly submit to her husband's will, despite his best efforts and the expectations of her society.

The couple had five sons, but their first child died, a tragedy from which Kasturbai never fully recovered. Mohandas left to study in London in 1888, Kasturbai having sold her precious gold to fund his education, despite being completely uneducated herself (unlike many of the female nationalists of the day). Kasturbai and their sons remained in India, (mistakenly) believing that he would soon return. They finally joined Mohandas in 1896 but they struggled to adapt to the Western lifestyle which he attempted to enforce upon her and their children. He continued to torture her and recalled one incident where, upon a dispute about household chores, he grabbed her by the wrist and tried to throw her into the street to which she begged him to release her from the marriage or at the very least treat her with respect and stop making a scene publicly. She won that argument, and many others, he reported. Whether or not Kasturbai agreed that she was indeed the winner of this situation and shared his belief that their marriage was ultimately peaceful we will never know. She was certainly not afraid to stand up for herself, as is evident from one argument the couple had when he sold jewellery that was given as a gift to her without her consent. When she asked what right he had to her necklace and he said it had been donated for *his* service, she replied: 'Service rendered by you is as good as rendered by me. I have toiled and moiled for you day and night. Is that no service? You forced all and sundry on me, making me weep bitter tears, and I slaved for them!'.[35] Thus, even before the nation acknowledged that hers was a life of service, Kasturbai had asserted so herself.

In 1906, having now adopted a life of ascetism and *ahimsa*, Mohandas took a vow of *brahamacharya* (chastity/celibacy) without consulting his wife. Some claimed that Kasturbai opposed his vow as she felt it was a neglect of his husbandly duties, but she strongly denied this and gave it her public support. Considering his later confession about his early sexual treatment of her, it is not unthinkable that she did not mind. Having suffered with respiratory issues since birth, in 1908 she fell gravely ill after contracting pneumonia. This was aggravated by her determination to fast while her husband was imprisoned. She haemorrhaged and was forced to undergo surgery without anaesthesia as she was too weak to withstand the effects of chloroform; witnesses remarked on how she did not even shed a tear in pain. This brush with death seemed to be a wakeup call for Mohandas, who apologized to his wife for his abusive treatment and promised that he would be faithful to her even in death. In future bouts of illness, Mohandas personally nursed her, and they prayed together for her recovery. Perhaps strengthened by the new support of her husband, Kasturbai recuperated and survived with a passion for justice that was more ferocious than ever.

Kasturbai had a long and active career alongside her husband which demonstrated that she was as devoted to her country as she was to her husband. Her first brush with politics came in 1904 when, while living in South Africa, Kasturbai established the Phoenix Settlement (a community based on self-reliance) near Durban. One of her supporters remarked that despite having no formal education, she was at least equal if not superior to her peers in her comprehension, her logic, and her patriotism. In 1913, she broke taboos by peacefully protesting a new law which deemed only Christian marriages to be legally registered. Thus, while her husband is often lauded for his assertion of the equality of all religions, it was his wife who first publicly defended this belief. In fact, their grandson remembered that her determination to oppose the law was a point of contention between the Gandhis, as Mohandas was reluctant to allow his wife to intervene. Kasturbai won the battle, and was among the first group of women to protest the law in 1913. For their protests, Kasturbai and her comrades were sentenced to three months of hard labour. Kasturbai was particularly targeted because of her high-profile husband and her refusal to break her strict religious diet to eat the poor food provided. Regardless, she channelled her passion into productivity and used her time in prison to lead other women in prayer, and urged the educated prisoners to teach the illiterate to read and write. Kasturbai's arrest and mistreatment caused an outcry across the ocean in India, where INC leaders chastised their fellow politicians for wasting time postulating while women languished in jail with the lowest scum of society. This was the first – but certainly not the last – time that Kasturbai would prove an inspiration for her male counterparts.

In 1914, the Gandhis left South Africa and returned to India to join the independence movement of which Mohandas would become the primary leader. Despite continuing to suffer from chronic bronchitis, Kasturbai threw herself into protesting and often stood in for her husband during civil disobedience demonstrations while he was incarcerated. She also took over running their *ashrams* (spiritual retreats or monasteries). This was a significant endeavour which required her to rise before dawn to prepare food for an army of people after her daily devotions. One guest at her *ashram* wrote in 1925 that she demonstrated an almost militant organization. In the *ashrams*, she was known as 'Ba', meaning mother, because she took on a motherly role of feeding and caring for the guests. The *ashrams* proved a breeding ground for some of the most influential activists of the movement, including women who were directly inspired by Kasturbai's spirit.

In 1917, Kasturbai accompanied her husband to Champaran, Bihar, where she busied herself teaching women to read and write and guiding them in the necessities of hygiene. In 1922, despite another particularly poor episode of her health, she participated in a non-violent protest in Borsad. Two years later, she stood in for her husband while he was jailed in Poona. The women of Borsad, who had been brutally beaten with lathis, wrote to her specifically, begging her to represent them. Kasturbai eagerly responded to their plea, and they rejoiced that despite her ailing lungs, she engaged with her usual fire. She led numerous marches (some comprising crowds of up to 25,000 people) of her own volition and was jailed at least four times.

Kasturbai spoke of the need for unity between all communities, asserting that non-cooperation with the government would have no effect unless Indians cooperated with each other. She was an outspoken advocate of wearing and spinning only *khadi*. In all her speeches, she stressed the importance of women's involvement in the nationalist movement. She also shared her husband's fight to empower the Dalit community and frequently spoke out in their defence. Like many other female nationalists, she was deeply concerned with women's rights and closely equated the freedom of women with the freedom of the nation. She condemned child marriage and purdah and argued that until such customs were ended women could never be considered free. Thus, Kasturbai was not afraid to lay the finger of blame for some of India's problems at its own door, and asserted that only Indian themselves could fix them.

In 1933, Kasturbai was arrested for addressing a meeting from which the British had banned her husband. She was jailed for only one month, while her fellow activists were jailed for three. She disputed this favourable treatment, and the British granted her wish; she was jailed for the full three months. This demonstrates that for Kasturbai, these protests were not about fame or heroics, nor just about her country, but also its people, who she regarded as true comrades. Immediately upon her release, she joined another demonstration and was sent back to prison for a further six months.

In 1939, Kasturbai was asked again to advocate for women, this time by a group in Rajkot who had been beaten by police. Her husband and his friends tried to dissuade her from getting involved – she was now seventy years of age, and Mohandas was unwell. In fact, he was saved only when his wife persuaded him to begin taking milk, pointing out that he had only sworn off cow's milk and not goat's – thus preventing his starvation. Despite warnings against intervention, Kasturbai refused to turn her back on the women. She was arrested for speaking out against the 'reign of terror' that the Rajkot rulers had released on peaceful protestors. She felt a strong emotional connection to these women, herself being descended from Rajkots, and thus would not abandon them in their hour of need. This episode is crucial in understanding Kasturbai as a dedicated freedom fighter in her own right – here she demonstrated that she was not just an obedient wife participating when instructed to by her husband. Rather, her first loyalty was to her fellow women, and to attaining justice for the people of her country.

In the following years, with her husband away, she travelled all over the north of India, speaking in favour of Hindu and Muslim unity, and urging people of all classes to take up the wearing of *khadi* and boycott foreign goods. In 1942, Kasturbai was arrested on her way to stand in for her husband in an address to the nation. As she was taken away, she shouted: 'The women of India have to prove their mettle. They should all join in this struggle irrespective of caste or creed. Truth and non-violence must be our watchwords'.[36] She was sentenced to a month's solitary confinement but was released when her health worsened. From behind bars, she continued to advise her husband and their followers. She persuaded Mohandas to free her fellow prisoners from their vow not to write letters home to loved ones (Gandhi himself having promised to cease writing letters given that he was banned from writing about politics), convincing them that their mothers would worry and deserved to know that their children were alive and well. This reminds us that while she was a spirited activist, she was also a loving mother and cared for her followers as people and not merely as soldiers in the fight.

As Kasturbai's health increasingly deteriorated, British physicians prescribed life-saving penicillin. However, her husband refused the prescription on the principle that it was foreign medicine. He claimed that it was Kasturbai herself who refused the treatment, entrusting herself wholly to God – however, all witnesses attest that it was Mohandas who gave the order to cease medication. Consequently, Kasturbai suffered two heart attacks and became bedridden in constant pain. Her husband remained always at her side and refused to leave even to attend to political emergencies. He asked that she be allowed to see a traditional doctor, to which the British eventually agreed, although they refused to release her on medical grounds. While the treatment seemed to initially improve her condition she soon relapsed. This time, she did not have the strength to fight, and she died in prison at Pune on 22 February 1944 aged seventy-four. It is tragic to think that had she not been denied treatment by her husband she may have lived to see her dream of Indian independence fulfilled.

The British forbade Kasturbai a public funeral, fearing it would incite a riot. Instead she had a private cremation in which prayers from Hindu, Christian and Muslim communities were heard alongside tributes from her followers. She was described in a heartfelt eulogy by S.C. Bose as a martyr for the cause and mother of the Indian people – years before her husband was described as the nation's father. Bose used the overwhelming public grief at her loss to rally the people against the British for revenge, arguing that only repulsion of their rule could avenge Kasturbai's death (which he viewed as a murder at British hands).

Mohandas was devastated by his wife's death and established The Kasturbai Gandhi National Memorial Trust Fund dedicated to helping women and children in rural India as Kasturbai had tried to do throughout her life. Today, her birthday is marked by National Safe Motherhood Day in India, so that her dedication to women, especially mothers, lives on. She continues to be remembered as the dutiful wife of the great Mahatma Gandhi (an honorific title which his wife never received), and much is made of their supposedly equal and loving partnership. However, she deserves to be remembered as more than just a devoted wife and mother (although she was undoubtedly both).

Unfortunately, Kasturbai remained largely illiterate for her entire life, so almost all that we know of her comes from the stories of others, primarily her husband. Kasturbai repeatedly demonstrated that she was just as dedicated to the cause of Indian freedom as her husband, and often directly disobeyed him in her activism. In fact, many of her greatest moments came when her husband was absent. Gandhi himself acknowledged that all her political activism was undertaken of her own volition. While the suffering she endured at British hands should not be understated, neither should the pain that her own husband inflicted upon her and the hardships that she endured for his sake. Although her marriage should not define her, her story is important to complicate the enduring image of Gandhi as a peace-loving saint who did nothing but empower women. That women wrote to her, and not her husband, for help speaks to the respect that she enjoyed in her own right. Kasturbai translated the nationalists' ideology into more relatable and palatable language than her husband, who often got lost in philosophical debates which meant little to the common people. Kasturbai was described as the invisible string which held the entire movement together. She deserves to be visible once and for all. Kasturbai's great-grandson, Tushar Gandhi, has written of his dismay that his grandmother's story has faded into the shadow of her husband, lamenting that: 'We have all collectively neglected Ba and decided that she needs to be kept in the background'.[37] Strange that this should have become the case when Mohandas himself stated she was above him in all things. It is time that we put her back in the spotlight and remember her not as Gandhi's subservient wife, but as his guru.

Manu Gandhi (1927–1969)

Another Gandhi who is forgotten in Mohandas' shadow – perhaps even more so because she represents one of the darker aspects of Gandhi's legacy – is his grand-niece, Manu. However, Manu wrote herself into history by keeping a diary of her life with the Gandhis, right up until Mohandas' assassination in 1948. Yet, the few sources that do mention her refer to her as 'Gandhi's walking stick', as she was dubbed during his life, or – as one article remembers her - 'a lonely spinster'.[38]

Mridula (more commonly known as Manu or Manuben) Gandhi was born in 1927. She was the youngest daughter of Mohandas Gandhi's nephew. When Manu's mother passed away when she was twelve, Mohandas and Kasturbai agreed to raise her and she came to regard them as her mother (Ba) and father (Bapuji). Despite barely having reached her teens, Manu decided the time had come for her to join the movement when, at daybreak on 9 August 1942, Mohandas was arrested and taken to the Aga Khan Palace in Poona with several members of his household. She described the day as such:

'It was decided that we, the women, were to join the struggle. I jumped with joy. There were three or four other girls of my age … who were also very eager to go to the prison … Since all the women were about to proceed to prison, men realized that they would have to roll rotis and for this reason they took over the kitchen work. They did not know how … We offered to teach them, but why should the proud men learn from us?...

'Many told me that I looked much younger in a frock and hence would not be arrested. That day I wore a saree for the first time. I was fourteen years of age … seven of us including a Muslim woman set out for Wardha … we made speeches and shouted slogans. A motor van came. There were about 40 policemen in it. They made loud noises of the petrol motor, the louder the noise the greater our energy. They made the noise so that people would not be able to hear our speeches. To harass them people would enter narrow lanes, they would be forced to come out of the police van and follow after us'.[39]

In order to allow the crowds to safely support them, the protestors asked a wedding band to follow them in their procession because then they could not be beaten as protestors but could claim they were marching as part of a wedding procession and were thus protected from the police.

The women were eventually arrested and taken to Wadha jail before being moved to Nagpur in September. Manu wrote extensively about her experiences in jail, discussing how she could not eat the food she was given without vomiting, how she lay awake with a fever among over a hundred women who were crammed into tiny cells with no sanitation facilities. She also tells how she was only permitted to wash her sari when the warden made an exception for her on account of her tender age and her relation to Gandhi. However, despite these conditions, which must have been exceptionally hard for such a young girl, her accounts of this time are relatively cheery, discussing how women of all ages kept a sense of comaraderie by spinning, singing nationalist songs in a show in defiance, and playing games in a spirit of childlike celebration. The matron assigned to watch over the women, Manu reveals, was a secret Gandhian herself and because she was illiterate, Manu shared with her Gandhi's teachings and lifestyle, showing that Manu was not merely a follower of Gandhi's message, but an active apostle of it.

The only time that Manu recalls feeling any anguish in jail was when she learned that her beloved Bapuji had begun a hunger strike. She recalls that it had been started because the British had molested women in a reign of terror in Chimur. Manu resolved to perform her own fast in solidarity. The British warned her that she would be force-fed if she followed through on her threat, but she was not afraid and refused all food and water for three days, a remarkable feat for a teenage girl. This inspired her fellow inmates and the women fasted in cycles, so that in twenty-one days, forty-two women fasted. When not fasting, they took vows of silence, and did spinning relays. They only relented when Gandhi finally gave up his own hunger strike – for which he has received lasting acclaim while the women received little thanks for their discipline.

In February 1943, reports emerged that Kasturbai had suffered a massive heart attack and that her husband's health was also ailing. A British guard informed Manu that she would be allowed to join her family on account of her high regard. During the transfer, she showed her deep compassion when, after speaking to a follower while her elderly British guards slept, she became anxious that she had gotten them in trouble and begged her follower not to tell the papers that he had spoken with her. Eventually, after nine months in jail, Manu was reunited with her beloved guardians when she was moved to the Aga Palace to serve as a nursemaid to her aunt.

It was at Poona that Manu's first diary entry was recorded on 11 April 1943. From her diary, we learn that Manu's entire life, from the moment she woke up at five o'clock in the morning for prayers to when she went to bed in the evening was dedicated to caring for her Aunt Kasturbai. She wrote of her daily interactions with other female companions of Gandhi and of her lessons in Hindu philosophy. From her writings, it is clear that the approval of her great-aunt and uncle were Manu's primary concerns and that – despite her self-confessed struggles with some of the more regimented aspects of her life such as the early starts – she was happy to be in their service. For example, on one occasion she recalls her dismay at sleeping through her aunt's cries of pain and makes a concerted effort to wake up during the night to tend to her, showing her complete devotion. Although she wrote of her grief at her real mother's death, and was in frequent contact with her natal family, she writes of how Kasturbai helped to heal her aching heart by acting as her surrogate mother.

It is easy to forget how young Manu was during this stage of her life and how difficult it would be for many teenagers to willingly submit to such a restricted existence of subservience and austerity. Thus, we see in Manu not just a deeply compassionate and caring young woman, but also a remarkably strong one who was wise and disciplined beyond her years. She relished the opportunity to be a small part of this movement. When Gandhi suggested that she be 'released' from her duties, she was horrified and worried endlessly that they did not understand her devotion or were not pleased with her work. She wrote of how much she enjoyed being in their service, even during imprisonment, and how grateful she was to be able to play such a role in the movement.

Given the clear bond between them then, we can only imagine the grief that Manu felt when Kasturbai passed away in 1944, thus condemning Manu to send a second mother to the funeral pyre. She recorded her heartbreak in her diary, as well as her gratitude for all Kasturbai had done for her and the nation. After Kasturbai's death, Mohandas begged that Manu be allowed to stay with him and resolved to further Manu's education now that she was released from the responsibilities of nursing her aunt. Together they read the Hindu scriptures, and he instructed her in geometry and grammar until they were released from prison. Interestingly, Manu records in her diary that following Kasturbai's death, Mohandas took over the maternal role in her life, fulfilling every need that a mother would have traditionally provided. Such a statement may seem strange to modern readers, but it is clear to see why Manu so craved someone to fill the mother-shaped hole in her life and how she understood this not as a gender role but rather a nurturing and caregiving role which her great-uncle clearly assumed. However, in his time, Gandhi with his fragile frame and peaceful ideologies was also criticized for being effeminate by those who favoured a more masculine, military style of nationalism and by agents of an empire which equated masculinity with violence and dominance. Therefore, Manu's statement could also be seen to paint this stereotype of Gandhi in a more positive light and portray it as a strength rather than a weakness. However, it is also an opening into a more controversial aspect of Gandhi and Manu's relationship, and one which has haunted Gandhi's legacy ever since; Gandhi's decision to sleep in the same bed as Manu.

In late 1946, the seventy-seven-year-old Gandhi announced that he intended to sleep in the same bed as young naked women to 'test' and 'prove' his celibacy, on which his entire ideology rested. Manu was not the only young woman to participate in this experiment – his other great-niece, Abha, as well as young women beyond his family circle also acted as bedfellows for him during this time. When his son expressed disgust at Gandhi's request for Manu to sleep with him, Gandhi responded: 'Do not let the fact of Manu sleeping with me perturb you. I believe that it is God who has prompted me to take that step'.[40] Elsewhere, however, he told an acquaintance that the experiment was designed to test Manu's claim to be asexual and celibate, devoid of lust. Supposedly, when a man proposed marriage to Manu – a proposal which she could not accept if she was truly to be regarded as a *satyagrahi*, completely devoid of sexual feeling – Gandhi demanded that she prove her 'purity' by agreeing to sleep naked next to him. While this would explain why Manu only partook in the experiment for a short time, withdrawing once she had proven herself, it seems a weak explanation given that she was not the only one subjected to this experiment. Even if this explanation were true, it reeks of misogyny and a particularly Hindu brand of misogyny which regards all women as powerless to their overwhelming sexual desire which can only be controlled by the strict handling by men (as exemplified by the Goddess Kali who destroys the universe until her husband stops her). It is also extreme arrogance on Gandhi's part to presume that if she could resist him – not only a man fifty years her senior but also one to whom she was closely related – then she could resist any man.

Much is made of the fact that Manu fully consented to this experiment, stating that it was as harmless as a young girl sharing a bed with her mother – perhaps another reason for her emphasizing the maternal role which Gandhi played in her life. It is also said that the pair slept soundly in a totally chaste and peaceful night, supposedly proving the innocence of the experiment. However, she later revoked her consent for this experiment, as did several other of the participants. We do not know why, and it is important that we do not try to fill in the gaps with speculation. As soon as Manu withdrew her consent, Gandhi ceased the experiment and – as far as we know – she was never forced into the arrangement again. However, the fact remains that regardless of how Manu may have viewed their relationship, there is something highly questionable about a grown man asking a young naked woman to sleep beside him, especially when that woman is a blood relative. No mention is made of what would have happened to these girls had Gandhi's experiment failed and he had proved unable to resist his lust – would the girls have been allowed to rebuke his advances? Kamala Nehru, someone who was well-acquainted with Mohandas, said of him in a letter to her husband: 'There is no one else like Gandhi in the world but as regards women's rights he is no better than other men'.[41] This casts doubt over the view that everyone who knew the couple failed to see this incident as anything but innocent – and shows that women who were perhaps older, and less naive to the ways of men than Manu, had legitimate cause for concern regarding her involvement. Whatever we think of Gandhi's intentions, Manu was just twenty years old when this episode took place, so regardless of the motivations behind it, it must have had a lasting impact on her.

However, the pair retained a deep bond for the rest of their lives. In fact, following Kasturbai's death, Gandhi and Manu became inseparable. As Gandhi aged, he began to lean – literally and metaphorically – on his great-nieces wherever he went (hence their nicknames as walking sticks). In May 1947, Gandhi wrote to Manu discussing his death in a strange foreshadowing:

'But if I should die of lingering illness, it would be your duty to proclaim to the whole world that I was not a man of God but an impostor and a fraud. If you fail in that duty I shall feel unhappy wherever I am. But if I die taking God's name with my last breath, it will be a sign that I was what I strove for and claimed to be'.[42]

Some have taken his confession as a sign of something sinister between the two, however others have interpreted it as the humble ponderings of a frail old man. Eerily, his wish that he should die with God's name on his lips would soon come true.

On the evening of 30 January 1948, the seventy-eight-year-old Gandhi was taking an evening walk in Delhi, leaning as usual on Manu and Abha. When Gandhi stepped onto the prayer platform, a sinister figure in khaki separated from the crowd. He pushed Manu aside and shot Gandhi three times in the chest. As Gandhi had wished, he whispered the name of the God Ram, and collapsed. Manu, his grand-niece, devoted follower, and confidante, cradled him as he died. As she had been pushed out of the way by his murderer, she had dropped the diary in which she had chronicled her leader's last years. She would never write in this diary again. Instead, she spent the rest of her life eulogizing the life of her adopted parent and continued sharing his story and teachings until her death in 1969 at the age of forty-two.

The twelve volumes of her diaries were preserved in India's national archives, and only recently has the first been published in English. It is remarkable that someone who wrote a narrative of a life so closely intertwined with the life (and death) of arguably the most famous man in modern history, should have been completely forgotten until now. Yet her diaries preserve her resilient, kind, devoted, fiery spirit, and provide one of the most intimate looks at the inner workings of the Indian nationalist movement and its most influential figures.

Sushila Nayyar (1914–2001)

Another woman who shared Gandhi's achievements (and his bed) but has lived in his shadow ever since was his personal physician, Sushila Nayyar. Sushila was born on 26 December 1914 in Kunjah (today in Pakistan). She had met Gandhi several times as a child when her brother was his personal secretary, and thus she grew up believing in Gandhian philosophy. She later wrote that she saw Gandhi as a paternal figure after losing her father when she was four. After school, she moved to Delhi to study medicine, all the while keeping regular contact with the Gandhis. In 1939, she followed her brother to Gandhi's *ashram* at Sevagram where she was welcomed into the Gandhis' inner circle. She immediately volunteered her medical expertise when a cholera outbreak erupted in Wardha and was credited with almost single-handedly managing the epidemic. Gandhi was so impressed by her capability and strength during this time that he asked her to be his personal physician, believing there was no one in the land he could trust more with his wellbeing – a great honour given his obsession with his health.

When the Quit India Movement was launched in 1942, Sushila was arrested and placed in prison alongside Gandhi and his family at the Aga Khan Palace. Upon her release in 1944, she established a small pharmacy at Sevagram, but soon the demand for her services became so large that it was deemed to impeach on the peace of the *ashram*, and she was forced to relocate her dispensary to a guesthouse in Wardha. In 1945, this enterprise officially became the Kasturba Hospital, named after Sushila's hero, Kasturbai. Incidentally, this hospital has since been renamed the Mahatma Gandhi Institute of Medical Sciences – another example of how history has erased the significance of women in the nationalist movement to present Mohandas Gandhi as the one and only hero of the era. During this time, many attempts were made on Gandhi's life and given her physical proximity to him at all times, Sushila was often called upon to testify in the trials of these attempted murders. On one occasion, she testified regarding an incident in Panchgani in 1944 when Nathuram Godse had attempted to stab Gandhi with a dagger. Four years later Godse achieved his goal and successfully assassinated Gandhi. Sushila's intimacy with Gandhi also led to her taking part in his controversial celibacy tests, as previously discussed.

Her proximity to Gandhi and his wife enabled Sushila to become one of their most prolific biographers, writing several works on both Gandhis from 1944 until her death. Her biography of Mohandas alone runs to nine volumes. She also wrote treatises relating to her work, particularly on women's reproductive rights. Sushila championed Gandhi's campaign for prohibition, but not out of a sense of moral superiority. Rather her medical and social work had opened her eyes to the plight of impoverished women whose lives were blighted by an epidemic of alcoholism among their husbands. Having witnessed the abuse that they suffered as a result, and the economic toll of alcoholism on families who were already struggling, she believed that a complete ban on alcohol would drastically help India's most vulnerable communities. Her concern for women's rights was also seen in her emphatic campaigning for birth control and family planning support, which she saw as essential to the empowerment of poor women who could not – and should not be forced to – care for large families which further contributed to the physical and economic burdens placed on women.

When her beloved Gandhi was assassinated in 1948, Sushila left India and headed to America where she graduated with a further two degrees in public health. She returned to India in 1950 to establish a tuberculosis hospital in Faridabad, the refugee resettlement colony established by Kamaladevi Chattopadhyay (whose story we will hear later). Sushila also established a leprosy sanitorium in Gandhi's memory. However, she had not completely abandoned her political leanings. In 1952, she was elected to the Legislative Assembly of Delhi, and until 1955 served as Health Minister in Nehru's new government. She then served as speaker of the Delhi Vidhan Sabha (as the State Assembly had been renamed) for a year before being elected to the Lok Sabha as a member for the Jhansi Constituency for the next fourteen years. From 1962–1967 she served as Union Health Minister again. However, she disagreed with Indira Gandhi, India's first female prime minister, and joined the Janata Party which successfully ousted Gandhi from power. Having finally had enough of the political drama, she retired from politics and dedicated the remainder of her career to her medical pursuits at the Mahatma Gandhi Institute of Medical Sciences. After a lifetime of service to her country and its people, Sushila suffered a heart attack and passed away on 3 January 2001 at the age of eighty-seven.

Sushila's life was remarkable for many reasons, one of them being that she never married and yet managed to have a life-long successful career, which was seen as virtually impossible for a single woman at the time. She rebutted any conventions which looked down on elite women getting involved with the messy work of healthcare and threw herself wholeheartedly into every aspect of medicine, never afraid to get her hands dirty no matter how grim the situation. Her writings provide a legacy of what Sushila really stood for but also demonstrate her complete devotion to the Gandhis and their struggle. While she loved and admired Gandhi as a person, Sushila emphatically endorsed his ideology regarding celibacy and physical labour as being key to disciplining both body and soul. Throughout her life, she was extremely disciplined in everything she did – a trait which also made her critical of those whom she saw as lax in their routines or work ethic. Thus, the only complaint anyone had of her was that she expected everyone to be as self-sacrificing and embrace a life of public service in the same all-encompassing way that she had, which was not always possible, even for the most dedicated nationalists and social workers. Nonetheless, her many pursuits show that she had a deep commitment to the rights of women, and to caring for the poorest and most downtrodden of India's communities. She used her privilege to help uplift women from dire circumstances through education, healthcare, and campaigns to address social issues which directly affected women.

Avantika Bai Gokhale (1882–1949)

Many of the women Gandhi associated with throughout his life went on to become his biographers. Another was Avantika Bai Gokhale. She wrote his biography, and was a constant companion throughout his struggles, but again her name has been lost to history – unlike her male counterpart Gopal Krishna Gokhale.

Avantika was born to Brahmin parents in Tasgaon and lived in Indore. She was a child bride, married at only nine to Baban Gokhale. Her husband arranged for her to be educated but spent much of his time overseas. Avantika took charge of her own education and achieved a first-class degree in midwifery in 1901. When her husband lost two of his fingers in an accident and was unable to work, she became the primary breadwinner of the family and thus the couple decided that they could not afford to have children. However, Avantika later adopted a daughter who she trained as a nurse and who worked alongside her. Avantika became a renowned midwife, and in 1912 she joined the Social Service League. A year later, she accompanied the Raja of Ichalkaranji to London to learn the practices of London midwives. During this trip, she met prominent Indian nationalists who introduced her to the world of nationalism for the first time.

On returning to India, Avantika was introduced to Gandhi and in 1916 she visited him at his Sabarmati Ashrma, where he stayed from 1917 to 1930. She adopted the Gandhian principle of wearing only *khadi*, which she upheld throughout her life. Having spent close time with Gandhi, she went on to write his biography in Marathi which was published in 1918. She remained close to him throughout her life.

Her most prominent nationalist effort was her participation in the Salt Satyagraha of 1930. She was one of the first women to join Gandhi in these marches, and she organized many public salt-making events in Bombay. Avantika branded their work the 'salt of freedom'. On 26 October 1930, Avantika joined other female freedom fighters in raising the Indian flag, against police orders, at the Azad Maidan. This stunt cost her a year in prison. She also joined her fellow activists in helping to form the DSS. This organization brought together women who were willing to picket foreign goods stores. Krishnabai's sister, Indirabai, distributed propaganda for the organization. The DSS began with arranging daily meetings of women to spin and discuss nationalist politics. When women were called upon to directly join the Swadeshi movement, DSS members went door to door preaching the message, selling *khadi*, and exhibiting their wares. Led by Krishnabai, they then went on to join their male comrades in picketing foreign clothes shops, an act that was considered among the most dangerous forms of protest and thus one which women had until now been reluctant to engage in. DSS members, including Krishnabai, stopped customers as they entered shops and urged them not to further India's oppression by opting for foreign rather than homemade goods. Like many others, Avantika partnered her nationalist work with an interest in women's rights. In 1918, she began the Hind Mahila Samaj, through which she taught women to sew and embroider. She also worked for the Bombay Municipal Corporation from 1926, an organization which worked to improve the conditions of young girls living in slums.

Renuka Ray (1904–1997)

A woman whose autobiography reveals much about the nationalist movement from the very centre is Renuka Ray, another of Gandhi's close companions. When Renuka Mukherjee was born in 1904, she was welcomed by her progressive middle-class family, full on both sides of men and women who considered themselves feminists and nationalists. Her parents paid little regard to caste or religious prejudices and condemned patriarchal customs regarding dowries and widowhood – views which Renuka attributed to their belonging to the Brahmo Samaj. She claimed to have been completely unaware that social divisions ever existed until she was much older. In 1911, the family moved to England, where she was surprised to find the English were welcoming and congenial, unlike the British living in India who Renuka found arrogant and unfriendly. On returning to India, Renuka experienced racism for the first time from her white classmates. This coincided with her awakening to the division within India, and the role that Britain played in fostering it. She was filled with righteous rage at the British's condescending and contemptuous attitude which, she noted, even the most subservient of Indians resented. Respectful Brits, she found, were grossly outnumbered and thus most Indians came into contact only with the those who were cruel, haughty, and prejudiced.

In 1920, Renuka and her friend, Lalita, became the first two girls in Calcutta to leave university to join the non-cooperation movement. The girls were desperate to become Gandhi's disciples, equating this with serving the nation, although their admiration for Bengali revolutionaries somewhat challenged their dedication to Gandhi's non-violent ideology. Renuka was permitted to attend the 1920 INC session, one of the few women to attend despite being just sixteen. Having refused to return to university, the girls were taught Hindi and spinning by Gandhi himself. Their daily routine included going door-to-door trying to collect funds and enlist women to the cause. Calcutta was a fairly conservative city, and they struggled to get access to many women who observed purdah. However, those they did meet were receptive and often donated their jewellery if they had no access to cash.

Renuka and her friends succeeded in recruiting enough women to host a women's nationalist meeting at which Gandhi could address the crowd. This was a huge achievement as it marked the first time that such large numbers of women had forgone the seclusion of purdah to attend a political meeting. Gandhi told the women gathered that he expected more of them than their male counterparts because history had taught women how to suffer in silence and restrict their emotions. Although he went on to blame mothers for spoiling their sons, he urged women to let go of patriarchal customs which had kept them from political engagement and to ensure the good behaviour of their men. Despite the patronizing tone which placed the onus on women to control men, the meeting concluded with a mountain of jewellery being laid at Gandhi's feet as donations to the cause. Renuka called this the start of a nationwide revolution through which rural and secluded women, that previous generations of social reformers had failed to reach, began to mobilize and act to directly improve their circumstances.

Having found her calling living the austere but fulfilling life of a *satyagrahi*, Renuka was devastated when she was informed that her father and Gandhi had decided that despite her pleas, she was to be sent to England to continue her education because juvenile and uneducated girls were of no use to the movement. Seventeen-year-old Renuka arrived in London in August 1921 to study at the London School of Economics. Despite her initial reluctance, she greatly enjoyed her studies – although she recalled her indignation at some lectures which glorified the British empire. She joined and began to lecture for the League Against Imperialism, through which she met nationalist S.C. Bose who introduced her to her heroes among the Bengali revolutionaries. Her cousin attempted to recruit her into the IRA, and even went so far as to provide her with a gun so she could learn to shoot. However, she decided against enlisting because she knew that her family, and worse, Gandhi, would not approve.

While at university, Renuka fell in love with fellow nationalist Satyen

Ray. When he proposed, she was hesitant as she feared that marriage would restrict her political freedom, but Satyen promised that she would maintain her independence, and the two were engaged. When they returned to India, Gandhi warned Satyen that Renuka's top priority would always be her country. Satyen replied that he knew that all too well and that they would work through any issues her politics presented with perseverance and bravery. Having received everyone's blessings, Renuka and Satyen were married on 26 October 1925.

After their marriage, Renuka accompanied Satyen on his Indian Civil Service postings which exposed her to rural India for the first time. Although she did not speak the local languages, she was able to observe the problems facing the rural and tribal communities. British industrialization had robbed these areas of their traditional trades by outpricing them and heavily taxing indigenous goods. This rampant abuse by the British, Renuka observed, had resulted in an unemployed and landless generation. Through social work based on Gandhian ideals of self-sufficiency, she focused primarily on improving women's lives through addressing matters such as maternal healthcare, education, and childcare for local women. As she later recalled their goal was to use the momentum of the freedom struggle to bring around a total social reform of women's rights.

Since her return to India, Renuka had been a member of the AIWC and was made its president in 1932, organizing many successful marches and protests. In the 1940s, Renuka was offered the position of woman representative for the Central Assembly but was unwilling to work alongside the British. Yet, with all other potential candidates imprisoned, she reluctantly accepted in February 1943. However, the AIWC made sure to include a caveat stating that she could not be forced into supporting the government on any position. In her maiden speech, Renuka asserted that full equality would not be possible until women were represented, in a government led by the Indian people. The British men present stormed out and many formally denounced her. However, her speech made national headlines and INC leaders wrote to her from jail congratulating her on her bravery. Renuka recalled that she found it difficult to find her voice in that assembly owing to its 'overwhelmingly masculine' atmosphere.[43] However, she soon got over her timidity, and during the Second World War she successfully shamed the British government into reinstating a ban on women working in underground mines. She caused further upset when she refused to support the British budget, despite their threats and bribes towards her and her husband. Her refusal had no effect because the Viceroy could pass the budget regardless, but he saw her actions as a humiliating defiance. She was not re-nominated for the assembly but considered her term a success for rallying public opinion against the colonizers and in proving her own integrity.

On one occasion, Renuka was accused of sedition for refusing police access to an all-women's meeting, telling them that their presence was inappropriate for the women observing purdah. They only backed down when Renuka's husband stepped in. While Renuka thanked Gandhi for publicizing the fight for women's rights, she also stressed that women themselves must be credited for their huge contribution to the nationalist movement, not only through direct activism on the streets but also through influencing their husbands, brothers, and sons within the home towards the freedom struggle. Renuka firmly believed that unlike with other minorities, the British had failed to cause division among women because, unlike men, all women were united by their shared oppression. She explained that no one wished to turn women into men, but rather to let women realize their full potential for the benefit of the entire nation.

While not arrested during the Quit India movement – despite being frequently interrogated and harassed – she contributed to the movement by distributing funds among the families of incarcerated freedom fighters, and by helping to harbour and act as messenger for those in hiding. Renuka drew attention to the women among the many unarmed protestors who were shot dead by British police for protesting Gandhi's imprisonment. In Calcutta alone, she witnessed almost a thousand people shot dead by police.

However, the event which truly hardened Renuka's heart against the

British was the famine of 1939 which she regarded as one of the deepest stains on the British Empire. It was, she said, outrageous that Indian troops were dying in a war they had been forced to join while their families starved, and their country was stripped of its resources on Churchill's command. Soon after she joined the Central Assembly in 1943, she left Delhi to investigate the actual situation in Calcutta. She was horrified by what she saw, as the meagre AIWC resources were completely overwhelmed. Renuka returned to Delhi to inform people of the situation which was being drastically under-reported by the national media. When the reality of the disaster began to unfold, food collections were made but, criminally the government stopped it reaching East Bengal where it was most needed. Indian parties were not completely innocent in this situation, as Renuka discovered when she returned to Calcutta to question the Food Minister of the AIML as to why the shipments were not getting through. He suggested that the entire famine was a myth perpetuated to discredit the party and told her not to interfere. The British Governor of Bengal also refused to intervene. Both later conceded and sent meagre relief efforts in September 1943, but by then countless more had died. Renuka travelled to Midnapore where she saw ineffable scenes as emaciated people mobbed the train begging for food for their children.

Renuka believed that the famine was British revenge on the people for their support of the Quit India movement. She appealed for donations both nationally and abroad and established orphanages for those whose families had perished. Years later, she could not shake the haunting scene of seeing the roads lined with corpses, with those who clung to life looking just as skeletal. By this point, twenty million people were also succumbing to disease. INC leaders were powerless, having been jailed for demanding that the Allies send food to the worst-hit areas. The British had also unleashed a campaign of propaganda, fearing that this humanitarian crisis would damage the reputation of the Empire. They were right to be worried, as Renuka attested that the plight of Bengal proved the fallacy of Allied claims to be acting in the interests of freedom and democracy. As well as the war and the famine, Renuka also blamed the British policy of 'divide and rule' for the communal divisions within India. In her view, India's religious communities had lived together harmoniously for centuries. It was during the 1857 war, Renuka believed, that the British became aware of the danger posed by a united India and began actively working to divide its people. This began with blaming the 1857 uprising solely on Muslims, who resented being unduly punished compared to other communities. The British then switched and began showing preference for Muslims, disproportionately punishing Hindus for nationalist activities. When Hindus and Muslims asked to work together, the British made this difficult by implementing policies which fostered distinct religious communities, a policy which Renuka argued was the root cause of interreligious strife in India.

When these communal tensions escalated to interreligious riots in Calcutta, Renuka was part of the Relief and Rehabilitation Committee. She and her husband worked relentlessly to provide relief despite having no police protection or support from a government who were content to leave bodies rotting in the streets. She helped organize women volunteers from the AIWC. She accompanied Gandhi to one of the worst-affected areas, Noakhali, where girls had fled into hiding after being raped, leaving the villages filled with nothing but corpses. Her job was to coax women out of hiding, assuring them that they were now safe. Renuka and her female comrades were often challenged by armed mobs but were protected by Gandhi's presence. With him, they walked from village to village, singing nationalist songs and establishing camps to provide psychological and physical treatment to the victims of the riots.

One day, their supply jeep crashed on a road that had been destroyed in the fighting. As she plummeted down the cliff, her last thought was that she would not live to see India's emancipation, proving that India's freedom was still her most cherished dream. Thankfully, Renuka was rescued but spent three months recuperating in a cast, traumatized by nightmares of the crash, and was never again fit to return to her relief efforts as she could not walk the long distances required.

Aside from the obvious human tragedy of these riots, Renuka was dismayed by the political implications; now the British could use the chaos of Partition to prove that South Asians could indeed not govern themselves peacefully, retrospectively justifying the centuries of British interference. While she cast blame on political leaders who refused to heed Gandhi's warnings about the disastrous consequences of Partition, she realized the circumstances were impossible. She called the creation of Pakistan 'the final blow of the British' and mourned the mutilation of her beloved India. The public, she recalled, were reconciled to Partition as they believed their leaders' assurances that this was the only way to rid themselves of the British and restore harmony between religious communities, for even the leaders could not have imagined the barbarity to come.

Renuka's autobiography ends with a condemnation of how far India had strayed from Gandhi's ideals following independence. However, she again lays the blame for this at the feet of the British who knew that the more damage they left behind, the less threat these new countries would pose to them and Western world order. Renuka lamented that the years since independence were a testament to the immense challenge India and Pakistan have faced in restoring peace and prosperity in their lands in the wake of Partition. However, she was unwaveringly optimistic that future generations would be able to reunite their country, and it was with this optimism that she took up the seat offered to her in the Constituent Assembly, determined to help bestow a sense of justice in the new nation she had indeed lived to see. She recalled her pride at seeing the national flag being hoisted for the first time and singing the new Indian national anthem which she saw as a memorial to all those who had lost their lives during the *satyagrahi* campaign for freedom. She was also happy to watch as Hansa Mehta, whose story we will hear presently, presented the Indian flag on behalf of all the women of India.

Renuka sat as a member of the Constituent Assembly of India from 1946–1947. In the first government of independent India, she was appointed as Minister of Relief & Rehabilitation from 1952–1957, which allowed her to continue her social work and do her best to reunite the warring communities of West Bengal. She served as a member of the Lok Sabha from 1957-1967, and in 1959 headed a committee on Social Welfare and Welfare of Backward Classes, which is popularly known as the Renuka Ray Committee in honour of her life-long dedication to *all* the people of India. She lived until she was ninety-three, having been awarded the Padma Bhushan, the third-highest civilian award, for services to her country.

Her autobiography, a seminal account of the nationalist movement, was published in 1982. It provides a crucial insight into the motivations and actions of its key figures, offers an explanation of some of the key grievances the nationalists had against the British, is a crucial eye-witness account of the humanitarian crises of the 1940s, and outlines the issues facing South Asian women in the years up to – and following – the nation's independence, as well as the movements to improve them. If this book were studied in schools with the same attention that 'heroes' of British imperialism such as Churchill have been, then a new generation would grow up with a much more balanced view of the circumstances that changed the world forever in 1947.

Sarojini Naidu (1879–1949)

Perhaps one of the few Indian women nationalists who has been somewhat remembered by history is Sarojini Naidu. Dubbed by Gandhi as the 'nightingale of India' for her beautiful poetry, Sarojini used her eloquence to champion women's rights, caste, and religious equality, and of course, the case for Indian home rule. Born Sarojini Chattopadhyay in Hyderabad on 13 February 1879, she grew up in current-day Bangladesh. Sarojini was the eldest of eight siblings, many of whom shared with their parents a passion for poetry and patriotism. Sarojini reportedly wrote her first poem – in Persian - aged just twelve. Having graduated top of her class, she went on to study at the University of Cambridge in 1885. Here she became aware of the women's suffrage movement which ignited the spark of activism within her. After touring Europe, she returned to Hyderabad in 1898. On her return, she married Govindaraju Naidu. By all accounts theirs was a long and happy marriage, and together they had five children who were strongly encouraged to join their mother in the nationalist movement.

From 1904 onwards, Sarojini became an increasingly prominent public speaker, giving lectures on everything from independence to women's rights. Sarojini was unconventional in that she wrote her poems in English and was greatly inspired by British Romantic poets – which was somewhat at odds with the contents of her works which denounced the British and their oppression of India – but maybe she just wanted the British to understand the critiques she levelled at them. Her first poetry collection, *The Golden Threshold*, was published in London in 1905. Her second, published in 1912, was the most explicitly nationalist of her works. In 1911, she was awarded a medal for her relief work during catastrophic floods, and she frequently addressed both INC and AIML meetings.

In 1914, Sarojini met Gandhi for the first time, and became a public supporter of him and of Kasturbai, who Sarojini held as the pinnacle of Indian womanhood. In 1915, she addressed the Hyderabad Ladies' War Relief Association where she recited one of her most famous poems, *The*

Gift of India, which condemned the British exploitation of Indian soldiers. In the same year, she gave her famous address calling on the INC to encourage Indian unity.

In 1917, she co-founded the Women's Indian Association (WIA) before returning to London with her friend, Annie Besant, to promote universal suffrage. She also attended the Madras Special Provincial Council where she spoke in support of the Lucknow Pact. A year later, she gave another speech in Bombay where she promised the 5,000 delegates that women's enfranchisement would not distract them from their traditional responsibilities or take power away from men, because while men and women had naturally different roles to play in society, it was mothers who could instil nationalism into the hearts of new generations. The speech – which concluded in the passing of the resolution for women's suffrage with a seventy-five per cent majority is emblematic of her lifelong efforts to reconcile her dedication to women's political engagement with upholding women's traditional roles and her belief in the fundamental differences between men and women.

Around this time, she formally joined Gandhi's *satyagraha* movement, but continued to travel and make powerful speeches at home and abroad. In the 1920s, Sarojini took centre stage in Gandhi's non-cooperation movement. In 1920, she publicly condemned the British administration in the Punjab for their deplorable conduct towards women following the Jallianwala Bagh massacre – a charge that Edwin Montagu, Secretary of State for India, vehemently denied. Sarojini replied with ample evidence of gross misconduct among British soldiers, taken from reports conducted by the INC, and she especially chastised the British for failing to respect the boundaries of purdah. The British did not know how to respond but reports of British brutality towards Indian women continued until and even after independence.

When the INC declared 6-13 April 1921 'Satyagraha Week', Sarojini was nominated president of the Rashtriya Stree Sangha (RSS), a new independent women's organization which by November had over a thousand members in Bombay alone. Its stated goal was emancipation of women and of India. In 1924, Sarojini represented the INC at its East African meeting, and a year later she was elected the INC's first Indian woman president. In 1927, she became a founding member of the AIWC.

In May 1930, Sarojini was elected leader of a raid on the Dharasana salt works. When Gandhi expressed fear for her safety, she replied: 'I am here not as a woman but as a General'.[44] The British were astounded to see a woman leading such seditious behaviour, and she was quickly released amid British confusion about how to treat a female prisoner. However, when she led a second raid on 21 May, they hardened their stance and jailed her for a year. Hundreds of women took to the streets in protest, one of the first instances of a visibly large-scale revolt against the British by Indian women.

When Gandhi himself was arrested on 6 April 1930, he appointed Sarojini as his successor. Between 1930 and 1932, three Round Table Conferences were held during which Indian and British politicians came together to discuss constitutional reform in India. Having boycotted the first in protest at Gandhi's arrest, Sarojini joined other INC representatives at the Second Round Table Conference in 1931 during which major changes were made to how the British operated in India, including the first discussion around India being given dominion status. A year later however, Sarojini herself was imprisoned again for her continued resistance to British occupation.

Throughout her life, Sarojini was especially passionate about women's right to education and constantly asserted that India would never be free until women were restored to their rights and uplifted by society. For Sarojini, women's rights superseded all other issues because the patriarchy is the one unchanging issue throughout place and time. Sarojini concluded that men – especially politicians such as Nehru - wanted Indian independence for their own gain and not for the betterment of society. Her worldview rested on the belief that women were the backbone of Indian civilization. The true glory of India's past, she frequently asserted, was the power and privilege it gave to women under both Hindu and Muslim rule, and all the damage that had befallen India – culminating in its domination by the British – was a direct result of the mistreatment and neglect of women and their rights. She also made much of the fact that women were the first teachers of men, and that since even the most illiterate of women are trusted with teaching their sons the basic necessities of life, they should be trusted with other duties too. Thus, one of Sarojini's great strengths came from using history to justify future progress, especially where women's rights were concerned.

While others – including Gandhi – were calling on women to join the nationalist movement alongside (and only with the permission of) their husbands, Sarojini placed the onus on India's men to prove that they were worthy of a woman's blind devotion and highlighted that men's efforts were in vain without the help of their women. Yet it is worth noting here that at an AIWC conference in 1930, Sarojini gave a famous speech in which she rejected the label of feminist because she saw no need for such a term in a country where, in her view, women were naturally equals to men in all walks of life. Therefore, one should be wary of assigning modern labels to a figure who did at times propagate gender roles which are slightly jarring to the twenty-first-century ear. For example, she repeatedly equated womanhood with motherhood, and even on occasion claimed that as a woman she could not comprehend politics. She was also not afraid to echo the cries of male nationalists that the greatest role a woman could play in the freedom struggle was merely to support her husband. However, her overarching ethos is arguably feminist, at least in the pure sense of celebrating the sisterhood of all women, a bond that no one can understand unless they have lived as a woman in this world. This shared experience made women the superior – and natural – nationalists, Sarojini concluded.

Perhaps unsurprisingly given her belief in defined gender stereotypes, another common theme in her writing is that Indian men have been emasculated by British rule. In justifying her involvement in politics, she scathingly replied that if men had stepped up and adequately defended their country, there would be no need for women to get involved. Sarojini's belief that India had allowed itself to become emasculated led her to lay most of the blame for colonial oppression not with the British but with the Indian people themselves. Given her belief that Indians were the cause of their own suffering, she said that only they can deliver themselves from it. She repeatedly offered herself in sacrifice for the nation and urged others to do the same.

Another key theme of Sarojini's ideology was the necessity for Hindu-Muslim unity in the fight for Indian freedom. Her views centred around three arguments: that Hindus and Muslims share the same history and same basic principles of faith, that both religions have something worthy to contribute to India, and that they both have a shared goal which can only be achieved by their unity. She rebuked the idea that Hindus and Muslims were different races, emphasising that both religions are based on a love of God and service to humanity. She devoted a lot of attention to praising the Muslim Mughal rulers for the assimilation that they fostered between Hindus and Muslims, stating that all the freedoms which Indians now sought to wrestle from the British were first bestowed upon them by the Mughals. This view is revolutionary even today when Hindu nationalists are working to erase Mughal history from Indian curriculums.

While some nationalists were (understandably) reluctant to concede that the British (and even Mughals) had brought any benefit to India, Sarojini was keen to emphasize that India's strength lay in its ability to pick and choose the best of foreign traditions while still maintaining the integrity of its own. While she was keen to stress that this did not mean submitting to being completely overruled by foreign systems, she believed that every religion had value to bring to the nation.

As well as dismissing religious differences, Sarojini was also highly critical of casteism, a surprising stance given her own dominant-caste birth. While eloquently justifying why the caste system had once had a place in Indian society, she condemned those who now used it as a source of antagonism which hindered India's progress. She also defended the rights of the rural and illiterate communities. Although English was her chosen medium, she acknowledged that the nationalist movement would always be limited unless it embraced and used the vernacular to recruit and educate the masses. This was a key insight, as most prominent Indian nationalists had been educated in Britain, or at least taught English, making the movement somewhat elitist and exclusionary to most Indians who could not read or understand English. Thus, while Sarojini herself was born into this elite society and benefitted from her own British education, she was not blind to this privilege and used it to further the cause among *all* Indians. While others based their patriotism on martial success or great ideological gestures, Sarojini believed that it was much simpler: equality and unity between every Indian regardless of gender, caste, class, or religion, without which India could never be free.

It is perhaps understandable, then, that Sarojini was frequently frustrated by the communal politics of her day, and with the politicians who benefited from it. Her speeches often disparaged the politicians (as well as the religious bigotry of the ordinary people) who stirred up religious discord and allowed man-made divisions to fester. Although she herself was politically active throughout her life, she advocated only politics that worked with and for the benefit of the people – not for personal gain or for the raising of one community against another. This is why Sarojini has been remembered as a *satyagrahi* and poet rather than a politician – she saw politics as a necessary evil which had more power to corrupt than to heal society and rather looked to religion and social work as better unifying factors than politics to heal her fractured nation.

Sarojini's nationalism was not based on irrational hatred of the British, personal political ambition, or a result of her own dire oppression. Rather, it was founded on a belief that freedom was a right which the British had no right to deny. In 1935, the British passed the India Act which promised to protect the interests of Indian minorities and to guarantee them the vote. However, women were not included in any such provisions. This was seen as a great betrayal by female nationalists, and there was particular anger that purdah had been used to justify the exclusion of women. Sarojini issued a furious statement to the British asking why women in purdah – who were themselves a minority within a minority – were not protected with other

Indian minorities – the conclusion being that only men were protected by the British and that women were irrelevant to the colonial government. She told the Joint Select Committee that only a tiny portion of upper-class women observed purdah but that even then, she had never seen purdah stop a woman doing anything they desired. In 1942, Sarojini was again sent to prison for two years for participating in the Quit India Movement.

Sarojini's life's work attests to her sincere belief in the brotherhood and equality of all India's faiths and communities, and seeing them literally massacre each other when India finally became independent in 1947 must have shattered her entire worldview. Her speeches from much earlier in the century seem to have even more pertinence when considered in the legacy of the carnage of Partition:

'When floods ... famines ... and plagues come, do not all of us suffer equally? What has the corpse of a Hindu or a Mussalman done not to deserve the same sense of honour from each of us who are equally created by God and who have been equally subject to mortality'.[45]

Following independence, she was appointed the governor of the United Provinces (now Uttar Pradesh), becoming India's first woman governor. Having ignored doctor's advice to retire, she held the post until she died of cardiac arrest on 2 March 1949, aged seventy.

Perhaps the thing that separated Sarojini most from her peers – both male and female – was the onus that she placed on Indians themselves to take responsibility for their deliverance and overcome the divisions which they had allowed the British to exploit. Sarojini had all the makings of such prejudices, and yet her writings reveal a consistent dedication to asserting the equality of all Indians regardless of caste, gender, religion, class, or education. In 1903, she declared that her caste and religion did not matter, only her solidarity with all Indians against oppression of all kinds.

Sarojini had last published a book of poems in 1917, a collection called *The Broken Wing*. Following her death, her daughter edited and compiled a complete collection called *The Feather of the Dawn* which was published in 1961. During Sarojini's lifetime, her speeches were also collated into

The Speeches and Writings of Sarojini Naidu (1918), which has been in print ever since and is one of the best odes to sisterhood among women and brotherhood among religions ever published. While her body may have perished in 1949, Sarojini's writing and speeches survive as a testament to the progressive views that she held and advocated and tell us everything we need to know about why she deserves her exalted place in India's history. She advocated many of the same principles and practical measures that Gandhi has long been praised for – and in many cases doing so more eloquently and humbly – and yet she has achieved nothing like his level of fame despite having never been plagued by the controversies which have followed Gandhi to the grave. If Sarojini had been born a man, it is likely she would be as much a household name as Gandhi and Jinnah are today. However, had she not been born a woman, she would likely have not possessed the lucid insights into the intricacies of womanhood and the complexities of nation-building which made her one of the greatest activists of history.

Dame Amrit Kaur (1887–1964)

While Mohandas Gandhi became renowned for his eloquent writings and speeches, few know the name of his private secretary, Dame Rajkumari Bibiji Amrit Kaur, who worked alongside him for an incredible sixteen years and most likely helped him pen some of his most poignant correspondence. Amrit Kaur, as she was most widely known, was born on 2 February 1887 in Lucknow. Her father, Raja Sir Harnam Singh Ahluwalia, was born into the ruling family of Kapurthala, but left the land after a succession dispute. He was converted to Christianity by a Bengali missionary, whose daughter, Priscilla, he later married. Amrit was the youngest – and only girl – of their ten children.

Amrit was sent to Dorset, England, to be educated at a Christian school, and then completed a degree at the University of Oxford, returning to India in 1918 and immediately throwing herself into the freedom struggle. She had grown up around nationalist leader Gopal Krishna Gokhale, a close friend of the family. Through Gokhale, Amrit was introduced to the teachings of Gandhi, whom she first met in 1919. She was soon appointed as his private secretary, a post she held for the next sixteen years. The Jallianwala Bagh massacre was the catalyst for her formally joining the INC and vowing to incorporate her desired social reforms in her fight for Indian independence.

In 1927, Amrit co-founded the AIWC. The organization grew into a national one which achieved many reforms in social welfare and established many schools and other educational establishments exclusively run by and for women. Amrit was appointed its secretary in 1930 and its president three years later. In 1930, she was at Gandhi's side as he led the Dandi March. It took the British authorities three years to finally catch and imprison Amrit for participating in this march. She was released in 1934 and went to live at Gandhi's *ashram* where she gladly adopted the prescribed life of asceticism, despite her royal roots.

In 1937, Amrit was imprisoned again for sedition, this time for attending a meeting in Bannu as a representative of the INC. However, the British soon realized that perhaps it was better to have her as a friend than an enemy and appointed her as a member of the Advisory Board of Education. She accepted but resigned the post as part of the Quit India Movement in 1942. This resignation earned her another spell in a British prison. She later served as the chairperson of the All-India Women's Education Fund Association and as a member of the executive committee of Lady Irwin College in New Delhi. In 1945 and 1946 she served as the Indian delegate at UNESCO conferences, and as a member of the board of trustees of the All-India Spinners' Association, in ode to her Gandhian proclivities.

When India finally won its independence in 1947, Amrit was elected as the United Provinces representative for the Indian Constituent Assembly. She was also a member of the Sub-Committee on Fundamental Rights and the Sub-Committee on Minorities. Amrit worked tirelessly to ensure that the constitution guaranteed universal suffrage, and protected the rights of women, children, and religious minorities. In this world-changing year, she was named *TIME* Magazine's Woman of the Year, a testament to the incredible legacy that her career left on the world.

After India's independence, Amrit joined Nehru's first Cabinet – the first woman to hold cabinet rank, serving for ten years. She was assigned to the Ministry of Health, in which position she led several major campaigns including the world's largest-ever vaccination programme. She and her brothers also gave up their ancestral land to serve as holiday homes for doctors and nurses. She was a key component in the founding of the Indian Council of Child Welfare and served as the chairperson of the Indian Red Cross Society for fourteen years. She also led campaigns to fight malaria, typhoid, and leprosy, and promoted birth control.

Although a dedicated nationalist, Amrit was never distracted from her mission to advance the position of women in her society. She championed the cause of universal suffrage and testified before the Lothian Committee on Indian Franchise and Constitutional Reforms, and before the Joint Select Committee of the British Parliament on Indian constitutional reforms. She openly criticized purdah, campaigned against child marriage, and pushed to abolish the *devadasi* system (which will be explained later). She also sought to improve literacy, particularly among women and caste-oppressed communities among whom literacy rates were especially poor. Amrit died in New Delhi on 6 February 1964. Despite being a practising Christian her whole life, she was cremated following Sikh custom in line with her family's faith. She never married, and had no children, but left a legacy on India and indeed the world.

Latika Bose (1902–1987)

Many women (and their families) were reluctant to involve themselves in the freedom struggle because it clashed with their cultural and religious notions of women being relegated solely to the private realm. However, leaders such as Colonel Latika Bose proved adept at combining effective mobilization of women into the political sphere without compromising conservative ideals of what a woman should be and do.

Latika Ghose was born in Bengal in 1902, the niece of famous Indian philosopher and nationalist Aurobindo Ghose. She was well educated, having graduated from the University of Oxford before returning to India to work as a teacher. Like many of her contemporaries, she was a keen believer in Gandhi's *satyagraha*. In November 1927, the British government appointed the so-called Simon Commission, a group of seven British men, to report on the workings of the Indian constitution established by the Government of India Act of 1919. The Simon Commission caused widespread outrage in India due to the exclusion of Indians from the entire process. Latika's first notable political endeavour was the organization and stewarding of a women's protest against the Simon Commission. S.C. Bose was impressed with her efforts, remarking that if he had only ten more women like Latika, he could progress women's status by a century.

Having seen her capabilities, Bose asked Latika to start the *Mahila Rashtriya Sangha* (MRS, meaning, Women's Political Association) in 1928. Latika was initially hesitant as she knew that for an English-educated woman such as herself, her best employment prospects lay with the British government and aligning herself with the nationalist movement would destroy those prospects. However, she quickly decided that her devotion to the cause of women's and India's emancipation mattered more to her than her ambitions, and she agreed to establish the group. While Bose had wanted Latika to lead the movement, she instead appointed his mother, Prabhabati Bose, as the first president and her own sister-in-law, Bivabati, as the first vice president. She argued that having the mother of one of the most popular and prominent male activists would add legitimization to the movement and that having a woman with more traditional values, as opposed to a Western-influenced leader, would make the group more palatable to conservative Bengalis. The MRS was split into *shakti mandirs* (temples of female power) which functioned as working cells that would go into the community to spread the MRS mission. Latika took the role of secretary and India's first organization, with the sole goal of engaging women in political activism, was born. The key principle of the MRS was that the goals of women's empowerment and Indian home rule were inseparable. It focussed specifically on opening women's eyes to their double oppression – that of women and as colonial subjects. Thus, the MRS was propagating awareness of intersectionality over a century before Kimberlé Crenshaw first coined the term. Educating women was the crux of the MRS mission, and from its conception, it focussed on organizing educational groups. Although officially taking a 'backseat' as secretary, Latika was instrumental in forming the values and vision of the MRS. She was also a natural at mobilizing women and inspiring them to take up the fight for freedom.

Latika's was a particularly Hindu vision; she drew similarities between the current struggle for women's rights and the battles waged between the gods and demons in Hindu mythology. She frequently evoked one story in which the warrior goddess Durga appeared as *shakti* (in this context meaning specifically divine feminine energy) and defeated the demons who had been triumphing over the gods. She also urged women to channel the spirit of self-sacrifice demonstrated by historical Rajput queens who died by suicide after their menfolk left for battle to avoid capture by the enemy. She urged her followers to be inspired by the spirit of their foremothers, telling them that they were the *shakti* of the nation and that they should let go of everything except love for their nation. Her impassioned campaign worked, and she was able to recruit hundreds of women to the MRS. The initial recruits were primarily the wives, sisters, mothers, and daughters of INC members whose own activism allowed their women to join the activities without being seen as disobeying male authority. However, the

MRS hoped to raise the political consciousness of all Bengali women. As well as being educated about the arguments for independence, women were also taught crucial skills including reading and writing, childcare, first-aid, and self-defence. Thus, the MRS became a very attractive prospect for young women who may otherwise never have received such education.

The MRS' first opportunity to publicly showcase itself came in 1928 when Bose asked the women volunteers to march alongside their male counterparts in an inauguration process for the annual INC meeting in Calcutta. He assigned Latika the rank of colonel and asked that the women wear a military uniform like their male colleagues. However, Latika rejected this request as it was considered a radical suggestion for the women to wear trousers, and instead mandated that the women should wear red-bordered dark-green saris with white blouses. She argued that these uniforms – in the INC flag colours – would make the women a striking sight, while maintaining the femininity and modesty of the women. She also took other precautions – such as not asking the women to camp overnight and refusing to put them into dangerous armed situations – that helped keep her women safe, and silenced opponents who argued that such public involvement of women would be alienating to more conservative communities. Their new uniform was agreed upon, and Colonel Latika led at least 300 women, mostly students and teachers, in procession alongside the male volunteers. Latika apologized for her failings as a military leader, believing that she could not march in time or salute correctly. However, these were trivial matters compared to all she had achieved. As per her wish, her women marched as clear equals of the men in this historic procession. Witnesses recorded how Latika and her followers changed their ideas about women's suitability for political activism:

'As the ladies clad in their saris marched past to the sound of the bugle and the beating of the drum, there could be traced not a touch of all the frailties that are so commonly attributed to them. No faltering, no hesitancy, no softness associated in popular minds with the womanhood of Bengal but chivalry written on every face and manifest in every movement.'[46]

Kamala Nehru (1899–1936)

Another remarkable woman who has been left hidden in her husband's shadow is Kamala Nehru (1899–1936). An independence activist in her own right, and outspoken supporter of women's rights, Kamala was not only the wife of India's first prime minister, Jawaharlal Nehru, but also mother to India's first female prime minister, Indira Gandhi.

Kamala Kaul was born on 1 August 1899 into a dominant-caste family originally hailing from Kashmir but now residing in Delhi. She had two younger brothers and a sister. Hers was a traditional and religious upbringing, and when she married her husband at the age of just sixteen, she found herself ill-prepared for the modern notions of his family. While Nehru has survived in history as a hero of the freedom fight and the founding father of modern India, the couple's marriage was not always an easy or happy one. Her husband abandoned her shortly after marriage, taking off on a trip to the Himalayas, himself admitting in his memoirs that he had neglected and underestimated his wife, regretting that he had often taken his political frustrations out on her – while ordering her to stay out of his business despite her repeated attempts to help both him and his cause. He was a well-known womanizer, most famously rumoured to have had an affair with Lady Edwina Mountbatten, the last vicereine of India. Kamala did not speak publicly of her husband's infidelity, but she suffered from ill health throughout her life and often fell into deep depression, writing to her friends that she was unworthy of love and that the world would be better without her. Her husband paid no attention to her ailing health or her mental turmoil and instead stated that she had all the freedom to think and act as she willed and thus, he had no more obligation toward her. Indeed, when he was offered the chance to return to his wife, on the condition that he ceased his political activity, he refused (unlike his political rivals M.K Gandhi and M.A. Jinnah who both abandoned their political pursuits to nurse their wives through illness). Kamala, however, was left to fend for herself. Only her closest confidantes seemed to notice or care about the tragic state she was in. Her only child, Indira, later recalled how her mother's suffering had instilled in her a determination to steel herself against the world – indeed Indira would later become known as 'India's Iron Lady'. Kamala made sure to raise Indira to be a strong and independent woman, who could succeed with or without a husband, and she took great care to ensure that her daughter was given the best education and care, perhaps aware that given her ill health, she might not live to care for Indira herself.

Yet despite her deteriorating health and her husband's cruelty, Kamala never allowed herself to lose sight of what mattered. Aside from caring for her daughter and her mother-in-law, Kamala joined the fight for freedom, independent of her husband's political agenda. While her husband was a resolute politician, she preferred the path of a *satyagrahi*. She was closely involved with the movement of Gandhi's son, Harilal, and quickly emerged as a leader alongside him. In 1921, as part of the non-cooperation movement, she organized groups of women to picket shops selling foreign goods and alcohol in Allahabad. Despite their troubles, she supported her husband politically – selling her jewellery to secure his release from prison and help fund the cause. When Jawaharlal was arrested to prevent him from giving a national speech, Kamala took it upon herself to go in his place and triumphantly read the speech to a large crowd of supporters. This alerted the British to her huge popularity with the people, especially Indian women, and she was arrested at least twice. She also turned her house into a dispensary where wounded activists came to be treated in secret along with their families. Her house was turned into a proper hospital, named in her memory by Gandhi following Kamala's death. She also spent time at Gandhi's *ashram*, where she became close friends with his wife, Kasturbai, and the wives of other nationalists. She was not afraid to speak up on women's issues, and frequently addressed the poor status of India's women, closely equating the fight for India's independence and the improvement of women's status.

Despite her passion for activism, her health continued to deteriorate, and she was often forced to leave India to seek treatment in Europe. In 1935, she was taken to Germany by S.C. Bose while her husband was in prison. This time, perhaps sensing that the condition was serious, Nehru asked to be released from prison to be with his wife. Faced with the prospect of losing her, Nehru later recalled, he finally began to appreciate all she had done for him, and the couple's bond was restored. Despite their happy reconciliation, Kamala's health once again declined. She died of tuberculosis on 28 February 1936 in Switzerland, with her teenage daughter and her mother-in-law by her side. She was just 36 years old.

Following her death, her husband added a prologue to his autobiography in which he recalled his devastation at his loss and his regret at having treated her so poorly during their marriage. Her unwavering loyalty both to her husband and her country, despite the great personal sacrifice both required of her, especially given her ill health, is a testament to the strength of Kamala Nehru, who deserves to be as well remembered as her husband, given that she was driven by patriotism and compassion for her fellow women, rather than personal ambition.

Swarup Rani Nehru (1868–1938)

During her short life, Kamala had been greatly inspired by her mother-in-law, Swarup Rani Nehru, another formidable Nehru lost in Jawaharlal's shadow. Swarup Thussu was born in Lahore to a Kashmiri Pandit family. We know little of her life before she married Motilal Nehru, whose first wife and child had died in childbirth. Soon after their marriage, the couple lost a child of their own, and they were supposedly told by a holy man that they were cursed to never have a son. However, ten months after this holy man's demise, they delivered a son, Jawaharlal Nehru on 14 November 1889. They later had two more children, Vijayalakshmi and Krishna, and both survived.

From the early days of her marriage, Swarup suffered from poor health and thus was cared for throughout her life by her elder sister, Rajvati. On 5 May 1905, Swarup and her family left Bombay for London. They intended to find a good English school for their son, but Motilal also wanted to consult British doctors about his wife's treatment to heal her various ailments. They secured a place for Jawaharlal at the prestigious Harrow to study alongside the British elite and then undertook a trip around Europe before returning to India in November 1905. Tragically, they lost another son soon after this but in 1907 welcomed their second daughter.

Motilal was happy for his family to be anglicized, allowing his daughters to be given English nicknames by their British governesses and his son to be dressed in English attire for family photos as well as receiving a truly British education. However, Swarup was determined to maintain their Hindu Indian heritage. Perhaps understandably, given the loss of two children, she frequently fretted about the effect of the 'evil eye' on her children, and marked a black dot on their forehead for protection. When her son reached a marriageable age, he wrote to his mother requesting that he not be forced into an arranged marriage – expressing a preference for the life of a bachelor. However, Swarup did not approve of this choice, and in line with Hindu tradition, secured a priest to find an astrologically compatible wife for her son. This is how Jawaharlal came to marry Kamala Kaul on 8 February 1916. It was later said that the conservative Swarup Rani was upset that this marriage bore no sons, only one daughter, Indira Gandhi. However, Indira herself always spoke fondly of her grandmother, who seems to have spoiled her whenever she could.

During the First World War, Swarup Rani joined a group of both Indian and British women who knitted woollen garments for the troops, showing that unlike many nationalists she was happy to work and live alongside the British. The affluent neighbourhood in which they lived had many British residents, living luxurious lifestyles in mansions complete with tennis courts, swimming pool, electricity, running water and stables. They were one of the first families in Allahabad to own a car, and her husband and children were always clad in designer attire. Thus, in many ways, the Nehrus had more in common with the British elite than with most of their countrymen.

However, this prosperous lifestyle was set to come to an end in the 1920s. One can only wonder what Swarup felt when she discovered that her husband and son had both given up their successful legal firms to join the non-cooperation movement. Subsequently, Swarup's jewellery was sold, her daughter was taken out of school, and the family was ordered to live a life of (comparative) austerity in line with Gandhi's *satyagraha* ideals. Soon, the house became frequented more by INC leaders and *satyagrahis* than by English aristocracy. There is little evidence of whether she had any say in this drastic change in lifestyle, but she soon proved herself an enthusiastic supporter of the movement – although she did later chastise her daughter-in-law for strictly adhering to the ascetic lifestyle and complained that she should at the very least don a few simple pieces of jewellery, suggesting that she was perhaps not totally ready to let go of the trappings of privilege.

On 7 December 1921, Motilal and Jawaharlal were arrested and imprisoned under British justifications of maintaining law and order. When questioned on how she felt about their arrest, she 'rejoiced in the great privilege of sending my dear husband and my only son to jail'.[47] A year later, she led a meeting in Idgah on 26 January 1922, where she instructed the 100 people present to recruit more women into the INC. This was a drastic move for Swarup who had lived her life in seclusion but now took to the streets wearing *khadi* in a show of support for the movement. In 1930, in the midst of the Salt Satyagraha, Swarup flouted the British laws and instructed women to prove their patriotism by making their own salt. Such messages could have got her arrested and imprisoned, but she showed brave defiance and was more than willing to join her husband and son in jail. Her influence was hailed in one of the popular women's songs of the era, *Song of Jawaharlal Nehru's Mother Calling for Participation in the Holy War*. Her daughter, Krishna, expressed her admiration for her mother's actions: 'That was one of the most extraordinary things. A tiny fragile Hindu lady, born to the luxury and seclusion of strict orthodoxy, suddenly became a revolutionary orator. Her fiery speeches swayed and roused the crowds to a high peak of emotion'.[48]

Swarup was by her husband's side when he died on 6 February 1931, and remained deeply devoted to her son. On one occasion, she visited him in prison but refused to use a fan despite the sweltering heat. A witness reported that 'the mother's heart was touched, and henceforth she refused to enjoy the comfort of an electric fan while her son rotted in the hot prison cell'.[49] Despite such devotion, Jawaharlal himself admitted that he often took advantage of his mother, stating in his autobiography that 'I had no fear of her, for I knew that she would condone everything I did, and because of her excessive and indiscriminating love for me, I tried to dominate over her a little'.[50]

However, perhaps she was not as easily manipulated as her son thought, as Swarup did not let her grief or motherly concern distract her from her activism. In April 1931, she was injured after being beaten by British police during a demonstration. She proudly reported the incident to Jawaharlal writing, 'the mother of a brave son is also somewhat like him'.[51] Perhaps this was a subtle reminder that despite his efforts to control her, Swarup was an independent and indomitable freedom fighter in her own right.

Despite her lifelong battles with her health, she lived until the age of 70 when she died on 10 January 1938, with her beloved sister, son, and daughters at her side. Her sister, who had devoted her entire life to caring for Swarup, died the following day – a tragic testament to the bond they must have shared. There is no doubt that Swarup raised a remarkable son, but it should be remembered that – in more ways than one – there would have been no Jawaharlal Nehru without Swarup.

Krishnabai Rau Nimbkar (1906–?)

One woman whose life is shrouded in mystery, despite her active role in the nationalist movement is Krishnabai Rau Nimbkar. All we know of Krishnabai's childhood is that she was born in Madras around 1906. Her first known political act was her establishment of the Madras Youth League as a student; during this time, she gave evidence before the Joshi Commission, established to debate the criminalization of child marriage. She later went on to become a lecturer in a girls' college in Allahabad, a post she resigned from in response to Gandhi's call for civil disobedience. She returned to Madras where she became a member of the Women's Swadeshi League, which required women to vow to live the life of a *satyagrahi*, spin a mandated amount of thread per month, and preach the value of *khadi*.

Krishnabai had a reputation as an able orator and a strong leader, and she put these skills to use when she co-founded the Desh Sevikas Sangha (DSS, meaning Women Serving the Country), under the protection of the Swadeshi League. This organization brought together women who were willing to picket foreign goods stores. Krishnabai's sister, Indirabai, distributed propaganda for the organization. The DSS began with arranging daily meetings of women to spin and discuss nationalist politics. When women were called upon to directly join the Swadeshi movement, DSS members went door to door preaching the message, selling khadi, and exhibiting their wares. Led by Krishnabai, they then went on to join their male comrades in picketing foreign clothes shops, an act that was considered among the most dangerous forms of protest and thus one which women had until now been reluctant to engage in. DSS members, including Krishnabai, stopped customers as they entered shops and urged them not to further India's oppression by opting for foreign rather than homemade goods.

Now presumably married, having changed her name to Krishnabai Nimbkar, she led civil disobedience demonstrations in Madras, for which she was jailed by the British. This is where the historical record seemingly ends. We do not know where or when Krishnabai died, whether she lived to see Indian independence or what further role she played in achieving it. However, her leadership of the DSS has never been erased, and her devotion to non-violent principles and her belief in the value of her country live on.

Lilavati Munshi (1899–1978)

The DSS had many outspoken leaders in its time, another being Lilavati Munshi. Lilavati was born on 21 May 1899 in Gujarat. Her family were Jains, a small but influential religious community who espoused extreme non-violence. She married Lalbhai Sheth at a young age, but he died in 1926. She remarried, wedding Gujarati writer, Kanaiyalal Munshi, with whom she had two sons and four daughters. Despite her large family, she was actively involved in the independence movement throughout the 1920s and 1930s. She joined Gandhi in the Salt Satyagraha and was arrested several times by the British for her participation in the civil disobedience movement. Lilavati came to be regarded as one of the movement's most influential figures, and when she was released from prison on Gandhi's birthday alongside two other women, Perin Captain and Mrs Lukanji, she was met by a mile-long procession of over 5,000 women. These women were all members of the DSS and struck an imposing image marching with placards and flags in their saffron saris (saffron being the colour of Hindu nationalism). The crowds at the end of the parade numbered up to 10,000 – an unprecedented show of women's support for their female leaders.

When Lilavati later became a leader of the DSS, she used her eloquence to highlight and protest the brutal treatment of women by the British forces. Across Gujarat, the British were attempting to intimidate protestors with threats of violence which were often followed through. For example, in the Bardoli district, peasants who had stopped paying taxes were viciously beaten. Women, however, were particular targets of the authorities. In one village, an old lady was locked in her house without food or water. In Bombay, three young women filed a complaint against their arresting officer, Sergeant MacKenzie, alleging that he and his male colleague had visited their cell in the night and made inappropriate gestures. Similar, and much worse, stories were heard across India. A huge rally was held in Bombay to protest the policy of British police to abandon women protestors in the jungle at night. One demonstrator, Lady Jagmohandas, equated this policy with rape and screamed that any regime that so insulted India's women would not reign for long. Another protestor, Mrs Annapurnabai G. V. Deshmukh, drew comparisons between these female activists and the heroines of the Hindu epics, using them to prove that the gods would always intervene to protect Indian women from evildoers.

Lilavati made it her mission to lay bare the barbarity and hypocrisy of the British police. During a speech honouring the imprisonment of Jawaharlal Nehru, she mocked the suggestion that the British had ever acted as protectors of Indian women (as they frequently claimed). Their chivalry, she argued, was reserved only for white women. She pointed to a recent example where British authorities had paid thousands of rupees to rescue a white woman from Indian abductors, but the British cared little for the plight of Indian women save for where it justified their colonial oppression (for example being used as an excuse to outlaw certain religious practices or to more heavily police native men). Lilavati was not altogether uncritical of Indian men either, however. She warned women that they could not rely on their own men to defend them against the British and that as this was an issue that uniquely affected women, women themselves must stand up and fight for their freedom. She reminded them that the elite (both British and Indian) showed little respect for them and that they must demand respect for themselves.

From 1937 to 1946, Lilavati was a member of the Bombay Legislative Assembly. When India finally achieved its independence, she served as a member of the upper house of the Indian Parliament from 1952 to 1958 as a member of the INC representing Bombay. She was also a prolific Gujarati writer and published several works of different genres which live on long after her death on 20 February 1978.

Lilavati is remarkable in that she not only resisted the everyday realities of British oppression, but she also challenged the very notions on which British colonialism was based. The British Empire made 'Christianising and civilising' the natives its justification and often exaggerated or misinterpreted the plight of women in conquered lands as a validation for

British interference. Given that a queen sat on the throne of Great Britain as Empress of India, it was easy to assume that her soldiers would protect the rights of all women under her care. Lilavati made public how far that notion was from the truth. Not only did Victorian gentlemen share many of the same pejorative views of the women (that they were an inferior and hysterical breed whose place was in the kitchen and not in the streets) they claimed to be protecting, but British soldiers were often active oppressors of women – beating, raping, torturing, and imprisoning Indian women to the same extent, if not more so, than their male counterparts. Thus, Lilavati should be saluted not only for mobilizing so many women into peaceful protests, but for helping to shatter any illusions that British rule was of benefit to Indian women, and for proving that only the women themselves would fight to their death for their rights.

Kamaladevi Chattopadhyay (1903-1988)

Kamaladevi Chattopadhyay was many things – an artist, an actress, and an activist. Born Kamaladevi Dhareshwar in Mangaluru on 3 April 1903, she was the youngest of four daughters of a wealthy Brahmin family. Her life was marred by tragedy in her early years. When she was just seven, her father died. A few years later, Kamaladevi's older sister also died and in her, she lost her best friend and inspiration. However, Kamaladevi was not short of women to look up to. Her paternal grandmother was an expert in the ancient Indian epics. Her mother, meanwhile, was an intelligent and independent woman. When Kamaladevi's father died, he left no will and thus his entire estate passed to his son from a previous marriage, bypassing his wife and daughters completely. Her mother refused the monthly allowance that she was half-heartedly offered in compensation and instead supported herself and her daughters using the large dowry that she had brought with her to the marriage. Kamaladevi later recalled how her mother tried to instil in her daughters that same sense of independence – making them face their fears head-on by travelling alone from a young age to prepare them for adulthood. Kamaladevi was also introduced to many of the prominent women nationalists and thus witnessed firsthand women taking centre stage in the freedom struggle. Therefore, she grew up with a firm belief in the rights of women and with the desire to fight for herself and others. This spirit was to reveal itself at an early age – as a child, she refused to stop playing with the servant children who she told her mother were much more interesting than the children of the elite with whom she was expected to socialize. This refusal to overlook inequality or injustice wherever she saw it was something that would only develop as she grew older.

Kamaladevi was married when she was fourteen, but her husband died just two years later and she thus became a widow before her sixteenth birthday. Unusually, she was permitted to continue her education after her widowhood, attending college in Chennai, having been an able student throughout her early education. She was a keen scholar of ancient Sanskrit, no doubt influenced by her grandmother's knowledge of the Hindu scriptures. While at university, Kamaladevi met Suhasini Chattopadhyay, Sarojini Naidu's younger sister. Suhasini introduced Kamaladevi to her brother, Harindranath (known as Harin), a famous poet, playwright, and actor. Given her interest in literature and the arts, Kamaladevi was immediately impressed and the two quickly fell in love. At the age of twenty, Kamaladevi married Harin in 1923. This caused a huge scandal in her conservative Brahmin society, where widows were expressly forbidden to remarry. The ever-independent Kamaladevi was completely undeterred by her community's disapproval, and she bore Harin a son one year later. Together, the couple worked writing plays and supporting each other in their other artistic pursuits. Shortly after their marriage, she joined her husband in London where she received a degree in sociology.

Ironically, it was in London that Kamaladevi first heard of Gandhi's non-cooperation movement. Keen to support this venture, she returned to India in 1923 and joined the Seva Dal – a social work organization which had turned its attention to the nationalist movement. Not long after her return, she was made leader of the women's branch and helped recruit an army of *'sevikas'* from across India who were trained and organized in the fight for freedom. A few years later, Irish-born Indian nationalist Margaret E. Cousins suggested that Kamaladevi throw in her hat as a member of the Madras Provincial Legislative Assembly. Although she narrowly lost, she made history as the first woman to run for a legislative seat in India. In 1927, she co-founded the AIWC, serving as its secretary. During this time, she travelled across Europe learning from similar organizations and representing Indian women.

In 1930, she was one of the seven leaders appointed by Gandhi to prepare salt on the beach in Bombay as part of his Salt Satyagraha. She was the only woman, apart from her friend Avantikabai Gokhale, to do so. She recalled this day in her autobiography:

'This was [women's] first appearance in any modern militant political campaign and I could hardly suppress my excitement at the enormity of the occasion and my own good fortune to be among the first as I attached my name to the pledge to devote myself to my country's freedom battle. My hand shook a little under my tumultuous emotions. It seemed such a stupendous moment in my life, in the life of the women of my country. I felt I was tracing not the letters of my name but recording a historic event'.[52]

She also recorded the police brutality towards all protestors regardless of age or gender that followed this protest and recalled the irony of the police offering to help her to the hospital after she sustained injuries in the assault.

Not content with her part in this historic protest, she took it upon herself to set up a salt stall near the High Court of Bombay, where she stopped a passing magistrate and asked him if he would like to purchase her Freedom Salt in a brilliant act of nonchalance, despite the knowledge that he could have her arrested for breaking the salt laws. This was around the same time she had made headlines when she had thrown her body onto an Indian flag to protect it during a skirmish between police and protestors, inadvertently becoming a symbol of the freedom struggle. She was indeed jailed several times by the British, but she recalled that she felt great happiness and pride at becoming among the first women political prisoners and that her only concern was that her organizations would be taken over by other factions who would care more about religious affiliation than patriotism.

As soon as the First World War erupted, Kamaladevi left England where she had been working and embarked on a world tour where she sought to convince foreign powers that India should be given its independence after the war as an acknowledgement of all they had contributed to the British war effort. On the US leg of this tour, she was stopped on a segregated train in Louisiana by a conductor who rebuked her for being in a white carriage. When realizing that she was not American, he hesitated as he was unsure where Asians sat on this racial divide. When he tried to find out exactly where she was from, she replied: 'It makes no difference. I am a coloured woman obviously and it is unnecessary for you to disturb me for I have no intention of moving from here'.[53] Flummoxed, the conductor decided it was not worth the fight and let her be. This was over a decade before Rosa Parks would earn her fame for refusing to give up her own seat on a bus.

Eventually, Kamaladevi's dream of Indian independence came true, but this dream swiftly turned into a nightmare as she witnessed the carnage that ensued. Thus, she threw herself into the efforts to rehabilitate refugees. Her first act was establishing the Indian Cooperative Union through which she determined to build a new town solely to accommodate refugees who had no other home to go to. Reluctantly, the new Prime Minister Nehru agreed to her plans but only if she did not ask for help from the state. She agreed to this condition and against all odds managed to establish the town of Fardiabad on the outskirts of Delhi where over 50,000 refugees were settled. Not only did she provide these refugees with new housing, but she helped them to make this a home by training them in new skills so that they could find work. She also established health facilities so that the town could flourish.

In addition to her political and social activism, Kamaladevi had two other passions. The first was acting. She starred in several films between 1931 and 1945 at a time when acting was considered a disreputable pursuit for elite women. Her first film was a silent movie produced in 1931, the filming of which she somehow managed to fit into her nationalist activities.

Her second and more famous passion was Indian handicrafts. While most Gandhian nationalists championed Indian homemade goods, Kamaladevi had a real dedication to reviving the lost arts of India and is credited with almost singlehandedly renewing and preserving India's arts and crafts heritage. Following independence, she grew concerned about Nehru's plans to modernize India's manufacturing using Western machinery, a fate which she feared would lead to the extinction of indigenous art forms. Since most traditional artisans were women, she felt a duty to protect the traditions not just for historical heritage reasons but also to save the livelihoods of Indian women. She publicly promoted Indian arts and crafts and established a museum to store and showcase some of the finest examples of India's native art to inspire future generations and preserve what she feared was fast becoming a dying trade. Similarly, she introduced the National Awards for Master Craftsmen and established the Central Cottage Industries Emporia which sought to restore India to its former material glory.

In 1955, Kamaladevi broke tradition again by filing for divorce from her husband of over three decades. Divorce was still extremely uncommon in India at this time, but for a woman to instigate it was almost unheard of. While the split was by all accounts amicable, it caused further outrage given that the marriage itself had already been considered scandalous owing to Kamaladevi's widowhood. Yet Kamaladevi cared just as little for public opinion as she had in her twenties and refused to be tied into an unhappy marriage just because of societal expectations. In the same year as her divorce, she was awarded the Padma Bhushan, showing that for once a woman's private life did not eclipse the acknowledgement of her achievements. She continued to channel her energy into her passion projects, and in 1964 she established a dance institute associated with UNESCO to keep traditional Kathak dancing alive for future generations – the institute is still running today. She either directly established or contributed to the founding of several other important schools, councils, and boards all of which aimed at preserving traditional art forms.

Kamaladevi died in Bombay on 29 October 1988 at the age of eighty-five. However, her voice lives on in the many publications she wrote throughout her life, many of which focus on the role of women in the Indian independence movement. She also published an autobiography two years before her death. In the final pages, she talks of how none of this life came easily to her – she was a self-professed introvert who hated crowds and public speaking and believed herself too intense and emotional. That she still pushed herself into the centre of a movement which made her a national figure in every sense of the word is then a great testament to the sincere passion she had for her country's freedom and ensuring the safety of her fellow Indians both before and after independence.

Jyotirmayee Gangopadhyay (1889–1945)

While the *satyagraha* movement may have been based on the principle of peace, this did not protect *satyagrahis* from being on the receiving end of violence, as is shown in the story of Jyotirmayee Gangopadhyay. Jyotirmayee was born in Calcutta on 25 January 1889, one of eight children. Her father, Dwarkanath Gangul, was a prominent nationalist who had helped found the Brahmo Samaj. Her mother, Kadambini Devi, was the first woman student to graduate with a medical degree from the University of Calcutta and was the first woman to address the INC. Having graduated with an MA in Philosophy, Jyotirmayee taught at a couple of schools in India before moving to Ceylon (now Sri Lanka) to become principal of a women's college. She had an active interest in social work and education and kept close contact with many colleges throughout her life.

Jyotirmayee envisioned an India in which women were empowered, the working classes were brought in line with modern standards, and in which Indians were educated about and proud of their history. In 1926, she organized a Students' Association for Social Service. She strongly believed that everyone should be educated in their mother tongue. She sought to encourage women into the workforce during India's industrial revolution, and she helped to establish the Aryasthan Insurance Company. When her attention turned to politics, she did her best to awaken national awareness among Bengali women through writings, speeches, and practical work.

In the early 1920s, Jyotirmayee joined the non-cooperation movement. Having been employed to teach by the government, she resigned her posts in accordance. She raised a women's volunteer corps for the INC and became the Vice-President of the Women's Satyagraha Committee. Her involvement with the Satyagraha campaign, specifically leading processions of women, earned her two stints in prison, one in 1930 and the other in 1932. In 1942, she was imprisoned again for her role in the Quit India Movement, during which she took part in anti-British demonstrations and gave speeches urging people to support the INC.

On 22 November 1945, Jyotirmayee's life was cut tragically short. She had joined a protest organized by the Forward Bloc to protest against the imprisonment of INA soldiers. Jyotirmoyee served as a representative for the protestors and demanded the release of all INA prisoners. When her request was denied, violence erupted in which two Indian students were killed. Their deaths caused a national outcry, and Jyotirmoyee led a procession in protest. Not having learnt their lesson, the British sought to violently repress this protest too. Jyotirmoyee was killed, thus becoming another martyr who would not live to see their dream of Indian Independence come true.

In the early days of the movement, there had been a belief that women were safer proponents of the nationalist cause because British sensibilities would not allow for women (especially those espousing non-violence) to be tortured or killed in the same way that male freedom fighters were. Jyotirmoyee's death was a shocking and tragic reminder of how wrong this assumption was.

Matangini Hazra (1870–1942)

Jyotirmoyee may have been one of the first *satyagrahis* to give her life during the movement, but she was certainly not the last. Another was Matangini Hazra. She was a close associate of Gandhi and was thus affectionately known as 'Gandhi buri', meaning 'Old Lady Gandhi' in Bengali, despite being no relation to the Gandhis.

Matangini was born on 19 October 1870 to a peasant family in the small village of Hogla near Tamluk. As with most girls of her class, she received no education and was married at just twelve to a sixty-year-old man. Her husband died when she was eighteen and she had no children. Having grown up following Gandhi's career, at the age of sixty-two, she took the INC pledge and dedicated herself to the cause of Indian independence. In 1930, she was arrested for the first time for breaking the Salt Act as part of the civil disobedience movement. Although swiftly released, she immediately joined the movement for the abolition of the *chowkidari* (farmers) tax. She joined a protest march against the illegal punishment of those who joined the movement and was arrested and imprisoned for six months in Baharampur. Undeterred, she joined the INC on her release, and began spinning her own *khadi*. In 1933, she was injured when a policeman beat her with a baton while she attended the subdivisional INC conference at Serampore. This only furthered her belief that the British were brutal invaders who would spare no one – not even aging women – from their wrath. In the 1930s, despite continuing impediments caused by the assault, Hazra threw herself into social work and began to champion the cause of the Dalits. When a smallpox epidemic broke out in Midnapore, she nursed the sick with little thought for her own health.

At the end of September 1942, peasant activists attacked police stations and destroyed telegraph lines across the Midnapur District as part of the INC plan to overthrow British authority in the area. The British did not take these assaults lightly and retaliated with brute force, causing widespread carnage as protestors clashed with police. Matangini asked that she be allowed to lead one of the protests. On 29 September, a crowd descended on Tamluk's court and police station. Greeted by armed soldiers, the mob hesitated in their resolve. It was at this moment that the now seventy-three-year-old Matangini stepped forward, raised the INC flag and addressed the people, urging them to proceed in Gandhi's name. In response, British soldiers shot the hand in which Matangini held the flag. Fearless, she stepped forward again, urging the police not to shoot unarmed protestors. Ignoring her pleas, she was shot in the other hand. Despite her injuries, she repeatedly chanted *Vande Mataram* (Hail to the Motherland). She was finally silenced by a fatal shot to her head. As she collapsed, the flag was still held high above her head. Her martyrdom incited open rebellion against the British government in the region and the revolution raged for two years before it was disbanded in 1944 at Gandhi's request. After independence, tributes were paid to Hazra across the region, and in 1977 a statue of her became the first statue of a woman to be erected in Calcutta. Today, there is also a statue marking the spot in Tamluk where she was murdered.

The image of a seventy-three-year-old widow being gunned down with the cry of her country on her lips is one of the most poignant of the Indian independence movement. She may have been known as Old Lady Gandhi, but while Gandhi's name lives on, Matangini's has all but been forgotten. She did more for her nation's freedom than many of the men around her – and she paid the ultimate price for a freedom that she would not live to enjoy.

Ambabai (c. 1900–c. 1970)

Many child brides found their power in the nationalist movement. One such young girl was Ambabai, a young child bride from Karnataka who refused to submit to patriarchal social norms which banished young widows to a life of marginalization and oppression and instead channelled her newfound freedom into fighting the British.

Ambabai had been married to a much older man, a policeman, at the age of just twelve, and was sent to live with him in Bombay. There, a neighbour introduced her to Gandhi's teachings. When she was sixteen, her husband died, leaving her a widow. She was sent back to her father's house in Udipi where she recalled spending five long years sitting in a room with nothing to do but pray. Her health – both physical and mental – suffered from this seclusion. While locked in this meditative state, she experienced a religious vision in which the Hindu god, Krishna, came to her, ran his hands over her body and told her not to be afraid for he would take care of her. Ambabai took this as a sign to cast off the shackles of widowhood and return to society with a bang.

Inspired by her neighbour from Bombay, she joined those picketing foreign clothes shops and liquor stores. She also participated in making and selling salt. This saw her brought before British magistrates and while she was released the first time, the second trial ended with her being sentenced to four months' imprisonment. Far from languishing in jail, she thrived and used it as an opportunity to rebuild her strength. Recognizing her passion and power, on her release INC leaders asked her to make public speeches on topics including sinning and the evils of alcohol (another important aspect of the *Satyagraha* ideology). She happily carried out these activities and for three months led *prabhat pheries* (singing processions) every morning. *Prabhat pheries* were an important platform for the less educated classes to participate in the movement. The songs sung during these processions were explicitly nationalist and religious, and the British came to view them as a threat to civic order, classifying the lyric pamphlets as seditious literature. The songs were officially outlawed in 1930. Thus, Ambabai was breaking the law in continuing to lead these processions, further showing her defiance of British authority. She later recalled these as the happiest days of her life. Thus, Ambabai fought not just against an invading foreign power, but against the weight of her own society, culture, and religion who sought to silence her and deemed her life at an end when she no longer served the purpose of wife.

Subbamma Duvvuri (1881–1964)

Another woman who rejected the social exclusion that traditionally came with young widowhood to instead pave the way for herself as a fierce nationalist was Subbamma Duvvuri. Subbamma was born into a middle-class family in Andhra Pradesh in 1880. She was married at just ten years old and was widowed less than a decade later. Her husband had been a poor man, and thus she was very vulnerable as a young, destitute, and childless widow. She threw herself upon the mercy of her relative, Tirupati Venkata Sastri, an esteemed poet and scholar. He taught her classical literature and she developed an impressive knowledge of Hindu epics.

Like many other women, she was drawn into the national movement as a devotee of Gandhi, speaking out all her life against the concept of untouchability which Gandhi regarded as a key issue alongside independence. She organized the Andhra Mahila Sabhas, a group that educated women about the independence movement. She put her excellent knowledge of Hindu mythology to good use by touring throughout Andhra Pradesh using their stories to evoke nationalist fervour by comparing the demons of these epics to the British. It was noted that she often moved people to tears with her emotional speeches. It is a tragedy that none of her speeches survive. She was frequently jailed for partaking in anti-British protests during the civil disobedience movement and was known for insulting her British gaolers and generally making mischief during her time in prison.

In 1921, she established the women's wing of the Andhra Congress and succeeded in mobilizing many women for the cause. A year later, she organized the Women's Congress Committee, and in 1923, her meeting in Kakinada attracted hundreds of women. In 1924, she founded a school for women, the Sanatana Stree Vidyalaya, at Rajamundry, where spaces were reserved for widows whose plight she could sympathize with all too well. She also encouraged her students to come out of purdah and participate in public meetings. In 1930, she spent another year in prison for participating in the Salt Satyagraha and was frequently jailed for participating in the Quit India Movement.

We know little of her life after independence, although she is said to have campaigned for Andhra to become independent from Madras. She passed away on 31 May 1964 at the age of eighty-three. Today, a statue of her stands in Freedom Park in Rajahmundry, a lasting testament to the widow who not only rejected the isolation and subjugation which was expected of her but also helped to raise other widows from it.

Jankidevi Bajaj (1893–1979)

Another of Gandhi's devoted female followers was Jankidevi Bajaj. Jankidevi was born on 7 January 1893 into a Hindu family in Madhya Pradesh. She attended school until the age of eight when she was married to twelve-year-old Jamnalal Bajaj in 1902. Some sources say that both she and her new family came from wealth, while others state that their later wealth was entirely a result of their own industry. Either way, it seems to have been a happy marriage and Jankidevi was a devoted wife and loving mother to their five children.

However, she was equally devoted to Mohandas Gandhi, and eagerly emulated his strict lifestyle. She and her husband were one of the first subscribers to Gandhi's non-violent campaigns. Jankidevi raised her large family to follow a simple life according to Gandhi's model and began to reject many of the customs she had been raised to follow as social evils which were blocking India from achieving its freedom. When she was twenty-four, her husband wrote to her asking her to relinquish all her gold because Gandhi saw gold as an evil that fostered jealousy and attachment. Jankidevi happily surrendered her gold and until her dying day never wore it again. In 1919, her husband also requested that she remove herself from purdah. This, like gold, was a symbol of affluence and social status which did not align with the couple's commitment to a life of asceticism and simplicity. Jankidevi called on her fellow women to similarly step out of purdah.

Aged twenty-eight, she threw herself wholeheartedly into the Swadeshi movement. She swapped her silk sarees for only *khadi*, which she spun herself. She taught hundreds of other women how to spin and collected all items of foreign clothes to make a huge bonfire which burned for several days. On 17 July 1928, she made a brave and public stand against untouchability by allowing Dalits into her family temple for the first time in its history. Influenced by Gandhi's support of Dalits, she hired a Dalit to serve her family meals – a radical breaking of caste taboos. From here on there was no stopping her. Empowered by a new sense of commitment to the cause, she set out on a march across hundreds of miles of rural India, where she enchanted thousands as she preached the Swadeshi ideology. She was imprisoned by the British several times, her longest stint being in 1932, but it never perturbed her or dulled her passion for the cause.

When India finally won its freedom, Jankidevi worked with Vinoba Bhave on the Bhoodan movement (the Land Gift movement, also known as the Bloodless Revolution), a reform movement urging the wealthy to voluntarily surrender a percentage of their land to the peasants who lived and worked on it. She also promoted the cause of women's education, and many educational establishments have since been named in her honour. In 1956, she was granted the Padma Bhushan. She published an autobiography in 1965 and passed away in 1979 aged eighty-six.

Jankidevi Bajaj is another woman whose life embodied her commitment to justice in all its forms. Like many nationalists, she came from a position of privilege, but unlike others who sought to gatekeep the movement from those less fortunate, Jankidevi used her position to empower women, Dalits, and the rural poor. This is important because it shows that even those giving their lives to India's freedom did not claim that it was a perfect land with no problems of its own. Rather, they wanted to create a new nation which was not only free of British oppression, but free of internal gender, caste, and class oppression too.

Gammididala Durgabāi Deshmukh (1909–1981)

One woman who was not afraid to stand up to authority – even within her community – was Gammiḍidala Durgabāi Deshmukh, also known as Lady Deshmukh. Gammiḍidala was born to a Brahmin family in Rajahmundry, Andhra Pradesh. At the age of eight, she was married to her cousin, Subha Rao. When she matured, she refused to live with him, rejecting the life that had been laid out for her. She permitted Subha to marry a second wife and left him behind to pursue her education. However, in an early display of nationalist fervour, she left school in protest when it became mandatory for children to be taught in English, and later went on to establish a Hindi-medium school for girls.

Gammiḍidala's first major contribution to the nationalist movement came in April 1921. The then twelve-year-old Gammiḍidala discovered that Gandhi himself would be visiting her hometown, Kakinada, and decided that he must meet the local *devadasis*. *Devadasis* are young girls who are given or sold to a temple at the age of around eight to become servants or wives of the temple god or goddess. This was once a prestigious position, but soon the girls came to be sexually abused by priests and other powerful men and grew up forced to earn a living as sex workers. Gammiḍidala made it her mission to educate the *devadasis* about who Gandhi was, and then approached his secretaries and asked if a meeting between Gandhi and the *devadasis* could be arranged. His officials did not take her seriously and joked that it would be possible if she donated 5,000 rupees to the nationalist cause. The *devadasis* managed to raise this money, and Gandhi arrived to find at least a thousand women and girls waiting to meet him. Gammiḍidala translated for them for over an hour, and many of the women donated their jewellery to Gandhi (a great sacrifice for such socially vulnerable women), adding another 20,000 rupees to his collection.

Two years later, the INC's conference was held in Kakinada. Gammiḍidala volunteered to support the conference and was assigned the role of managing admissions to the *khadi* exhibition. She was told not to let anyone enter without a ticket, a job she took so seriously that she denied entry to Jawaharlal Nehru himself. His aides arrogantly scolded her, to which she replied that she was only doing her job, and continued to refuse him entry until he presented her with a ticket. Far from being angry like his colleagues, Nehru praised Gammiḍidala for her courage in standing up to much older and more powerful men, and for her diligence of duty – two qualities which would continue to serve her and the nationalist movement as she aged.

Gammiḍidala closely adhered to the *satyagraha* ideals, never wearing jewellery or cosmetics. She was influential in organizing women *satyagrahis* to join Gandhi and his salt marches – the first women to be arrested in Madras were captured during salt marches organized by Gammiḍidala in the absence of any planned demonstrations in the region. She wrote to Gandhi for permission to organize a march led by T. Prakasam. Knowing that Prakasam would inevitably be arrested for heading the march, he assigned Gammiḍidala as 'dictator' of the movement in his absence.[54] For this, she was imprisoned three times between 1930 and 1933.

Just as she had not let a child marriage interfere with her education as a young girl, Gammiḍidala was not one to let the British keep her from her goals either. After her release from prison, she returned immediately to her studies, achieving an undergraduate and master's degree in political science. In 1942, she attained a law degree and became an advocate in the Madras High Court. She was later elected as the only woman on the panel of chairs in the Constituent Assembly of India. As well as several social reforms, she proposed Hindustani (a mix of Hindi and Urdu) be named India's national language – although she did acknowledge how problematic this would be in the southern states where Tamil is the primary language spoken. She thus suggested that a grace period would have to be introduced to allow for non-Hindi speakers to learn and adopt the language. Today, Hindi and English remain joint national languages in India.

Although failing to be elected to parliament in 1952, Gammiḍidala continued to wield influence on social welfare policies, resulting in the founding of the Central Social Welfare Board of which she was the first chairperson. Under her leadership, the Board focussed on reforms which benefited women and children through education, training, and healthcare. After visiting China in 1953, she advocated for their model of family courts to be established in India. After proposing the idea to Prime Minister Nehru and highlighting the importance of such courts to give quick justice for women in domestic disputes, the Family Courts Act was passed in 1984. She was the first chairperson of the National Council on Women's Education which was set up in 1958, and in 1963 she was sent to the USA to represent India at the World Food Congress.

Having left her first husband as a child, Gammididala did not remarry until 1953 when she met and married the Finance Minister of India, Chintaman Deshmukh. Prime Minister Nehru was one of only three witnesses to the marriage. The pair had no children (although Deshmukh had a daughter from a previous marriage). When her first husband died, Gammididala took in his second wife, Timmajamma. Rather than resenting each other, the two became firm friends, and Gammididala even arranged for Timmajamma to be given training to help her find employment (an extremely difficult task for widows in conservative Hindu society). Before her death, Gammididala published two books, one of which was her autobiography, *Chintaman and I*, published in 1981. She passed away in Narasannapeta at the age of seventy-two.

The thought of fourteen-year-old Gammididala barring the way of the famous and imposing Nehru is one of the enduring images of the nationalist movement because it speaks of the way that many women and girls were overshadowed by the more popular and more memorialized male nationalists, who used women to get them into positions of power and then left them behind. Gammididala knew that her worth to the movement was no less than that of her male counterparts – a testament to her character, but also symbolic of all the women in this book whose stories deserve to be given equal respect and celebration.

Accamma Cherian (1909–1982)

While many think of the *satyagraha* movement as a purely Hindu initiative, Christian women also took up the call, including Accamma Cherian who has been all but forgotten outside of her native state of Kerala but was instrumental in one of the most pivotal moments of the independence struggle and has been regarded as one of the most important politicians of her age.

Accamma was born in February 1909 to a wealthy Catholic family in Travancore (now Kerala). She received a degree in history and worked her way up to become headmistress of an English-speaking school. Inspired by Gandhi, in 1938 she gave up her job to join the Travancore State Congress (TSC) to fight for India's independence at the age of twenty-nine. Just a few months after joining the TSC, the organization was declared illegal by the British government and several of its leaders were arrested. Before his arrest, its leader, Kuttand Ramakrishna Pillai, placed Accamma in charge, demonstrating that despite being a relatively new recruit, she was already a trusted and capable member. In her autobiography, she recalled how eager she was to take on this role despite being fully aware of the risks. Under her leadership, a union was formed to mobilize people for a mass protest rally. On 23 October 1938, tens of thousands of people gathered outside the royal palace in Travancore to disturb the birthday festivities of the state's king and demand a retraction of the state's ban on the TSC.

Accamma stood at the head of this protest and was described as goddess-like as she arrived in an open-top jeep. In response to the protest, the British police were ordered to open fire on the protestors. Horrified, Accamma called the chief of police to kill her and spare the others. Her bravery compelled the chief to withdraw his order, and the protest continued until the government agreed to free the TSC leaders. When Gandhi heard of this incident, he dubbed Accama Tavancore's own Rani of Jhansi. However, despite her clear talent as a rouser of the people and a brave and defiant leader, she handed the presidency back to a man, Pattom Thanu Pillai, upon his release from jail.

The same year, under the direction of the INC, Accamma co-founded the

DSS and travelled across the state to encourage women to join the freedom struggle. One of her first recruits was her sister, Rosamma Punnoose. The sisters were arrested together in 1939 for participating in the TSC's first annual conference. Over the years, Accamma was arrested several times for repeatedly violating bans and agitating at protests; she often faced verbal and physical abuse in jail as fellow inmates were egged on by their jailors to target her. In 1942, she became the acting president of the TSC. One of her first acts was to welcome the Quit India resolution passed by INC at a session in Bombay. When India finally achieved its independence, Accamma was elected as a lawmaker in Travancore's first free election in 1947.

Despite all she had done for the independence movement, Accamma (like many other women) was sidelined following independence and her role in the struggle was downplayed. In the 1950s, Accamma quit the TSC after she was denied a ticket to parliamentary elections in India because the TSC president at the time believed that women in Travancore should be content to rule their homes and stay out of politics. She expressed her disgust at the exclusion of women from the INC following independence and lamented that women were denied leadership roles in the new nation they had helped to build. Her autobiography *Life: A Protest*, mentions two occasions when she was almost offered ministerial positions, but found that the highly idealistic male nationalists who had helped women stand at the forefront of the independence fight now trampled over them on their way to power. However, Accamma never gave up her fight for freedom and equality:

'Shakespeare has said that the world is a stage and that all the men and women are merely players; but to me, this life is a long protest. Protest against conservatism, meaningless rituals, societal injustice, gender discrimination against anything that is dishonest, unjust. When I see anything like this, I turn blind, I even forget who I am fighting'.[55]

Accamma went on to marry a fellow freedom fighter, V.V. Varkey Mannamplackal, with whom she had one son; she died in 1982.

Subhadra Kumari Chauhan (1904–1948)

As we have seen, Rani of Jhansi became an inspiration for many women nationalists in India, and one who immortalized this spirit in poetry was *satyagrahi* Subhadra Kumari Chauhan.

Subhadra Kumari was born on 16 August 1904, in a village in Uttar Pradesh. Her family was conservative and enforced strict gender and caste restrictions, which Subhadra often spoke out against – on one occasion chastizing her mother for discriminating against a caste-oppressed person. From the earliest days of her childhood, Subhadra showed a talent for writing and was often seen writing poetry while on the back of her horse-cart as she travelled to school. She wrote her first poem at the age of just nine, supposedly carving it onto a neem tree.

After leaving school at fifteen, she married playwright Thakur Lakshman Singh Chauhan of Khandwa in 1919 and the pair went on to have five children after moving to Jabalpur in the Central Provinces. In her husband, she found a like-minded and supportive partner, who shared her notions of social justice and encouraged her to continue her writing. He was a well-known social reformer who opposed the dowry system and disagreed with the imposition of veiling on women. Subhadra discarded her veil after marriage, causing great scandal in her conservative family. She and her husband were condemned by their family for 'debasing' themselves by attending the wedding of their domestic servant and eating alongside people of lower castes. Subhadra replied that if they were so offended, they were not obliged to visit her again. Both she and her husband supported their eldest child in choosing to marry into a different caste – a hugely controversial affair at the time.

In 1921, Subhadra and her husband again upset their family by joining the non-cooperation movement. By 1923 they had become leaders of the *Jhanda Satyagrah* (the Jabalpur chapter of the *satyagraha* movement). When she was eighteen, and pregnant, she was jailed as a *satyagrahi*. Some have argued that she was the first woman *satyagrahi* to be jailed, but it was more likely she was just the first in her region. Despite being heavily pregnant, she was shown little leniency in prison, although she was released before she gave birth. Throughout the 1930s, she led the women's section of the State Congress Committee of Madhya Pradesh and in 1936 was elected to the Bihar Legislative Assembly.

In 1942, her husband was arrested during the Quit India movement. Despite being left in sole charge of their five children and their household, Subhadra continued to fight. She herself was arrested shortly after, being marched to prison alongside her youngest, and desperately ill, child. In jail, she protested her treatment and that of her child for whose life she feared by going on hunger strike. We do not know how long she refused her food, but we know that she was only released when she fell deathly ill and needed life-saving surgery. Whether or not her condition was a direct result of her treatment by the British we do not know, but it is not an unreasonable assumption given the known conditions of political prisoners and the fact that she was driven to such desperate measures to protest her rights, and her child. Her health never fully recovered from this brush with death, but this did not keep her from her activism. She was again elected to the Bihar Legislative Assembly in 1946. When India won its independence in 1947, she joined her husband in working to promote peace in riot-ridden Bihar.

Her story ended abruptly when she was killed in a car accident on the way back from an assembly session on 15 February 1948, just a few weeks after the assassination of Mohandas Gandhi. She was only forty-four. While her life was cut tragically short, she lived on in her huge body of literature which included eighty-eight poems and forty-six short stories. Writing in the Khariboli dialect of Hindi, she wrote about everyday issues that everyone could understand and relate to. Aside from her children's poems, she primarily wrote about the trials of Indian women and their struggles to rise above gender and caste discrimination. Yet, her most famous poems are those which have an explicitly nationalist tone, odes which helped to inspire young people to take up the call of the freedom struggle. These poems centre women and the role that they played in reclaiming their nation for themselves. Undoubtedly her most famous poem is that dedicated to Rani Lakshmibai of Jhansi, published in 1930. This remains the most recited poem in Hindi literature and is still taught in many Indian curriculums today to inspire future generations. The poem, which runs to almost twenty stanzas, stood out not just because of its emotive rendition of a heroine of the 1857 movement, but because of its overwhelming popularity despite the dominance of men in the literary scene of colonial India. Such poems are a testament not just to the enduring legacy of Rani Lakshmibai, but to the spirit of Subhadra who worked in life and death to remind us of the central role that women – from caste-oppressed mothers to dominant-caste queens – had to play in the building of their nations.

Khurshedben Naoroji (1894-1966)

While many women found fame as Indian nationalists, renowned soprano Khurshedben Naoroji gave up fame to become one. Khurshedben was born into a Parsi family in Bombay in 1894, granddaughter of the first Indian to serve in the British Parliament and India's first nationalist leader, Dadabhai Naoroji. However, she did not initially follow in his political footsteps, and instead chose a career as a successful classical soprano. Nicknamed Bul (nightingale) by her family, she moved to Paris in the early 1920s to study music. Khurshedben struggled to adapt to the culture and found herself feeling lost and lonely in Europe, until she became friends with Eva Palmer Sikelianos, an American who had moved to Greece. The pair had long conversations about their respective cultures and established a music school in Athens which focussed on non-Western music. Happily settled in Greece, Khurshedben rediscovered her love of Indian culture, and began to wear saris and host Indian music concerts. From afar, she learned of Gandhi's home-rule campaign, and when Sikelianos proposed that they jointly host the first Delphic Festival, Khurshedben declined and opted to return to her homeland and join the fight for Indian freedom.

On returning to India, she moved into Gandhi's Sabarmati *ashram* in Gujarat. She was among the first to strongly encourage Gandhi to involve women in his cause. In a newspaper interview, she said that Gandhi's movement would lead to a 'great awakening' of women, and that – whether given permission or not – women were 'not going to stop their work so well begun'.[56]

Khurshedben worked primarily in the North-West Frontier Province, which is today the Khyber Pakhtunkhwa region of Pakistan. By the early 1930s, she had become a famous figure in regional politics and a close friend of Abdul Ghaffar Khan, who was known as the 'Frontier Gandhi' for leading peaceful nationalist politics among the Pashtun people. The British arrested Khurshedben several times, and she once joked in a letter to Gandhi that she had befriended the fleas, showing her unwavering spirit despite her poor conditions. In 1930, she was part of a group arrested for attempting to fly the Indian flag in a government college in Ahmedabad.

At Gandhi's request, Khurshedben made the unification of Hindus and Muslims her personal mission and attempted to promote the INC to Muslims who were increasingly favouring a separate Muslim polity. Communal harmony, however, was threatened by the fact that Hindu locals were frequently terrorized by Muslim bandits, famous for their kidnappings in the area of Waziristan. British and Indian authorities appeared reticent to challenge these dacoits, and thus they ran virtually free to commit campaigns of terror and violence. While her male colleagues and local police forces shied away from confronting these gangs, the brave Khurshedben decided to approach them directly and try to convert them to a path of *ahimsa* – no easy task. She toured the region on foot, meeting the bandits' mothers and daughters in the hope that they could dissuade their men from a life of banditry. Astonishingly, her method worked, and by December 1940, kidnappings had drastically dropped and Hindu-Muslim relations were consequently improved. Even the British reluctantly praised her for succeeding where they had failed, despite their superiority complex and their repeated claims that they knew how best to rule India and its people. This episode proved the influence that all women (not just the political elite) had on the activities of their menfolk, even where this has not been acknowledged by history.

Upon hearing that a group of Hindus were being held against their will in Waziristan, Khurshedben vowed to meet with their captors and try to negotiate their release. She knew that this put her at great personal risk, and she warned Gandhi that the bandits may demand a ransom for her release or even go so far as to remove a part of her body as a warning to other interferers. However, her bravery came to nought, as she was arrested and imprisoned by the British before she could even cross the border. She remained in prison until 1944, being shipped to numerous jails around the country at the whim of the British.

However, Khurshedben was alive and free to see India finally win its independence in 1947. Given her dedication to Hindu-Muslim unity, we can only imagine how distraught she must have been to see the communal carnage that followed. She worked for the government in various roles, but eventually returned to her singing career, happy in the knowledge that she left behind a free and (eventually) more united land. She is believed to have died in 1966, in relative obscurity despite not only her illustrious music career but also her courageous and compassionate national activities.

Satyavati Devi (1905–2010)

The freedom fighter who outlived all others was Satyavati Devi. But despite her illustrious 105-year life, she is more often discussed owing to her relationship to famous men (namely her grandfather, father, and son), rather than on her own merit. Now is the time to change that.

Satyavati Devi was born to a Hindu family in the Tarn Taran district of Punjab on 28 February 1905. She remembered that she was the most spoiled of her parents' seven children. The family lived with their maternal grandmother in Haryana. Traditionally, girls in her community did not attend school, but Satyavati was determined she wanted an education and begged to be allowed to go to school. Her father was always very supportive, and thus allowed her to attend school to learn Sanskrit, Urdu, Hindi and English, in addition to Gurmukhi which she learnt from her grandmother. Satyavati regarded her school years as the most formative of her later activism – she said that she decided to join the national movement aged just eight. She admired and emulated the Gandhian principles of her teachers, and all staff and students only wore *khadi*. She later recalled how she enjoyed being taught to spin, which would serve her well as a *satyagrahi*. The students were taught about the 1857 War of Independence but were well aware that this war was not yet over. Satyavati realized that women were easy targets for British officers and thus she and her friends would only travel in groups. The killing of one of her friends, Sushila Devi, also had a fundamental impact on her, and further fanned her determination to drive out the British and create a safer India for women and girls.

In 1925, she married medical student Lala Achint Ram who broke tradition by refusing a dowry and insisting that his wife never wear a veil – something that was extremely radical in rural Punjab at the time. Her new husband gave up his successful medical practice to join the nationalist movement, at Gandhi's personal request. Satyavati recalled that when Gandhi himself requested that they join the movement, her husband immediately burnt all his clothes as a show of his commitment. As well as her progressively minded husband, she came from a family of prominent Hindu reformers who had sought to encourage women's education and reform some of the more patriarchal traditions of the area. Satyavati took great pride in the peaceful demonstrations of her male relatives, but also asserted her own dedication to the cause despite her traditional role of housewife and mother. For example, she once addressed a crowd proudly claiming her place as one of millions of India's women who had left their domestic sphere behind for the first time to join Gandhi's fight in the struggle for the very life of their nation.

In refusing to allow women to use the excuse of motherhood to stand back from the freedom movement, she showed solidarity with the other women who had cast aside their silence to fight for their country. When her husband was arrested, she and her three children moved to her father-in-law's house in Amritsar. From there, she continued to join protest marches and was jailed several times – once alongside her daughters who were four and seven years old at the time. If the British thought that imprisoning Satyavati would silence her, they were sorely mistaken. She later recalled how prison did little to dampen her spirit and that the inmates would amuse themselves by taunting their jailors with nationalist chants and patriotic speeches. The British withheld food and water from them as punishment for their defiance. However, Satyavati again was undeterred by the British torture, later stating: 'We didn't care. Independence was all that mattered'.[57]

While she was in jail, a popular song became the rallying cry of local nationalists. It went:

'Jump into the burning fire, and stand firm in the holy war, do not retreat from the battle, so says Sister Satyavatiji. In the battle you must die before men. Don't be afraid of bullets or sticks. Move your head forward first. So says sister Satyavatiji'.[58]

The image of jumping into the fire evokes images of women committing *sati*. The language of a 'holy war' evokes the Islamic concept of *jihad* – a physical and/or mental battle of good over evil. In urging women to act first rather than waiting on the men to protect them, she again evokes the story of Sikh warrior queen, Mai Bhago. Thus, Satyavati knew how to unite women across religious and cultural divides (something which many of her fellow male nationalists failed to achieve) and urge women to engage in the battle for their nation's soul by whatever means necessary.

While in jail, she was struck down by pleurisy and then tuberculosis but continued to work with the INC throughout the 1930s and remained a well-respected — and well-heeded — member of the nationalist movement until and beyond her release. She harboured the wanted revolutionary Chandrashekhar Azad for three days before he fled to Lahore, sent supplies to Lala Lajpat Rai while he was in jail, and she personally cooked for Bhagat Singh. This shows that she was truly at the heart of the revolutionary movement, even though she, as a *satyagrahi*, preferred peaceful protest herself. On 26 August 1942, the twenty-seven-year-old Satyavati was again arrested, this time along with her three children — her daughter, Subhadra, was only thirteen at the time making her the youngest freedom fighter to be arrested. Her husband was also arrested. Satyavati, along with other women prisoners, erected the Indian flag in Lahore Jail, laughing in the faces of their jailors. She then went on hunger strike to protest the conditions in which political prisoners were being held.

When independence was finally announced in 1947, Satyavati was torn between ecstasy and terror. She was in Lahore, helping to cook for hundreds of women and children refugees who had fled the violence of Partition, a trauma that Satyavati could never bring herself to discuss. All she had to say was that she survived and found her way back to India in 1948 once the worst of the violence had subsided. Following India's independence, she and her husband took a keen interest in the Bhoodan Movement, exhorting landlords to give their land over to the people. In 1965, she donated all her jewels to the prime minister's National Relief Fund which was established to provide aid to those affected by national disasters.

From 1989 to 1997, her son Krishna Kant became the governor and then vice president of Andhra Pradesh. In both roles, his mother lived with him, ensuring that she remained at the heart of Indian politics even after her own activism had ended. In 2002, Krishna passed away and his mother refused to leave his side until he was cremated. In 2009, she and her eighty-year-old daughter, Subhadra, published a book called *The Illustrated History of the Freedom Struggle*, in an attempt to keep the memories of the nationalist movement alive. Satyavati continued to wear *khadi* and spin the *charkha* until she was over 100 years old when hip-replacement surgery hampered her movement. A year before her death, she was honoured by the President of India for her role in the independence movement. Satyavati died in Delhi on 26 October 2010, aged 105. At the time of her death, she was the oldest living Indian freedom fighter.

Satyavati, reflecting on her life when she was 104 recalled that she thrived on the struggles she had endured. She kept a close eye on Indian politics and society until her dying day, though she was less than impressed with what she saw. In 2009, she lamented that today's youth seemed to care only for money and power. Let her story be a reminder today to keep the courage and spirit of previous generations alive and fight for what is right, regardless of personal benefit.

Chapter three
Partners and politicians

'Nearly all the Indian leaders are surrounded by women members of their family, whether as wives, sisters or daughters, who exercise an extremely powerful influence on their careers. I had come out to India with the naïve impression that Indian women were completely submerged and had no say or interest in matters of State. This is certainly not the case ... a number of other women, Hindu and Muslim, are formidable personalities whose ambitions and interests measure up to those of their menfolk'.[59]

So wrote Alan Campbell Johnson, secretary to the Viceroy of India in 1947. While many women nationalists identified either as revolutionaries or *satyagrahis*, there was another group of women who – although often beginning their careers as *satyagrahis* and demonstrating revolutionary spirits – did not closely align themselves to either movement but rather preferred to fight the British through political means. These women used electoral reform, party politics, and legislation committees, employing many of the British's own political mechanisms against them to free India from within. These women played an instrumental role in ensuring that women's voices were heard at the highest levels of diplomacy, and in creating the very constitutions which would determine what independent India and Pakistan would look like. Political avenues were especially appealing to Muslim women who felt excluded from the explicitly Hindu-centric movements of Gandhi and who – as a religious minority – lacked some of the material power that other revolutionaries had at their disposal. These women have often been lost in the shadows of the men who not only claimed credit for the women's political ideas but also often discarded the women who had helped them get there as soon as they grabbed that power for themselves.

Rattanbai 'Ruttie' Maryam Jinnah (1900–1929)

The lives of all the women surrounding the male figures of the independence movement have been overshadowed, but arguably none have suffered such a severe erasure as Ruttie Jinnah, wife of Pakistan's founding father, Muhammad Ali Jinnah.

Rattanbai Petit was born on 20 February 1900 to an extremely wealthy Parsi family. Rattanbai was given the life-long nickname 'Ruttie', meaning 'happiness' in Hindi and 'lucky' in Urdu. She was said to be a rather spoiled child, but also extremely caring and passionate about a host of social causes, a trait which would only grow throughout her life. She was extremely well-educated and was known as a fashionista, a sportswoman, and a musician. Her greatest love was for her pets and her devotion to animal rights was something which she at times prioritized even above her marriage. Despite being politically engaged from a very young age, her true dream was to become a poet or a writer, but destiny had other ideas in store for her.

By sixteen, Ruttie had fallen for her father's charming and handsome friend, Muhammad Ali Jinnah, a man twenty-three years her senior whom she had known since birth. They shared a passionate nationalism and a fervent belief in gender equality. Jinnah found Ruttie wise and independent beyond her years, which she proved when she boldly proposed to Jinnah in 1916. He accepted, on the condition that she convert to Islam – which she did only after undertaking her own research on the faith, taking the Islamic name of Maryam. Her father strongly disapproved of the match and sought restraining orders against Jinnah which prevented the couple meeting for one year. Even when Ruttie was disinherited and disowned, their love endured and on 20 April 1918, the eighteen-year-old Ruttie married forty-one-year-old Jinnah in an Islamic ceremony. Ruttie had only a puppy to accompany her down the aisle. When her father again took Jinnah to court, Ruttie bravely addressed the judge herself, attesting that it was she who had kidnapped her husband and not the other way around.

As Jinnah became evermore embroiled in the politics of the day, every witness attested that 'his personal, political, and social life was always with Ruttie'.[60] Despite her concern for his workload, she shared his burdens and became his closest confidant and political advisor. As a young girl, Ruttie had written that she wished 'to find fulfilment in love' and it seems that she did.[61] However, this fulfilment came not just from being a companion to her husband, but in the opportunities the marriage gave her to assert her nationalist leanings. Years before her marriage she had written of her desire to fight 'pitched battles for freedom … with sword and dagger … sacrificing all at the feet of the motherland'.[62]

Although she turned down an offer to become the youngest ever vice-president of the All-India Trade Union Congress (AITUC) aged twenty, her moment to take a stand came in 1918 when the British proposed to raise a statue of the departing governor of Bombay. Their claim that the statue was raised on behalf of the people he had invaded was seen as a grave insult. Jinnah raised his objections at a public meeting of up to 20,000 people in December 1918. Ruttie, the only woman in attendance, joined her husband on stage and followed up his emotive speeches with a rousing 'Aye'. On 11 December, Jinnah left early in the morning to break into the Town Hall alongside fellow protestors. Furious at being left behind, Ruttie followed her husband and demanded entry to the hall, which was refused. Over 25,000 people had joined the protest, outnumbering pro-government factions by almost thirty to one. When the police eventually gained entry to the hall, they beat the protestors – including Jinnah. Many were shocked at this blatant display of police brutality, but Ruttie was not deterred. Rather, she was inspired to stand on a platform and begin addressing the crowds with cries of: 'We are not slaves! You have no right to stop me when I am exercising my right as a citizen of Bombay. Secondly, whatever you do, I am not moving from here'.[63] This was a dangerous gamble, as Ruttie was three months pregnant at the time. Drawing the line at beating a pregnant (and well-known) woman, the police instead turned a water cannon on her and the gathered crowd. Soaked through, Ruttie steadfastly refused to move and did not stand down until her husband emerged, only lightly injured from the police assault. For her part in this protest, Ruttie was dubbed 'the Indian version of Joan of Arc: beautiful, fiery, and defiant'.[64] As a result of the protests, the British abandoned plans for the monument. Instead, the public raised 65,000 rupees and built a different monument, one dedicated to the Jinnahs. At a speech given in a celebratory dinner a week later, it was stated that Ruttie had singlehandedly exalted Indian womanhood and both she and her husband were presented with medals of valour. This was a symbol of the respect with which she was held and the power she had to defy the British, even independently of her husband.

Another occasion on which she took a public stand against the British was following the arrest and deportation of her close friend, B.G. Horniman. Horniman was a freedom-fighting British journalist who had been working with the Jinnahs for some time. Jinnah had successfully defended him in court when the British had slapped him with fake sodomy charges in response to his publishing pro-nationalist articles. In 1919, Horniman was deported to Britain after he was believed to have leaked incriminating photographs showing the carnage the British had inflicted during the Jallianwala Bagh massacre. Seven months pregnant, Ruttie spoke confidently and flawlessly at a protest rally in Horniman's defence. The speech was completely spontaneous but was convincing enough that the AITUC launched a motion to demand Horniman's release. Despite medical advice against undertaking such a strenuous twenty-day journey in her advanced pregnancy, Ruttie insisted on travelling to London with her husband to fight for Horniman's release. She is said to have stated that freedom was more important than her health – a principle which she would dangerously hold to throughout her short life. In 1919, Ruttie delivered a baby girl named Dina, having gone into labour during a visit to a London theatre. While they both adored their only child, the Jinnahs were often accused of neglecting her to pursue their political goals. Prioritizing politics over motherhood must have raised more than a few eyebrows in an age when motherhood was deemed to be a woman's primary – if not only – duty, but the fact that she refused to be restricted to the role of mother is a testament to her strong ideals and her dedication to acting on them whatever the personal cost.

While Ruttie was not afraid to stand up to the British at an institutional level, she was defiant of them on a personal level too. She and her husband refused to dress according to either British or Indian standards. It was now commonplace among Indian nationalists to wear nothing but plain homespun cloth – which suited the British who believed this reflected their low status. The Jinnahs rejected both of these expectations and insisted on wearing expensive designer European clothes. Ruttie asserted her right to wear the same fancy clothes as her British counterparts. She purposefully dressed as garishly as possible, claiming she loved to embarrass the sanctimonious *satyagrahis* around her. On one occasion, she and her husband walked out of a dinner at the British governor's house when his wife, Lady Willingdon, scandalized that Ruttie had dared to wear a modern, Western-style dress to dinner, snidely suggested that she cover up or else she may catch a cold.

In early 1921, Ruttie refused to bow to the Viceroy but rather greeted him with closed hands in the Indian style. He chastized her saying that she should have greeted him in the British manner because when in Rome, one should do as the Romans do. She defiantly replied that he was in her country, and thus in this situation, *he* was the visitor, and she was the Roman. Five years later, she laughed when a later Viceroy said that he would not visit Germany because the Germans did not like the English. She sarcastically replied that if he wanted to be around people who liked the English, he should not be in India, much to the embarrassment of everyone present. Her humorous disdain for the British also manifested itself in her penchant for naming her dogs after British officials, a common method of insult in Asian culture.

In 1926, the Jinnahs embarked on a second honeymoon in Kashmir, by all accounts a truly blissful time in both their lives. However, one sticky issue arose when Ruttie became disillusioned with the number and needless bureaucracy of British checkpoints in the area. Eventually, she snapped and wrote on one form that the purpose of their visit was 'to spread sedition'.[65]

Her husband was highly unamused, given that she could have been killed for such a joke, but she did not care. She regarded any impudence against the British as a patriotic duty and would not be shamed for it. She also launched a campaign to destroy textbooks which glorified British colonialism, writing instead those that reflected the truth of British rule (a fight that sadly continues today).

Ruttie often combined her rebellion against the British with her conviction for gender equality, as demonstrated in two separate incidents. The first was her refusal to stand before British viceroys on the principle that a man should rise when a lady enters the room and not the other way around, regardless of what race that man might be. When asked why she would not rise for the Viceroy, she flippantly responded, 'He is a man, after all!'.[66] On another occasion, she loudly rebuked a British policeman whom she saw bullying an old lady on the street and knocking a basket of fruit from her hand. Ruttie ordered that he pick it up, apologize, and swore that he would live to regret defying her. Clearly mortified – and not a little intimidated – the policeman did as she said, and even promised never to insult an Indian woman again. Before departing, Ruttie gave the woman five rupees as compensation for her trauma. This shows that she took any insult to an Indian woman extremely seriously and was not afraid to put herself in danger to stand up for their rights. Furthermore, she stood for no illusions of superiority based on rank, gender, or race, as attested by her frequent visits to red-light districts while campaigning for the rights of sex workers and their children.

Sadly, however, Ruttie's political activities did not prevent her from becoming increasingly unhappy in the final years of her life. Her husband became fully engrossed in his politics and the neglect she felt culminated in her leaving their marital home in September 1927. She fled to Europe where she fell desperately ill, likely with a combination of colitis and severe depression (exacerbated by treatment with unknowingly toxic drugs). Jinnah rushed to her hospital bedside. Ignoring all pleas to return to India, he nursed his wife until she was deemed fit enough to return to India five months later. Although they never lived together again, Jinnah visited his wife every evening, discussing politics at her bedside. Everyone was sure that they would soon be fully reconciled. Sadly, they never got the chance.

On 19 February 1929, Ruttie was found unconscious and was rushed to hospital. The next day, her twenty-ninth birthday, her family came to wake her with a birthday cake. They found her lying dead on the bed. The doctors ruled that she had taken an accidental overdose. Jinnah was completely devastated by his wife's death. The famously unemotional leader broke down twice at her graveside and became reclusive in the years immediately following her passing. He remained devoted to her for the rest of his life, visiting her grave weekly (until he left India forever in 1947), playing her favourite songs when his dream of Pakistan came true, and carrying a trunk of her possessions wherever he went.

Ruttie died almost twenty years before Pakistan was born, but she undoubtedly helped to create it given that the Jinnahs were inseparable during the years that the very notion of it was conceived. Some have conceded that Ruttie must be applauded for her constant support of her husband's political endeavours. Others go so far as to attribute the very idea of a separate Muslim state to her. Some have argued that her biggest influence was accidental, given that her husband's vigil at her bedside in Paris coincided with the most crucial time of the nationalist movement when various developments destroyed any hope of Hindu-Muslim unity – Jinnah's refusal to return to India without her allowed the Hindu leaders to take control of the INC, causing the AIML to become more entrenched in their desire for a separate state. Similarly, Jinnah virtually went into hiding following his wife's death, again refusing to return to India at a time when crucial decisions about South Asia's future were being made. Thus, some have argued, if he had never loved or lost Ruttie, India may never have been divided. This also leads some to speculate that Jinnah, once the stalwart of Hindu-Muslim unity, became so embittered following his wife's death that he pushed ahead with his plans, even after the disastrous consequences became apparent. Some have blamed Ruttie's influence on Jinnah's obstinate trust of only Parsi doctors to keep his own terminal illness a secret, believing that if he had trusted Muslim doctors and made his illness public then the INC may have stalled their demand for independence, hoping to inherit a united India once Jinnah died.

None of these theories seem plausible on their own, although there is doubtless a little truth in each. What we can be sure of is that Ruttie agreed wholeheartedly with her husband's vision for the future of South Asia and that she undoubtedly influenced the creation of this new nation through Jinnah's political stance which was indistinguishable from that of his wife. In 1943, Jinnah must have been proud when over 5,000 women attended the annual meeting of the AIML, given that seventeen years earlier his wife was the only woman present. Thus, he watched in real-time as the example that his wife had set blossomed into a fully-fledged movement of women's political engagement for the first time in India's history. After assuming the position of Prime Minister of Pakistan, he continued to champion the rights of women and sometimes evoked his wife's memory to do so.

Given all that, it is absurd that Ruttie has been all but erased from history. There have been several explanations given for this. The obvious explanation is the regular misogyny of historians, journalists, and politicians who all conspired to generally erase women's contributions from the history of the Indian and Pakistani nationalist movements. Furthermore, Jinnah's relatives may have sought to discredit her to better their claims on his valuable inheritance. However, the factor most widely believed to account for the sparsity of evidence of Ruttie's life is the deliberate erasure of her story by her jealous sister-in-law, Fatima, who had the perfect opportunity, given her closeness to Jinnah, to destroy all Ruttie's personal belongings after his death. While there is little to be gained from feeding into narratives that pit one powerful woman against another, it cannot be denied that Fatima's dislike for Ruttie, and her determination to undermine the role that she played in Jinnah's life, must have contributed to her wider erasure from history. Fatima even went so far as to invent a fictional first wife in her autobiography to downplay the significance of his marriage to

Ruttie. Nonetheless, a woman as indomitable as Ruttie Jinnah was never going to be that easily erased. She was so widely written about – and almost overwhelmingly positively even by her adversaries – during her lifetime that it has proved impossible to condemn her to anonymity. Monuments still stand attesting to her bravery during anti-British protests and her influence is written into the very map of modern South Asia; Ruttie's legacy remains crystal clear for anyone who cares to look for it.

Jinnah often said that it was the biggest regret of his life that his wife did not live to witness his ascension as founding father of Pakistan. Given that Ruttie made such a mark on the world in just under three decades, it is tragic to think about what more she could have done had she lived to have the chance. Yet we can allay some of this tragedy by acknowledging the role she played in creating a nation, and in emulating her life of kindness, justice, and determination.

Fatima Jinnah (1893–1967)

Fatima Jinnah may have appeared as the villain in Ruttie's story, but the truth is much more complex. Fatima has seemingly been condemned to languish in the shadow of her older brother, M.A. Jinnah. Although earning the epithet 'Mother of the Nation' in Pakistan, since her death she has been remembered as little more than a devoted sister, despite her lifelong record of nationalism and political service.

Fatima was born in Karachi on 31 July 1893. Her parents were Isma'ili Shias from the Khoja community. This sect of Islam incorporated many Hindu beliefs and practices which – combined with the diversity of the places she grew up – gave Fatima an open-minded approach to religion. Neither Fatima nor her female relatives observed purdah. Her parents had moved to Karachi in 1875, following which they had seven children – four daughters and three sons. Their mother died in childbirth two years after Fatima was born so she was raised by her sisters and her paternal aunt. Her father controversially ensured that she was taught English. Her elder sister was forbidden to take part in these lessons by her husband, showing Fatima how restrictive marriage could be – perhaps explaining why Fatima, who valued education above all else, never married. When their father passed away in his forties, with her sisters all married off, Fatima was left to the care of her older brother, Muhammad Ali, a virtual stranger to her given that he was sixteen years her senior and had lived abroad studying in England for most of her life.

When she graduated school in 1912, Fatima moved in with her brother and their relationship began to blossom. They shared many hobbies, and she often helped him with his legal cases. When her brother was home, they discussed politics over breakfast every day, and she later expressed her gratitude that he always valued her opinion and never told her to mind her place. Tension arose between brother and sister however when he married Rattanbai Petit, a marriage she disapproved of for several reasons. However, the girls had once been friends so it is likely that Fatima was a little jealous of Ruttie usurping her role as her brother's friend and confidant. This jealousy might explain why she left her brother and went instead to live with her sisters.

In 1920, twenty-five-year-old Fatima, renowned for her beauty and intelligence, began her two-year training as a dental surgeon and in 1923 she opened a private dental clinic in Bombay, the first Muslim woman to do so. By 1927, she was also volunteering at a local clinic providing free dental care to women in purdah who could not attend private clinics. However, in 1929, things took a tragic turn when her sister-in-law, Ruttie, with whom Fatima had now reconciled, died on her 29th birthday. As well as the personal grief she must have felt, Fatima became deeply concerned for her brother who was distraught at her passing and she soon returned home to care for him herself.

Fatima accompanied her brother to London for the First Round Table Conference, although she did not attend the meeting itself. Jinnah decided that he could do more for his political goals in London where he was free from interference and decided to make a permanent move to Britain. Fatima made the difficult choice to join him, returning to India only to sell her practice and collect her niece. In London, she took up her own social work while overseeing the political activities of her brother. She asked him to become her political mentor and in response he appointed her his personal secretary, responsible for opening and replying to his mail, drafting his speeches, and summarizing all relevant newspaper articles. Therefore, much of the work which earned him his role as president of the AIML may have been written by his sister.

By the mid-1930s, the AIML was begging for the Jinnahs to return to India, which they did in late 1934. Her brother later credited her with persuading him that he had an indispensable role to play in carving India's future. Fatima must have been disappointed, then, to discover that on their return, she was relegated for the first time to little more than a housekeeper. Jinnah had now hired professional secretaries and was suddenly reluctant to discuss political matters with his sister, plagued by fears that he would be accused of nepotism. During one fight, he told her he was not obligated to discuss AIML business with her because he was not her political representative. In response, she began to directly participate in the party for the first time. In 1937, she attended the annual session in Lucknow, marking her formal debut into party politics. Her involvement deepened when her brother was first diagnosed with pleurisy in 1940 and she became his secret nurse because he did not want his political rivals to know about his ailing health.

In 1938, the Muslim League Women's Sub-Committee (MLWSC) was created, and Fatima was appointed its convenor, showing the AIML's trust in Fatima who was keen to arouse political and specifically national consciousness among Muslim women. By 1939, she had also become actively involved in the Bombay branch of the MLWSC, bringing her into conversation with all the main Muslim women's organizations across the country. While many men decried the founding of organizations which they feared would force women out of purdah, others encouraged their wives to shed their veils and step into the public sphere so that they could participate in this historic movement. While her brother sought to placate the male protestors, it was Fatima to whom the women turned for guidance and advice. Thus, for the first time, she was beginning to be respected as a politician and leader outside of her relationship with her brother.

In 1940, Fatima – clad in her trademark white sari – sat beside her brother on the stage at the Lahore session of the AIML when the Lahore Resolution (also known as the Pakistan Resolution) was passed in front of 60,000 members, unanimously endorsing the creation of a separate, independent Muslim state. From that moment on, Fatima joined her brother on stage at every session to come, causing widespread condemnation among the more conservative Indians. Her refusal to observe purdah despite public pressure forced the AIML to issue a statement asserting a Muslim woman's right to choose whether to adhere to purdah. Gradually, Fatima's appearances began to normalize the sight of women at political meetings. In 1942, Fatima helped to establish the Muslim Women's Students' Federation, acting as a liaison between women in purdah and male officials. One of the women involved in this endeavour later emphasized Fatima's role, stating that her contribution to mobilizing women was completely underestimated and that many of the women who found important work in independent Pakistan owed their careers to Fatima.

In the years immediately before Partition, Fatima and her brother were in constant touch and witnesses attested that their correspondence was almost completely political. In March 1946, she gave a speech in Lahore, thanking women for all they had done for Pakistan and asserting her certainty that the same women would help to make their dreams a reality. This was one of the few times she spoke publicly in favour of the creation of Pakistan, but that she did so completely independently shows that she believed in this new nation herself and was not merely agreeing with her brother in their private correspondence.

Several sources attest to the fact that Fatima was her brother's most trusted confidante. For example, she often answered questions on his behalf, and witnesses relayed how she proofread all his speeches and press statements, with his secretaries being ordered to run everything past Fatima before it was published. When later discussing this pre-Partition period, Jinnah recalled that his sister was the only one who had believed in him and his vision. She also stood in for him at AIML meetings, gauging the audience's reactions to his policies and reporting back to him. Thus, by the 1940s, Fatima had become his colleague more than his sister, and he would need her more than ever as Partition loomed.

At this time, Fatima became known as the First Lady of Pakistan, even before the state had been officially created. In late 1946, as communal riots began to sweep the country, she joined her brother in Karachi where she addressed a general meeting of the AIML. After Jinnah's departure, she remained as his representative, successfully convincing the party's warring members to reconcile and focus instead on bringing down the pro-INC leadership. Her influence was so great that India's first High Commissioner to Pakistan remarked that he believed Fatima to be the master behind all of Jinnah's plans. Likewise, the British Viceroy, Lord Mountbatten, was instructed that his wife should make it a priority to befriend Fatima because she had the power to sway her brother in any matter. This increasing influence is reflected in the fact that by early 1947, Fatima was now acting as a delegate of the Bombay Provincial Muslim League, showing that she was no longer confined to the women's branch of the AIML but was now a leading figure in the main male-dominated party.

Fatima was by her brother's side as he greeted the new Viceroy and Vicereine on 4 April 1947. Their first dinner was awkward, and Edwina Mountbatten later stated that the Jinnahs were the most challenging to deal with of all the Indian politicians but that one could not help but fall for their charisma and intelligence and admitted that she had great sympathy for many of their worries. Given the Mountbattens' closeness to Gandhi and Nehru (and in light of the rumours that Edwina and Nehru were more than friends), it is unsurprising that the Jinnahs may have shown some aloofness to the couple. In a speech at a Muslim women's organization in Delhi, Fatima expressed special pride in the Muslim women who had taken to the frontlines as equals with their brothers-in-arms. She called on those who would join the new nation of Pakistan to work hard for it while also asking those who remained in India to continue to care for and empower India's Muslim women.

When Fatima and her brother returned to their hometown, Karachi, to establish the new capital of Pakistan, they seemed rather melancholy having left behind the people and places they had loved all their lives. Fatima was given the responsibility of managing the diplomatic visits which would accompany Independence Day on 15 August. At one of the few celebratory parties the Jinnahs held around this time, Jinnah thanked Fatima for everything she had done for him throughout the struggle. While this speech moved Fatima, she responded not with a torrent of dedication to him, but with another speech applauding the nationalist contribution of women. This shows that contrary to popular belief, her brother's approval was not Fatima's *raison d'etre*. Rather, she saw herself as part of a wider movement of women's nationalism and as a fighter for women's rights.

Accordingly, it is fitting that Fatima had a front-row seat as power was officially transferred from British hands into her brother's. She was by his side as they greeted the Mountbattens for the official transfer of power. This occasion was solemn and awkward by all accounts, especially when Fatima rejected the gift that Edwina offered as a bribe to convince Jinnah to share some of his new power with Mountbatten. However, at one point, Fatima and Edwina were spotted holding hands and when they waved the Mountbattens off at the airport, Fatima even conceded to kissing Edwina on the cheek. Likely fearing for the lives of their beloved men and the future of their respective countries, for a moment they were merely women rather than representatives of opposite sides of one of the most monumental events in world history. However, when Edwina expressed a desire that the two should stay friends, Fatima did not return the wish.

This was the start of a new nation and in the absence of a Mrs Jinnah, Fatima now officially assumed the role of First Lady, one which she completed diligently. She travelled with her brother on all his official visits across Pakistan and kept up with her women's social work by inaugurating various medical and educational institutions specifically aimed at serving women. In November 1947, she delivered a speech in Lahore which encapsulated all she felt at the remarkable events of the last few years:

'We the Musalmans have been considered a backward race ... This complex had such an adverse effect on us that we ... also began to think Muslims quite unfit to handle any situation ... After the division of India ... now it is for you to show to the same people who thought we were incompetent, that we can more than manage our own affairs with efficiency and make Pakistan one of the world's most prosperous and strongest states. Let us now make one supreme effort by pulling together and thus succeed in our cherished dream.'[67]

She encouraged women to learn self-defence amid the unthinkable violence against them during Partition. She even worked with some of her former political enemies to establish a Woman's National Guard (WNG) to this effect. She took an active interest in relief efforts in refugee camps, although she refused an invitation by Edwina Mountbatten to visit camps on the Indian side of the border – a move for which Fatima was criticized by those who saw it as contributing to communal tensions. However, she did establish the Fatima Jinnah Kashmir Fund and the Women's Relief Committee Kashmir (Mujahidin) Fund, which focussed on helping ordinary people. She recalled her heartbreak at witnessing the plight of women and children especially and asked how any country could be expected to deal with such atrocities, while also asserting a confidence that if anyone could rise to the challenge it was her Pakistan. Thus, even after Partition, her care for women, her pride in her Muslim faith, and her patriotic dedication to the new Pakistan rang through in everything she said or did.

Fatima began to fret more than ever about her brother's health as she watched him deteriorate following Partition, attempting to dissuade him from his political activities. Her final recorded words to him expressed her desire that she could swap her life for his. He passed away on 9 September 1948. One can only imagine her heartbreak at losing her greatest friend, companion, comrade, and leader. However, this was not the end of her story. She continued to promote women's rights through education, medicine, welfare, political representation, legal rights, and emancipation from purdah. She continued to provide aid to refugees and other marginalized communities through fundraising, committee leadership, dispersing resources, and organizing relief efforts. She also continued to patronize schools and orphanages for girls. She constantly pushed for all sections of society, regardless of gender, ethnicity, wealth, caste, or religion, to work together to build a prosperous new nation. She even stood (unsuccessfully) as a presidential candidate aged seventy-one in protest at the current leader whom she regarded as a corrupt dictator. Now that she could no longer care for her brother, she turned to caring for her new nation and its people. As early as 1947, she had been referred to as the Madr-e-Millat, Mother of the Nation, a role she cherished and took extremely seriously. On 9 July 1967, Fatima Jinnah passed away at the age of seventy-four. She was buried next to her beloved brother in Karachi. Her official cause of death was given as heart failure, but many, including her nephew, speculated that she had been murdered by her political enemies.

While Muhammad Ali continues to be regarded as the architect of Pakistan, few remember his sister who was beside him in every sense. Not only did she fulfil her traditional domestic expectations as a homemaker and caretaker, but she encouraged and directly influenced the politics for which he has become one of the stars of the fight against the British Raj. However, more than just a great support to her brother, she was a great woman in her own right, repeatedly proving herself an ardent nationalist, a dedicated social worker, and a force of nature against whom no man – or woman – stood a chance. Thus, the next time you hear someone discussing the mighty Jinnah – you might ask, which one?

Vijayalakshmi Pandit (1900–1990)

Another woman eclipsed by her brother's shadow was Vijayalakshmi Pandit, sister of Jawaharlal Nehru. Born on 20 August 1900, Vijayalakshmi (then called Swarup) was eleven years younger than her elder brother Jawaharlal. In 1916, the teenage Vijayalakshmi attended the INC meeting and was awed by women nationalists Sarojini Naidu and Annie Besant. Four years later, she spent time in Gandhi's *ashram* and helped with the daily chores and spinning, as well as being given a chance to work in the office producing *Young India*, Gandhi's nationalist journal. Reminiscing about the impact Gandhi had on the movement, she recalled:

'When Gandhi spoke … he literally mesmerized the crowd, and when he appealed for funds all the *satyagraha* volunteers poured in, women took off their earrings, people took off their jewellery, and seemed to be compelled to do it. Here was this little frail, almost insignificant person, taking on the might of the greatest empire in the world, and what did he have at hand, he had a country where there was overwhelming poverty, illiteracy, superstitions of every kind, religious taboos, untouchability, in fact every dividing factor that you can think of was there, and yet out of this he welded a nation. And the greatest gift that he gave us was political freedom, freedom from fear. Because from that stemmed everything else.[68]

However, it was not just Gandhi who inspired the young Vijayalakshmi. She was also driven to action by the barbarity of the British, especially as exemplified by the Jallianwala Bagh massacre. She wrote that the massacre made it impossible for any Indian, whatever their political inclination, to deny the barbarity of the British. It was even more horrific given that so many Indians had just died for Britain during the First World War. The massacre seemed to Vijayalakshmi a slap in the face after everything Indians had given to the war effort and was the catalyst for finally revolting against the British regime. She singled out one particular policy: the order of General Dyer was issued when a missionary, Marcella Sherwood, was attacked six days after the Jallianwala Bagh masscare. Dyer ordered that no Indian was permitted to walk the street where this attack had occured. Rather, they were made to crawl. Those disobeying these orders were to be flogged. This encapsulated the humiliation that the British inflicted on the Indians:

'There was not anybody in India who was not conscious of the indignity that had been perpetrated upon [us] ... On that day British rule in India ended ... because one man had been made to crawl on his belly, the whole nation had crawled on its belly. And the humiliation of this was so great that India was a nation in mourning. There wasn't a home that didn't feel this. There wasn't a single individual who wasn't conscious that they had been personally humiliated and had lost their dignity and their self-respect by what had happened there. And I don't think any act that could have been thought up could have greater results in creating hatred and bitterness and opposition to British rule than this one crawling order in Amritsar.'[69]

It is not difficult to hear the truth ringing in Vijayalakshmi's words. Not only had the British massacred crowds of innocent people – including children – who were merely protesting the infraction of their basic human rights, but the British had then sought to silence and humiliate anyone who dared to speak against this barbarity. Dyer himself showed little remorse for the blood on his hands, despite facing criticism even from fellow British officers for the decision; this only served to convince nationalists such as Vijayalakshmi that Indians could never be safe while India remained under British control.

In 1921, Vijayalakshmi married Ranjit Sitaram Pandit, a successful barrister and classical scholar from Kathiawar Gujarat, Maharashtra. She was jailed for the first time in 1931, serving eighteen months between 1931 and 1933. In 1937, she became the first Indian woman to hold a cabinet post when she was elected an MP for the Cawnpore Bilhaur constituency. Once elected to the provincial legislature of the United Provinces, she became minister of local self-government and public health until 1938 (holding the post again in the year immediately before Partition).

While records are scant for many of these years, she had stayed active in nationalist activities, for she found herself again imprisoned for six months in 1940, and then for a further seven months in 1942 for participating in the Quit India Movement. When she was finally released in 1943, she dedicated herself to serving the victims of the Bengal Famine. She was also made president of the Save the Children Fund Committee which rescued destitute children from the streets.

If the plight she witnessed during the famine was not enough to further turn her against the British, in 1944 her husband was arrested and taken to Lucknow prison. He never left, and died in British custody, leaving behind his wife and their three daughters. While we do not know exactly how he died, the British's poor treatment of political prisoners is well documented, and thus it is not a stretch to suspect that his death was a direct result of his incarceration – at the very least through disease or starvation, if not directly through torture or murder. Her widowhood did not deter Vijayalakshmi from politics but rather seems to have emboldened her into action. While grieving her loss, Vijayalakshmi was also forced to deal with Hindu inheritance laws and the poor treatment of widows resulting from them. Rather than humbly accept them, she joined forces with the AIWC to campaign for these laws to be reformed so that women were not forced to suffer social oppression on top of their grief.

In 1946, Vijayalakshmi was elected to the Constituent Assembly as a representative from the United Provinces. When India achieved its independence a year later, she became a diplomat and served as an Indian ambassador to various countries across the world. Thus, not only did she help to create this new Indian nation, but she also took a central role in carving a place for it in the modern world and protecting its interests against ex-colonial powers who no doubt harboured resentment and suspicion of the dangerous precedent set by India's independence. For over two decades, she led the Indian delegation at the United Nations (UN) and became the first woman President of the UN General Assembly in 1953. Back in India, she sat as Governor of Maharashtra from 1962 to 1964 and returned as an MP from 1964 to 1968. She was highly critical of her niece, Indira

Gandhi, during her tenure as prime minister, especially during the state of emergency in 1975. In 1977, she openly campaigned against Indira, considering running for prime minister herself. She did not, but she was credited with helping Indira's opponents win the following election. In 1979, having retired from politics for a quiet life in the shadows of the Himalayas, she took to writing her memoirs. She passed away at the age of ninety, in 1990.

Vijayalakshmi's life is an insight into the motivations of nationalists who were not driven by personal power, but rather by genuine disgust at the injustices faced by Indians under the British Raj, and a sincere belief that not only did the British have no right to rule over India, but that they were cruel and hypocritical oppressors who must be driven out. However, her later diplomatic efforts show that rather than holding a grudge for the death of her husband or the widespread suffering she had witnessed at British hands, she had worked to chart a new relationship between India and the rest of the world – including Britain – in which India could sit as an equal and not a subject. While she has been lost in the shadow of a brother, we should remember his equally remarkable younger sister who used her privilege and power to secure global peace, a better world for the generations of women after her, and for those who like her who had suffered firsthand the tragedy of British subjugation.

Begum Jahanara Shahnawaz (1896–1979)

As well as brothers and husbands, some women also had to escape their father's shadow to become prominent activists in their own right. One such lady was Begum Jahanara Shahnawaz. Jahanara was born in Lahore on 7 April 1896 to a famous Punjabi family, the daughter of Mian Muhammad Shafi, one of the founders of the AIML. Jahanara began her education by learning the Qu'ran (as was the case for most Muslim children of the day). As well as attending a local school, she was taught English from an early age by her grandfather, a renowned Muslim reformer. When she was fifteen, she was married to a Punjabi lawyer, Mian Muhammad Shahnawaz. However, she refused to let marriage – or birthing a daughter in 1912 – get in the way of education and she graduated the same year her daughter was born. Both her natal and marital families encouraged equal gender relations. Jahanara and her family had always worn burqas as this was seen as an accommodation which had granted them the freedom to attend school and engage in politics. It was not until 1920 that Jahanara first revealed her face in public, having done so at the request of her father who wanted to bring Muslim women in line with the Hindus who had been casting off their veils in ever greater numbers. After this, Jahanara more freely interacted with organizations including the WIA, the AIWC, the AIML and *Anjuman Khawateen-e-Islam*, an organization founded by Jahanara's female family members with the primary goal of female education and social reform among Muslim women. It was even said that Jahanara's wedding doubled as a meeting for this organization. Thus, Jahanara was raised with the belief that both genders were equal in their ability and worth, an attitude she would fight to maintain her entire life.

Jahanara played an active part in the fight to raise the age of consent, as well as successfully petitioning to outlaw the practice of polygamy which she saw as detrimental to women. She contributed to the movement to address Muslim women's social concerns through Urdu literature by publishing articles challenging perceptions of and about Muslim women in

British India. She had written her first article aged just nine, titled *Talim-e-Duktaaran* (a Female Education). In 1916, she wrote an Urdu novel, *Hasanara Begum*, which propagated the idea that the only evil within the Indian Muslim community was ignorance. She used the novel to challenge social taboos and to highlight the importance of female education – and the role that women themselves could play in fighting for it. Not limited to Urdu, she also wrote important works in English, most notably her autobiography, *Father and Daughter* (1971), which documented her social and political struggles and those of her countrywomen.

Having had her interest in politics piqued by her parents' visits with prominent nationalists, Jahanara was delighted when the All-India Women's Association was founded in 1917 and she was elected to be a member representing Punjab. Jahanara was one of two women chosen to represent the interests of all-Indian women at the First Round Table Conference in London on 12 November 1930. They argued that women needed reserved seats so that they could speak for the rights of the 120 million Indian women who had no control over their own lives. Addressing the first session, Jahanara said that 'the social reform of a country depends mostly upon women'.[70] Her speech was well received by the audience and the press, and she got many statements of support from influential figures on both the Indian and British sides of the table. Most notably, Lord Irwin, then Viceroy of India, wrote to her, congratulating her on her work and expressing hope that the constitution could be built on the foundations that she had begun to lay. She was asked to report back to numerous delegations about the discussions at the conferences and detail the new constitution being proposed for India.

In 1932, at the Third Round Table Conference, she was the only Indian woman in attendance. A year later, she was nominated as the only female member of the Indian delegation to the Joint Select Committee. In her opinion, she was single-handedly responsible for protecting the interests of all women in India. She gained the support of British women activists with whom she had much in common, despite coming from different sides of the empire. She left London on 17 August 1933, but the fruits of her efforts were not seen until the details of the 1935 constitution were published, in which women were given an electorate of 600,000 voters. This was a key moment in Indian history, as it opened the way for women to become active in regional and national politics.

In 1937, eighty women, including Jahanara, were elected to Provincial and Central Parliaments and India became the third best in the world for its female representation. The same year, Jahanara was elected to the Punjab Legislative Assembly and was appointed Parliamentary Secretary for Education, Medical Relief and Public Health. She drew attention to the fact that she was the only female member of the AIML council, and it was subsequently decided that every province should be asked to delegate two women. Thus, Jahanara directly ensured that more women could be included in the conversations that were shaping the freedom struggle. This continued when in 1938 she became a member of the Women's Central Subcommittee of the AIML. In the five years she spent in this post, she pressured the AIML to address women's issues, in particular healthcare. In 1940, Jahanara attended the historic AIML session during which the Lahore Resolution was passed. She also hosted all-women delegates in her own house, ensuring their safety as well as their participation.

Jahanara's dedication to the nationalist cause was brought into question during the Second World War when she was nominated by the Viceroy to be a member of the Defence Council for India. She chose to continue in this position despite the AIML's decision not to support the British war effort and she was thus expelled from the party. Jahanara argued that it was more important for her to remain on the council to protect the representation of Muslims. She was asked by the National War Front to encourage the participation of women in the war effort and consequently took up leadership of a women's branch. She travelled across India addressing crowds of diverse genders and backgrounds. During this trip, she noted that attitudes – especially among women – were increasingly favouring independence. She continued to press the government to seek out women's opinions on how their lives could be improved and wrote articles highlighting key developments in the women's movement.

In her capacity on the Defence Council, she travelled to the Pacific Relations Conference in Canada and the US in 1942. Here, she reported her surprise that anti-Muslim sentiments had spread and that many told her that Muslims should surrender India since they had no right to call themselves citizens. She also realized how misinformed outsiders were about how many Muslims there were in India, among other lies and misunderstandings. On her return, she begged Jinnah to readmit her to the AIML, and advised that he must directly work to counteract this widespread propaganda about Muslims. Jinnah agreed to reinstate her, and she immediately began working to mobilize women in Delhi. She succeeded, for she stated in 1945 that Muslim women showed more dedication to and impatience for the creation of Pakistan than men.

Thus, despite her support for the British war effort, Jahanara again found herself aligned with nationalists and became active in the movement for Pakistan. She was one of thousands of Punjabi women who fought to create a new nation in which their rights as Muslim women would be better respected. In 1946, shortly after rejoining the AIML, she was elected to the Central Constituent Council. She was soon sent on another mission to America to elucidate the AIML's goals to the UN. Again, she found that Americans were completely deluded about the situation in India and that even Muslim Americans were firmly in favour of the INC. She also found herself repeatedly snubbed by UN delegates, even those from Muslim countries, who stated that they feared making an enemy of India.

While she left New York thoroughly despairing of international aid, Jahanara was more convinced than ever that the AIML's cause was a righteous one. In Punjab, a government had been formed of INC and Sikh parties, despite the AIML having won almost all Muslim seats and the population being mostly Muslim. By late January 1947, public demonstrations against new legislation led the newly assembled governors to call for the closure of all AIML and Muslim National Guard (MNG) offices in Lahore. Immediately upon hearing this, Jahanara and her daughter, Mumtaz, rushed to their nearest AIML office to join their male leaders in resisting the closure. Mumtaz led another group of women to the MNG offices to put up similar resistance. When the male leaders looked about to surrender, Jahanara shouted: 'Let all the men give up. We women shall start the civil disobedience movement'.[71] Eventually, all seven of the leaders, including Jahanara, were taken into custody.

These arrests triggered bigger demonstrations which spilled beyond Lahore and left the government with no choice but to retract the ban on the MNG. A few days later, Jahanara, Fatima Jinnah, and several other women were teargassed and arrested for further protesting this makeshift government. They were incarcerated for five days but immediately joined another protest on their release, participating in sit-ins in government buildings. Despite frequent arrests, police intimidation and even the murder of some protestors, the women were not dissuaded. When students of Lahore's Islamia College extended the protests to the countryside, their college principal was arrested. Jahanara responded by heading to the college herself to urge all staff and students to protest in support. Two professors and some students followed her as they returned to Lahore to join a demonstration of almost 100,000 led by Jahanara's mother, daughter, and sister. Jahanara's sister, Geteara Bashir, organized grand daily (sometimes bi-daily) processions of women calling out the government for denying the rights of Muslims in their own nation. During one of the processions, their mother led the charge and was beaten with lathis by the police. On another occasion when, for once, police showed some hesitancy about beating the women, the police commissioner turned to Jahanara to quell the crowd before further violence erupted. She said that she would only help them if they allowed her a free platform to speak. He reluctantly agreed, and she publicly called for the government to resign before asking the crowd to peacefully disperse. In return for her cooperation, Jahanara was arrested along with sixty other protestors.

In the absence of their leaders, the people continued their disobedience campaign – picketing, sitting in, boycotting, and breaking into properties. In a show of defiance, three teenage girls wearing burqas scaled the walls of the prison where Jahanara was being held and hoisted an AIML flag on the roof. The British jailors beat them and threw them into a cell next to their leaders. This brutal treatment of young girls provoked further outrage, and eventually, the whole city was placed into lockdown in an attempt to restore order. Far from languishing in jail, the women continued to provoke their jailors. Mumtaz and her friends, for example, made an AIML flag out of their dupattas and placed it on the roof to replace the one erected by the girls. For this, Mumtaz was beaten unconscious. She and her mother were eventually released on 2 March 1947, and again immediately took to the streets to join another protest of hundreds of thousands of people. That same night, the defeated government of Punjab finally resigned.

By July 1947, Fatima Jinnah had launched a mission of AIML's Women's Sub-Committee members to fan out across the province to awaken Muslim women's political consciousness. Jahanara proudly recalled how Mumtaz had undertaken a tour of Peshawar while refusing to wear a burqa despite all the other women relenting to public pressure and veiling themselves. Jahanara followed her daughter's example and addressed a crowd of 20,000 people without her veil, with little opposition from the spectators who she reported were largely supportive of both her and the notion of Pakistan. Given her experience, she persuaded her fellow speakers to cast off their burqas and show their faces with pride. The efforts of these women directly contributed to the success of the referendum in which AIML members voted to endorse the idea of a new Muslim nation.

When India was finally partitioned in 1947 and Jahanara's dream of Pakistan came true, she and her daughter returned to Lahore after celebrating in Karachi and were horrified to discover the hundreds of thousands of refugees and the widespread slaughter of men, women, and children of all communities. They immediately joined their colleagues in providing financial and social aid. Jahanara personally contacted key politicians on both sides of the border, including Nehru, to demand that they help with the situation, and they all responded, showing her repute across the divided subcontinent. Jahanara led efforts to collect and distribute vital supplies to the refugees. Her daughter joined the Women's Volunteer Service which did work ranging from canvassing for donations to disposing of the dead. Indeed, oral histories show that it was women who were charged with rescuing babies from the arms of their dead mothers as the rest of their families lay slaughtered all around. Given that women have a reputation for swooning at the sight of blood, it is telling, though not surprising, that some of the most harrowing jobs were undertaken by women while the men busied themselves with propagating further violence. Jahanara noted with disgust the sheer incompetency of government responses to this carnage and was not afraid to tell the new leaders where they were failing. To counteract the government's inadequacies, Jahanara suggested that the WNG be established to better organize relief efforts and to train women to use weapons so that where necessary they could defend the innocent masses when the government failed to do so. The first meeting of this group was held at Jahanara's own house.

When the dust of Partition began to settle, Jahanara returned her focus to women's rights and in 1948 she headed a protest of thousands of women who marched through Lahore in anger that a bill to improve women's economic prospects had been discarded by the Pakistani government. The women succeeded in having the Muslim Personal Law of Shariat of 1948 passed, legally recognizing a woman's right to inherit property – a right they had been denied under the British.

Jahanara Shahnawaz remained active in politics for much of her life before finally passing away on 27 November 1979, aged eighty-three. She was survived by her two sons, but not her daughter who had been killed in a plane crash shortly after Pakistan's creation. Although she faced criticism at the time for dividing women by supporting separate electorates and thus working against Hindu-Muslim unity, Begum Jahanara Shahnawaz is largely remembered as a woman who spent her life in pursuit of the upliftment of her Muslim sisters and her country. The crucial role she played in representing Indian women, and Muslim Indian women in particular, at a time of great transition and chaos, cannot be understated. She knew that practical measures and challenging social taboos were needed more than empty promises and influenced the necessary changes. She was not afraid to stand up to male authority to ensure these came to pass.

Abadi Bano Begum or Bi Amma (1839–1924)

A Muslim woman who worked extremely closely with Gandhi to dispel the notion that only Hindus had a place in the freedom struggle was Abadi Bado Begum, also known as Bi Amma, who was dubbed 'The Burqa-Clad Freedom Fighter'.

Abadi was born in 1839 in Amroha, a small village in modern-day Uttar Pradesh. Nationalist spirit was in her blood, as her family had been persecuted by the British for their participation in the 1857 War of Independence. At a very young age, Abadi was married to a senior civil servant, Abdul Ali Khan. Together they had six children – one daughter and five sons. Her husband died young after contracting cholera, and Abadi was left to care for her large family alone. She raised her children with strong Islamic values, teaching them stories of the Prophet Muhammad – whose life of political activism (in which his wives and womenfolk played a substantial part) encouraged her family's strong sense of justice and political consciousness. Showing her resourcefulness in adversity, Abadi pawned her jewellery to pay for her children's education after their uncle refused to educate them himself. Although illiterate and uneducated herself, Abadi placed a high value on education and ensured that her children were sent to English-speaking schools which were considered the best with the greatest opportunities. While this meant living on simple food with simple clothes, her priorities paid off and she must have been extremely proud to see one of her sons go on to study at the University of Oxford, while many of her other children became prominent nationalists alongside her.

Her sons, Maulana Shaukat Ali and Maulana Muhammad Ali Jauhar, found their fame as 'The Ali Brothers' – founders of the Khilafat Movement (sometimes known as the Caliphate Movement or the Indian Muslim Movement), a pan-Islamist campaign launched by Indian Muslims to restore the Ottoman Caliphate and to unite Muslims in the nationalist struggle while representing their specific interests. Her sons were not shy to admit that it was their mother who stoked the fire of their nationalist fervour. One remembered how their mother told him that he should be prepared to sacrifice his life for his country. Her words became famous across India, and the fact that she valued India's independence more than her son's life is illustrative of her passion for the cause and her willingness to make personal sacrifices to see it realized. While the movement fortunately did not require her sons to become martyrs, it did find them incarcerated.

In 1917, their seventy-eight-year-old mother headed agitation to free her sons from prison. She also campaigned on behalf of fellow nationalist Annie Besant while she was in prison. Impressed by her contribution to these demonstrations, Gandhi approached Abadi and asked her to speak out publicly in support of the freedom movement and to garner support among women especially. During the 1917 sessions of the AIML, she gave a rousing speech calling Indian Muslims to action and stressing the importance of unity in the face of British oppression. As well as the stirring content, her speech drew attention because she became the first (recorded) Muslim woman in India to give a public speech while wearing a burqa. Abadi adhered strictly to purdah but did not restrict herself to the house and broke all boundaries by giving her speeches while veiled. This shattered the stereotype that all women who practice veiling are silent and oppressed – rather, they can be at the forefront of political activism and be some of the most important voices. She urged other women to abandon their traditional relegation to the domestic sphere and publicly join the fight for freedom. At an AIWC meeting in Ahmedabad, Abadi spoke to an audience of 6,000 women, urging them to enlist as INC volunteers and to protest the arrest of their male loved ones by keeping up momentum in their absence.

With her sons and many of the most famous nationalist leaders including Gandhi, in jail, Abadi took up their mantle and travelled throughout India rallying support and raising money for the freedom struggle and the Khilafat Movement. Along with other women activists, she often addressed women-only gatherings where she urged the avoidance of foreign goods, extolled the virtues of homemade attire, and exhorted women to donate to prominent nationalist, Bal Gangadhar Tilak's, Tilak Swaraj Fund.

When the possibility arose that her son, Mohammad Ali, would be freed from prison, she reportedly warned, 'Mohammad Ali can't even think about begging forgiveness from the British. If he does so, then my old hands have enough strength to strangle him.'[72] Once again, this demonstrates her dedication to the cause and her absolute disdain for the British – and the spirit that still raged within her ageing body. One wish that she expressed countless times was that even the cats and dogs of her country 'should not be under the slavery of the British'.[73] Abadi was a fierce believer in the importance of communal harmony and was considered one of the most prominent proponents of Hindu-Muslim unity, despite her passion for protecting Muslim interests.

Abadi Bano Begum passed away in 1924, twenty-three years before her dream of Indian freedom was realized. However, given her belief in Hindu-Muslim unity, perhaps it was well that she was spared the heartbreak of witnessing the communal carnage that erupted after Partition. Sixty-six years after her death, the Pakistani government acknowledged her contributions by portraying her on a postage stamp. In India too, a girl's hostel in New Delhi was named in her honour. Aside from this, however, her story has largely paled in public memory, hidden in the shadows of her sons. However, her sons were always keen to pay tribute to her contribution and spirit. Maulana Mohammad claimed that despite her gender and her illiteracy he never met anyone 'that I could call wiser and certainly that was more truly godly and spiritual than our mother.'[74]

Amjadi Bano (1885–1947)

Abadi inspired many women, but most closely her daughter-in-law Amjadi Bano who should be one of the most recognizable names of the nationalist movement and yet is almost impossible to find in most historical records.

We know little of Amjadi's life before 1902 when she married her cousin, Maulana Mohammad Ali Jauhar (cousin marriage being a common practice among South Asians at the time, especially among Muslims) aged seventeen. Her husband was a well-known Muslim leader and activist and from the very start of their marriage, she became his political as well as marital companion and travelled with him on all his political tours. Even more than her husband, her greatest inspiration was her mother-in-law, Abadi (Bi Amma) who led Amjadi and their fellow women into the heart of political life. The British Governor of the United Provinces complained: 'Even the women of his [Maulana Mohammad Ali] household collect donations and go on the rampage of inciting unrest'.[75]

Their 'rampage' continued from 1919 when Amjadi and Abadi joined the Khilafat Movement, motivating many other Muslim women from elite families to join them in their campaigns. Some of these women, such as Noor-us-Sabah Begum, later credited Amjadi with transforming their lives. In 1920, Amjadi was made secretary of the women's wing of the Indian Khilafat Committee. During this time, she also attended AIML sessions. During her husband's four years imprisonment for his role in the Khilafat Movement, Amjadi addressed crowds in his place. Things continued to get worse for the family when the British confiscated her property in Rampur and shut down her husband's publications, resulting in a complete loss of income for the family and their two daughters. Both daughters predeceased her, a devastating blow that only seemed to make Amjadi more resilient. In the November 1921 edition of *Young India*, Mohandas Gandhi dedicated an article named *A Brave Woman* to Amjadi, showing the high regard in which she was held by Hindu and Muslim leaders alike.

In 1930, Amjadi accompanied her husband to London for the First

Round Table Conference, making her one of only two Muslim women in attendance. Tragically, her husband died in 1931, leaving her a widow. However, rather than bowing out of politics, she remained resolutely independent, choosing to live alone in Delhi – a highly controversial statement for a young woman at the time. Having continued her activism since her husband's death, in 1938 she was made president of the AIML's women's sub-committee which she founded to work under the main body of the AIML during the Lucknow session of 1938. This is seen as a crucial step towards the political mobilization of Muslim women, especially in terms of their involvement with the AIML.

AIML leader M.A. Jinnah had a great deal of respect for Amjadi, and it was through his recommendation that she was nominated as the only woman among the twenty-five members of the Special Working Committee of the AIML. Together, this committee drafted the Lahore Resolution. Hers is the only woman's signature on this historic document which would change South Asia forever. Moreover, several witnesses attested that it was Amjadi who first dubbed the Lahore Resolution the 'Pakistan Resolution', during an address she gave to the women's central sub-committee at Islamia College, Lahore on 23 March. This became the phrase chanted by millions of nationalists as they demanded the creation of Pakistan and even today the resolution is more commonly referred to by the name she bestowed upon it.

Amjadi's dedication was such that, so legend says, she was visited on her deathbed by Jinnah himself where she asked him one final time to guarantee her that her dream of Pakistan would come to fruition. He promised her that it would. Amjadi passed away on 28 March 1947, and Pakistan was officially born five months later.

In the photographs taken by the AIML Working Committee which passed the Pakistan Resolution, Amjadi can be seen centre stage, fully covered by a burqa. Upon discovering this photo, it took hours of research to even find the name of the woman beneath the veil. While pages and pages have been written about the other twenty-four members of this world-changing committee, Amjadi is all but anonymous, less than a century after she was hailed by some of the most well-known men in the movement for her character and activism. The fact that she was able to claim her seat at a table so dominated by men is a testament to her tenacity and dedication. The British (and even many Indian reformers) believed then – as many still do today – that the burqa is a symbol of oppression, of a silent subaltern with no power – or even desire – to contribute to the political work of nation-building. Amjadi betrays the fallacy of this view. She not only carved out a political career for herself, a career that altered the world map forever, but she helped pave the way for millions of other Muslim women to join her on that journey. She and her mother-in-law were certainly a formidable duo, but as politically conscious Muslim women, they were by no means a minority.

Shareefa Hamid Ali (c. 1883–1971)

Another Muslim woman who combined her nationalism with her fight for women's rights was Shareefa Hamid Ali. Shareefa was born into a political Muslim family; her father was a devout follower of Gandhi and her mother was one of the first upper-class women to abandon purdah. Shareefa and her sisters were sent to school without veils, a radical digression at the time, which the young Shareefa defended by arguing that purdah was a sign of social division and women's oppression. Shareefa did not let her controversial dress distract from her studies – she became fluent in six languages: Urdu, Gujarati, Persian, Marathi, English, and French. She also had a creative spirit and dedicated her free time to painting, playing music, and sketching. When she was twenty-five, she married her cousin, Hamid Ali, and the couple moved to Bombay, where she continued to cultivate her education and hobbies. Shareefa's interest in politics was reignited in 1907 when she attended an INC session. She developed a passion for the cause of the Dalits and established nursing centres and education classes for women in rural villages to empower women who did not benefit from formal education.

Shareefa's first political success came from her campaign for Har Bilas Sarda's Child Marriage Restraint Act, also known as the Sarda Act (or Sharda Act), which sought to diminish the number of girls getting married under the age of fifteen. Ali organized a campaign in Sindh, gathering women to pressure policymakers into setting the marital age to one where young women would be more mature and better educated. This campaign succeeded in uniting women from all religious, caste, and class backgrounds, an impressive feat in an increasingly divided India which shows that womanhood always proves a unifying bond. The women's insistence that they did not live and die to be housewives but wanted to receive an education and live a life before marriage and motherhood embarrassed the British government which constantly painted Indian women as little more than passive housewives. The government eventually ceded, and in 1929, passed an act setting the minimum age of marriage in India to fourteen for girls and eighteen for boys. This was still highly problematic and did not hit the bar of eighteen which Shareeda had argued for. However, it did outlaw marriages of girls as young as seven or eight which was not uncommon in colonial India, and thus the campaign was still seen as a success. Buoyed by her success with the Sarda Act, Shareefa continued to pursue her women's activism. When Sarojini Naidu was imprisoned, Shareefa took over as leader of the AIWC and helped establish several branches across India. She was also chairwoman of the governing body of the All-India Women's Education Association.

In 1933, Shareefa testified to the Joint Select Committee on Indian Constitutional Reform in London. She spoke against the establishment of a separate electorate for Hindus and Muslims, stating that it would bring about an unbalanced power bias in the Hindu community's favour and that it would hinder the reform of inheritance laws. Her rivals in the AIML, who were advocating for religiously separate electorates, posited that Muslim women would not support Shareefa if she did not win the support of the Muslim men, specifically those in the AIML. Even Shareefa conceded that the reforms proposed by the AIWC were more beneficial to Hindu than Muslim women. The AIWC portrayed itself as apolitical. However, its leading members (except Shareefa), were INC members who openly praised and supported Gandhi and Nehru (both Hindus). Muslim women repeatedly reported feeling patronized and ignored by their Hindu counterparts. However, Shareefa and two other Muslim women, Hajrah Ahmed and Kulsum Sayani, remained loyal to the AWIC, perhaps because they saw it as one of the few organizations explicitly looking out for the rights of Indian women. In 1934, Shareefa served as AIWC representative at the Istanbul Congress of the International Alliance of Women, and in 1937 she partook in the Congress of the Women's International League for Peace and Freedom in the Czech Republic.

In 1939, Shareefa was elected to the women's sub-committee of the National Planning Committee, designed to investigate the socio-economic and legal status of women and make recommendations to improve equality. Two other Muslim women who were assigned alongside Shareefa both resigned in protest at not having their voices listened to. As the only remaining Muslim representative, Shareefa encouraged the committee to consult with Muslim legal authorities. To her annoyance, this was dismissed, and she stated that the draft report had so many inaccuracies regarding Islam – despite her having sent over comprehensive evidence to be included – that she refused to sign off on it, finally doing so only at the personal request of Jawaharlal Nehru.

A few months before India gained its independence, Shareefa was one of fifteen Indian women representatives at the first UN Commission on the Status of Women. These women established the UN's duty to foster and protect the equality of women of every race, religion, and background in line with the rights of men. These values are still upheld by the UN today, and Shareefa's work in India in the decades following independence directly inspired the UN's Universal Declaration for Human Rights and minimum marital age legislation.

Shareefa was a devout believer in Indian independence, but she strongly opposed the division of India along religious lines. While it is often assumed that all Muslims were in favour of the creation of Pakistan, Shareefa had always fought for unity among Indians. Her main complaint with the AWIC and many other prominent nationalists was their ignorance of Islam and their sense of superiority over Muslims. She, like most other women in the AIWC, blamed the AIML for creating division among Hindu and Muslim women, a fate which dismayed Shareefa as she had seen from her success with the Sarda campaign that women's greatest chance of success came when they were united against patriarchal injustice rather than divided by communal infighting. Sadly, however, Shareefa's dream of a free and united India was not to be, and she must have been dismayed by the interreligious violence that erupted when India and Pakistan were declared independent (and separate) countries in August 1947.

Sucheta Kripalani (1908–1974)

Many *satyagrahis* later turned to politics and one such woman who became a lifelong politician was India's first female chief minister, Sucheta Kripalani. Sucheta Majumdar was born in Ambala (now in Haryana) in 1908 to a Bengali Brahmin family. She moved around a lot as a child owing to her father's job as a medical officer and thus attended many different schools. She later described herself as a reserved and insecure child, who felt she was not as beautiful or as smart as her peers. However, she need not have doubted herself – she graduated with an MA in history and political science from St. Stephen's College, Delhi. She went on to become a teacher at a school in Lahore and then got a lecturing position at Benares Hindu University.

Sucheta's nationalism blossomed at an early age. She later recalled how, when she was just ten, she and her siblings overheard her father discussing the Jallianwala Bagh massacre. They were so incensed by what the British had done that they went to school and insulted some Anglo-Indian classmates – not having an opportunity to direct their anger towards anyone else. Soon after, the Prince of Wales visited Delhi and Sucheta and her classmates were taken to line the street to welcome him. Sucheta was outraged and wanted to refuse, but did not have the power to do so. She later recalled how her complicity had a lasting effect on her and her sister. She wrote that the fact that they were helpless to resist 'did not absolve our conscience from feeling shame. We both felt very small of our cowardice'.[76] She also remembers another incident where her Bible teacher criticized Hinduism and Sucheta and her sister complained about it to their father. He taught them some of the key tenets of Hinduism, and when they returned to school the next day, they quoted the Bhagavad Gita and humiliated their teacher with their knowledge of the Hindu scriptures. It is not surprising then that this intelligent, spirited, and politically conscious young girl would turn into a fierce freedom fighter in her adulthood. Tragically, when Sucheta was twenty-one, both her father and sister died, leaving Sucheta to care for her large family and preventing her from dedicating herself to the fight for India's freedom.

In 1936, she controversially married J. B. Kripalani, a well-known nationalist and fellow Gandhian whom she met in 1934 while they were providing relief following the Bihar earthquake. Their marriage was opposed by both families and even Gandhi because Kripalani was twenty years older than Sucheta. Gandhi's approval meant a lot to Sucheta, as she credited him with uniting Hindu and Muslim women and encouraging them to join the movement. She also noted that 'Gandhi's personality was such that it inspired confidence not only in women but in guardians of women, their husbands, fathers, and brothers' because his respectable reputation assured everyone that they would be safe with him. However, her marriage seems to be the only time she stood against Gandhi. Gandhi feared that their marriage would distract J.B. from the cause and that he would lose his most able man and instructed Sucheta to find another partner. She refused, calling the suggestion wicked and unfair. She also pointed out that she was a dedicated nationalist herself, and that Gandhi would gain a loyal servant rather than lose one. The pair married, regardless of Gandhi's disapproval and he eventually relented and blessed the marriage. This may have been because they vowed that their marriage would be celibate, in line with Gandhi's *satyagraha* ideals. However, his opposition to the match sheds new light on the view – promoted by Sucheta herself – that Gandhi was a leading feminist who actively championed women's political involvement. Rather, he seems to have reduced women to a mere distraction from the more important work of men and overlooked the fact that they could be just as dedicated, if not more so, than men to the cause. However, this incident does not seem to have damaged Gandhi's relationship with either Sucheta or her husband, as both remained devoted Gandhians for the rest of their lives.

In 1939, the Kripalanis moved to Allahabad, where Sucheta got a job in an INC office. A year later, she founded the All-India Mahila Congress. In 1942, she was appointed to establish a women's department of INC.

However, before she could do much work, she was imprisoned by the British for offering individual *satyagraha*. In 1941, her efforts towards the Quit India movement began when she travelled to Delhi with Aruna Asaf Ali and other nationalists. They decided they must go into hiding, from where they could coordinate and organize resistance to the British war effort. However, Sucheta disagreed with Aruna about the best way to do this. She, like Gandhi, criticized Aruna's revolutionary methods, which they saw as going against the Gandhian ideal of peaceful protest. Thus, Sucheta established a separate campaign, seeking to connect with existing revolutionary groups and trying to steer them towards non-violent methods, stating that she aimed to paralyse the government by any means except violence. She travelled around India, acting as a messenger and advisor for various nationalist leaders, disguising herself to evade capture. However, in 1944, the British finally caught up with her and threw her in Lucknow jail, where she was labelled a high-risk prisoner despite her radical commitment to non-violence – a clear effort on the part of the British to demonize their opponents.

When she was released in 1945, Sucheta attempted to rejuvenate the women's department of the INC, but she realized that they were not interested in helping to organize social and political programmes for women. Thus, she turned instead to women's enfranchisement. In 1946, she joined the Constituent Assembly, helping to shape the future of India and women's position within it. When violence erupted around the time of Partition, she followed Gandhi to Noakhali and other rioting areas in eastern Bengal in an attempt to find peace. On 14 August 1947, she sang the new Indian national anthem, *Vande Mataram*, in the Independence Session of the Constituent Assembly immediately before Nehru's address.

While many women criticized the INC after independence for forgetting women's contributions and instead grabbing power for themselves, Sucheta ardently defended them as she always had. She stressed how far women's political engagement had come since the early days of the nationalist movement, pointing out that while women had been left on the sidelines of the 1930 Salt March, they were now imprisoned alongside their male comrades as equals. Her post-independence career did seem to prove her point – in the first Lok Sabha elections in 1952, she defeated the INC candidate as a member of a new party founded by her husband a year earlier. This party was short-lived, but Sucheta's political career was not, and she continued to serve in parliament for various terms until her retirement in 1971. She lived a quiet life out of the public eye until she died in 1974.

Sucheta's independent spirit was reflected in both her personal and political life, and she made considerable efforts to improve the status of women by helping to recruit them to the cause, assisting her fellow nationalists (both men and women), and in trying (albeit briefly) to incorporate women's social movements into the INC's plan of action. At the very least, no one can deny that she was an avid nationalist, a trail-blazing politician, and a brave fighter in the struggle for freedom.

Begum Qudsia Aijaz Rasul (1909–2001)

Begum Qudsia Aijaz Rasul was one of the few Muslim women who helped to draft the Constitution of India. Qudsia was born on 2 April 1909, the daughter of Sir Zulfigar Ali Khan, a descendant of the royal family of the state of Malerktola in the Punjab. Determined that his daughter should not grow up with religious bias, he ignored the advice of his community and sent his daughter to a convent school in Simla. Even his own family objected, and the local elders issued a fatwa (a ruling on a point of Islamic law given by a recognized authority) denouncing convent education as anti-Islamic. Defiantly, she stayed at the school and went on to graduate from Queen Mary's College in Lahore. However, her father was more traditional in other ways and insisted that Qudsia wear a burqa and observe purdah. In 1929, when Qudsia was just twelve, Sir Malcolm Hailey, a British peer and administrator, arranged her marriage to Nawab Aijaz Rasul, a member of the landed gentry. Two years after their wedding, Qudsia's father died, and she was taken to live with her in-laws in Sandila. She found that her mother-in-law was extremely traditional, but her husband was more progressive and opposed purdah. With her husband's support, Qudsia began to speak openly against purdah and cast aside her veil in public.

In 1935, Qudsia and her husband joined the AIML and took an active interest in electoral politics. A year later, Qudsia decided to contest a general (Muslim) seat for the United Provinces' Legislative Council, rather than pursuing one reserved for women. Once again, the Muslim elders were outraged and issued another fatwa warning of the danger of this shameful woman who refused purdah and openly competed with men. Unphased, Qudsia was triumphant, believing that her win by a large majority proved that Muslims were more liberal than their stereotypes suggest. Once elected, she caused further scandal by speaking in favour of birth control and highlighting the desire for women police officers.

Despite her elite background, she was known for her strong opposition to the *zamindari* system, a system introduced by the British under which a certain stratum of society, known as the *Zamindars*, was given the responsibility of collecting rent from peasants and handing it over to the British government, in return for being formally known as the landowners. Qudsia was strongly in support of the abolition of this system which directly placed Indian resources in the hands of the British at the expense of the poorest in society.

In 1946, while serving as secretary to the AIML, Qudsia was elected to the Constituent Assembly of India. She was one of only twenty-eight AIML members who eventually participated and was one of only fifteen women. She attempted to persuade Muslims to increase their demand for reserved seats. During conversations about the status of minorities, she opposed the idea of having separate electorates for Muslims which she deemed 'a self-destructive weapon which separates the minorities from the majority for all time'.[77] Eventually, many were persuaded by her appeal.

Unlike most Muslims, Qudsia Rasul and her husband decided to stay in India after Partition, a striking testimony to her belief that Muslims would be granted full citizenship. She remained a member of the Legislative Assembly until 1952. She held the office of the deputy president of the council from 1937 to 1940. After Partition, she acted as the Leader of the Opposition in the council from 1950 to 1952–54. She was the first woman in India, and the first Muslim woman in the world, to reach this position. She continued her political career until 1971, as well as travelling, writing, and being a trail-blazing sportswoman. In 2000, she was awarded a Padma Bhushan for her contribution to social work. She died on 1 August 2001, aged ninety-two.

Qudsia stands out among her contemporary women freedom fighters as she was one of the few who maintained her belief in a united India in which Muslims and Hindus could live harmoniously. However, like her peers, she provided a steadfast commitment to women's rights and improving the freedom of women both within the private and public spheres.

Hansa Mehta (1897–1995)

Another woman who helped to shape the newly independent India's constitution was Hansa Mehta. Hansa was born into a dominant-caste family on 3 July 1897. She studied philosophy at Baroda College, graduating in 1918, before travelling to England to complete further studies in sociology and journalism. While staying in London, Hansa was introduced to Sarojini Naidu, who first drew Hansa into the independence movement and introduced her to Gandhi in 1922. She married Jivraj Narayan Mehta, an esteemed doctor who went on to become the Chief Minister of Gujarat.

In 1930, Hansa was a founding member of the women's organization, Desh Sevika Dal. Two years later she was arrested alongside her husband and imprisoned for her role in the non-cooperation movement. Her political career developed in 1937 when she won a seat on the Bombay Legislative Council, having refused to contest a seat reserved solely for women. She stayed on the council until 1949.

From 1945-46, Mehta served as president of the AIWC. In her presidential address she offered a Charter of Women's Rights, demanding equality of human rights for all women. In 1946, she served as India's representative on the Nuclear Sub-Committee on the status of women. Thus, although having been jailed for her nationalist activities, women's rights occupied her mind and her time in the months immediately preceding independence.

Hansa continued to place women at the forefront of her politics for the rest of her career. In 1947–48, she served as India's representative at the UN Human Rights Commission. She is generally held to be solely responsible for altering the Universal Declaration of Human Rights from 'all men are born free and equal' to 'all human beings are born free and equal', highlighting the still precarious view of women as deserving of full personhood. She also teamed up with Eleanor Roosevelt to ensure that women were granted marriage equality. Thus, many of the rights that women across the world take for granted today are in place because of an Indian freedom fighter,

Hansa Mehta. Throughout her life, she also wrote and translated several books, including the Hindu epic, *The Ramayana*, as well as English classics like *Gulliver's Travels* and a selection of Shakespeare's works. Her later years were spent working in various universities, becoming the first female vice-chancellor in India. In 1959, she was awarded the Padma Bhushan. She died on 4 April 1995 at the grand old age of ninety-eight, leaving behind a legacy of almost a century of protecting the rights of Indian women, and India itself.

In 1947, Mehta had been one of fifteen women elected to the Constituent Assembly that drafted the Indian Constitution. She was a member of the Advisory Committee and Sub-Committee on Fundamental Rights. She was noted at the time for advocating strongly for equal rights and justice for Indian women in their new free republic. She played a central role on the day of India's independence itself; on 15 August 1947, she was given the honour of presenting the Indian flag for the first time. Her speech serves as a testament to the role that women played in freeing India, and to their love and commitment to their newly independent nation:

'It is my proud privilege on behalf of the women of India to present this flag to the nation ... There are hundreds and hundreds of other women who would equally like to participate in this function. It is in the fitness of things that this first flag that will fly over this August house should be a gift from the women of India. We have donned this saffron colour, we have fought, suffered, and sacrificed in the cause of our country's freedom. We have today attained our goals in presenting this symbol of freedom. We once more offer our services to the nation we made ourselves, to work for a great India, for building up a nation that will be a nation among nations. We pledge ourselves for working [sic] for a greater cause to maintain the freedom that we have achieved. We have great traditions to maintain, traditions that made India so great in the past. It is the duty of every man and woman to preserve these traditions so that India may hold spiritual supremacy over the world. May this flag be the symbol of that great India and may it ever fly high and serve as a light in the gloom that threatens the world today. May it bring happiness to those who live under its protecting care'.[78]

Conclusion

Throughout this book, we have heard the stories of women who contributed in a myriad of different ways to the Indian independence movement by standing up against the biggest empire in world history and winning. However, these women are but a drop in an ocean of millions of South Asian women who contributed to the movement, giving their time, their money, their voices, and even their lives for the freedom struggle, only to be almost completely erased from the history of that struggle. The women whose names and even faces that we do know are often those who benefitted from caste or class privilege, who were wealthy and well-educated enough to write themselves into the narratives, or who benefitted from association with famous male relatives in whose story they could be remembered, albeit as a footnote. These privileges allowed these women to effectively mobilize against the British and to defy the patriarchal customs of their own society, thereby more effectively mobilizing against the British.

This is not to negate the contribution of these women. The lives of dominant-caste or elite women were often more highly regulated than those of lower echelons of society because they were more likely to be expected to follow the segregation of purdah – a luxury lower classes could not afford. Wealth and status were not a guarantee of a good education either, as many women born into the most elite families were still expected to do little more than marry well and breed sons. In fact, these women often had more to lose by speaking out against the British, given that they were more likely to associate in British circles and to benefit from British education and protection, than those from the lower classes.

Many women from these upper classes chose to side with the government, or at the very least stay in the relative safety of segregation. Thus, those who did throw themselves wholeheartedly into the movement often sacrificed more than we can ever understand in the name of freedom and equality. These women were, in fact, instrumental in helping to mobilize those who had historically been less privileged and without these efforts the freedom movement would have suffered irreparably – as male nationalists such as Gandhi themselves acknowledged. Furthermore, as we have seen, many of these women used their privilege to uplift other women and other marginalized groups by combining their nationalism with social work which aimed at improving the lived realities of the masses and guaranteeing equality for everyone regardless of background in the free India or Pakistan of which they dreamed. Therefore, while the privilege of many women nationalists cannot be denied, this does not negate their bravery, their strength, or their dedication.

Nonetheless, these elite women, while influential figureheads, should not overshadow the contributions of those whose histories are even more hidden in an already invisible narrative. There were even those among the most admirable women nationalists who fought to silence or suppress the contributions of other women on account of their caste, class, or creed. They also tended to judge those whose values did not align with theirs, for example, by condemning those who chose to remain in purdah. Thus, an extra effort must be made for those who had to overcome the stigma and oppression they faced from their countrymen (and women) before they could ever hope to vanquish the British. These groups include, but are not limited to Dalits, widows, single mothers, the illiterate, those from religious minorities, those who did not speak Hindi or English, and the elderly. We have seen several examples of Dalit women who fought alongside queens in an age where the castes were often forbidden to share a meal; of widows who cast off their veils to take up arms against oppressors; those who rejected the traditional roles of wife and mother to take on the role of freedom fighter instead; those who died for a country whose name they could not have written; those who used their religion to empower them to fight for a unity in a country where religion was so quick to divide; and those who used their twilight years not to enjoy a quiet retirement but to fight for freedom until their very last breath. There are also many examples of women who proved that adhering to purdah restrictions or choosing to veil did not mean that a woman was not as dedicated, intelligent, impassioned, and enlightened as those who chose to cast their veils aside. Yet the few examples we do have of these remarkable women are probably not so very remarkable – it is just that history has not deemed the majority of them important enough to document. We may not know their names, birth dates, or faces, but their legacy can be seen everywhere, from the borders of the countries they helped to create to the spirit within the generations of South Asian women who followed them.

In modern-day India, Hindu nationalists have claimed power and Islamophobia is on the rise, so it is imperative to remember that without the contribution of Muslims and other religious minorities, India would not be the country it is today and may never have won its independence at all.

Similarly, Pakistan, while built to be an intrinsically Muslim nation, owes its very existence to Hindu freedom fighters who cast out the British so that all South Asians could decide for themselves where and how they wanted to live. Less than eighty years ago, Pakistan and India were one land, and the animosity which lingers between these two nations cannot be understood as anything other than the aftershocks of British policy that pitted communities against each other. The Indian independence movement – and the modern South Asian political landscape – has become a story of Hindu versus Muslim, which plays exactly into the hands of the British who installed this divide in a previously united country. Yet, as we have seen, women of all religious communities fought side by side. While the men of South Asia were increasingly divided – literally and metaphorically – by religion and nationality, the women remained united by their shared trauma, their universal sense of justice, and their deep devotion to their homelands.

Hopefully, this book has shown that women have all the same principles and skills as men. They had a passionate belief in freedom and justice. They wanted to raise the status of the oppressed. They were prepared to risk their life for their cause. They endured emotional and physical suffering on the streets and in jail. They had the political acumen to reason with a dictatorial regime. They had a vision for what a free independent country looked like and a plan for how to make it come true. They had a passion for protecting and safeguarding the rights of the country's minorities. They championed the power of education. They acknowledged the benefits of foreign rule while decrying the injustices of it. They lived in austerity. They fought for justice, not personal power (which cannot be said for many of the most prominent male activists). They raised their pens and their swords to banish the British. They gave powerful speeches and wrote influential treatises. They highlighted the importance of national, caste, gender, class, and religious unity to achieve their goals. They knew that freedom meant not just freedom from British rule, but freedom from all the injustices and divisions which threatened the peace of their land. They made huge personal sacrifices in the name of their cause. At every turn, where men fought, and spoke, and wrote, and picketed, and marched, and starved, and died – women were by their side – if not leading the way.

Furthermore, these women were at each other's sides for the additional battles that their male nationalists never had to face. They did all of the above and endured every hardship for which their male counterparts are still celebrated, but they did it while bleeding, while carrying children, and while recovering from the physical trauma of birth or miscarriage. They did it while caring for children and husbands, and while religious zealots and political elites even within their own communities denied their very humanity. They gave what they did not even own. They stood up to men within their families and beyond who could kill them, kidnap them, or rape them with no legal consequences. They endured being cast as victims by the British and as disposable accessories by their comrades.

And then, worst of all, when their dream was finally achieved when India was freed and Pakistan was created, they were not thanked. Instead, their male counterparts kept the spotlight for themselves and sought to banish women back to their kitchens, their nurseries, their menstruation huts, and their purdah. When Nehru and Jinnah took power, their mothers, wives, and sisters who had raised them to glory, were relegated back to mere accessories on their arms. When Gandhi was assassinated to national outrage and grief, no one looked to the women who had followed, emulated him, and guided him, to take up his mantle. Women had been allowed to fight for independence and had given equal dedication and sacrifice to achieve this dream, but this had not guaranteed them an equal place in the new India or Pakistan. Rather, they bore the brunt of the violence which welcomed this new dawn. Just as women endured the pain of childbirth, they endured the worst of the carnage that accompanied the birth of these new nations. Those women who lived to see their nationalist visions come true must have watched in horror as their dreams turned to nightmares. Their men had gone back on their promises to reward their contributions, and their vulnerability in a deeply misogynistic world was more evident than ever. Even today, India and Pakistan remain statistically two of the most patriarchal countries in the world, consistently sitting in the bottom five rankings of gender equality, especially concerning rates of female infanticide, domestic abuse, sexual violence, honour killings, child marriages, sexual exploitation, women's literacy, access to the labour market, and menstrual taboos. This is despite gender equality being guaranteed to some extent in the constitutions of both countries.

Yet women were not going to take this betrayal lying down (unsurprisingly given the spirit and determination they had shown over the past two centuries and beyond). As we have seen, many women nationalists spent the rest of their lives working to help shape their new nations into more just and equitable places. Within two generations, both Pakistan and India had record-breaking women prime ministers, Indira Gandhi and Benazir Bhutton, a direct result of the political power their mothers and grandmothers had carved for themselves. While India scores very poorly on many matrixes of gender equality, it is consistently in the top twenty in terms of women's political engagement – scoring well above many European countries including the United Kingdom. Consistently more women than men vote in India.

To keep improving the current situation, we need to remind today's generations that India and Pakistan were built on the shoulders of women.

These women not only had a front-row seat as the world was irrevocably changed forever but were instrumental in that change. Therefore, their stories provide insight and wisdom which can inspire and inform for generations to come. So many of the speeches and writings, especially those about the importance of unity across boundaries – given all those years ago are just as relevant today – if not more so. They witnessed first-hand the consequences of hatred and division and the avenues that these open for violence and oppression. They knew what it was to be denied your humanity on account of your race, religion, gender, or other uncontrollable characteristics, and therefore they know better than anyone how to avoid repeating the subjugation and agonies of the twentieth century. These women's beliefs in the equality of the genders, of the value of all religions, of the anachronism of caste and class discrimination, and of the glories of South Asia's shared past are all just as applicable, even without the involvement of British colonialism. Yet these women's stories are also a crucial testimony to the evils of colonialism – the legacy of which is still evident in much of the strife left in South Asia (and across the world) today.

There is rightly a great call to decolonize school and university curriculums in the UK which must include a real acknowledgement of the sins the British committed across the globe and the lasting impact of them both in Britain and beyond. However, another crucial part of decolonization is recognizing the achievements of other nations and their role in freeing themselves from the shackles of colonialism. Within that, women must be at the centre of this corrected narrative of world history. The histories of Britain and South Asia are inseparable, and the stories of their women are so deeply interlaced within those histories that you cannot leave them out without destroying the whole narrative. We owe it to these women and the generations who followed them to remember – and remind those who forget – that the world was changed forever because these women were victorious against the Raj.

Endnotes

1 Ajeet Javed (1998), *Secular and Nationalist Jinnah*, Kitab Publishing, pp. 148–9.
2 Shashi Tharoor (2017), *Inglorious Empire: What the British Did to India*, Penguin, 132.
3 Arunima Dey (2016), 'Women as Martyrs: Mass Suicides at Thoa Khalse During the Partition of India', *Indi@logs*, 3, pp. 7–17, 10; Yasmin Khan (2017), *The Great Partition: The Making of India and Pakistan*, Hampshire: Yale University Press, pp. 135.
4 Khan (2017), pp. 133.
5 Urvashi Butalia (2000), *The Other Side of Silence: Voices from the Partition of India*, Duke University Press, pp. 154–5.
6 Kavita Puri (2020), *Partition Voices: Untold British Stories*, London: Bloomsbury, pp. 133–4
7 Ibid.

Ranis and Revolutionaries

8 John Keay (2010), *India: A History: From the Earliest Civilisations to the Boom of the Twenty-first Century*, London: Harper Press, pp. 425.
9 John Malcolm (1824), *A Memoir of Central India, Including Malwa, and Adjoining Provinces: With the History, and Copious Illustrations, of the Past and Present Condition of that Country*, United Kingdom: Kingsbury, Parbury, & Allen, pp. 194.
10 Jawaharlal Nehru (1946/1985), *The Discovery of India*. Calcutta: Rajiv Gandhi, pp. 280.
11 Herpeet Kaur Grewal (2010), 'Rebel Queen – a thorn in the crown', *The Guardian*. Available: https://www.theguardian.com/lifeandstyle/2010/dec/31/rebel-queen-thorn-crown [Accessed: 12.5.23].
12 Priya Atwal (2020), *Royals and Rebels: The Rise and Fall of the Sikh Empire*. London: Hurst, pp. 182–3.
13 Anita Anand (2015), *Sophia: Princess, Suffragette, Revolutionary*, London: Bloomsbury, pp. 34.
14 Srikrishnan Sarala (1999). *Indian Revolutionaries 1757-1961 (Vol-1): A Comprehensive Study*. Prabhat Prakashan, pp. 40.
15 Biswamoy Pati (2012), 'India "Mutiny" and "Revolution," 1857–1858', in Kaushik Roy (Ed.), *Military History*, Oxford Bibliographies.

16 Ira Mukhoty (2017), *Heroines: Powerful Indian Women of Myth and History*, New Delhi: Aleph, pp. 145.
17 Michael Edwardes (1975), *Red Year: The Indian Rebellion of 1857*, London: Cardinal, pp. 114. (1975), pp. 111.
18 Government of India, 'Jhalkari Bai'. *Indian Culture*, Available: https://www.indianculture.gov.in/node/2790247 [Accessed: 17.1.23].
19 William Forbes-Mitchell (1910), *Reminiscences of the Great Mutiny 1857-1859*, London: Macmillan and Co., pp. 58–59.
20 Charu Gupta (2007), 'Dalit "Viranganas" and Reinvention of 1857', *Economic and Political Weekly*, 42:19, pp. 1739–1745, 1742.
21 Durba Ghosh (2013), 'Revolutionary Women and Nationalist Heroes in Bengal, 1930 to the 1980s', *Gender & History*, 25:2, pp. 355–375, 355.
22 Elita Karim (2010), 'A Long Walk to Freedom', *The Star Magazine*, 9:8. Available: https://archive.thedailystar.net/magazine/2010/02/03/cover.htm [Accessed: 16.3.23].
23 Tirtha Mandal (1991), *The Women Revolutionaries of Bengal 1905–1939*, Minerva Associates, pp. 4.
24 Kalpana Dutt (1945), *Chittagong Armoury raiders: reminiscences*, Bombay: People's Publishing House, pp. 20.
25 'Kalpana Dutt Caught At Last' (19 May 1933). *The Indian Express*, Chittagong: Free Press of India, pp. 6.
26 'India: I and My Government' (1932), *TIME Magazine*. Available: https://time.com/vault/issue/1932-02-08/page/17/ [Accessed: 21.3.23].
27 Meghna Guhathakurta, and Schendel, Willem van (Eds.) (2013). *The Bangladesh Reader : History, Culture, Politics*. Duke University Press, pp. 145.
28 Priyanka Dasgupta (2019), 'At 14, my mother had shot dead a British district magistrate. She said it was the need of the hour: Sunita Choudhury's daughter', *The Times of India*. Available: http://timesofindia.indiatimes.com/articleshow/67689187.cms?utm_source=contentofinterest&utm_medium=text&utm_campaign=cppst [Accessed: 21.03.23].
29 Sanchari Pal (2016), 'Remembering Madam Bhikaji Cama, the Brave Lady to First Hoist India's Flag on Foreign Soil', *The Better India*. Available: https://www.thebetterindia.com/69290/madam-bhikaji-cama-flag-stuttgart-india/ [Accessed: 29.12.22].
30 Meghna Banjan (2022). 'Gulab Kaur: The Sikh Woman Who Fought For India's Freedom From Manila'. *Feminism in India*. Available: https://feminisminindia.

com/2022/05/10/gulab-kaur-the-sikh-woman-who-fought-for-indias-freedom-from-manila-indianwomeninhistory/. [Accessed: 12.1.23].
31 Aruna Asaf Ali (1991), *The Resurgence of Indian Women*, Radiant, pp. 141–2.
32 Lakshmi Sahgal (2012), 'My days in the Indian National Army by Lakshmi Sahgal', *NDTV*. Available: https://www.ndtv.com/india-news/my-days-in-the-indian-national-army-by-lakshmi-sahgal-493887 [Accessed: 9.1.23].
33 Parvati Menon (2012), 'Captain Lakshmi Sahgal (1914-2012) – A Life of Struggle', *The Hindu*. Available: https://www.thehindu.com/news/national/captain-lakshmi-sahgal-1914-2012-a-life-of-struggle/article3672666.ece [Accessed: 9.01.23].
34 Ibid.

Stalwarts and *Satyagrahis*

35 M.K. Gandhi (1929/2007), *An Autobiography: The Story of My Experiments with Truth*, Penguin, pp. 209.
36 Joseph K. Siby K. (2020), *Kasturbai Gandhi: An Embodiment of Empowerment*, Mumbai: Gandhi Smarak Nidhi, pp. 122.
37 Mandira Nayar (2020), 'Shadow and Strength', *The Week India*. Available: https://www.discountmags.com/magazine/the-week-india-december-25-2022-digital-m/in-this-issue/iSXRrSQp_1671197448045 [Accessed: 24.8.23].
38 'Mridula Gandhi' (2018), *Indus*. Available: http://indpaedia.com/ind/index.php/Mridula_Gandhi [Accessed: 3.5.23].
39 Manubahana Gandhi and Tridip Suhrud (Trans) (2020), *The Diary of Manu Gandhi:1943-1944*. New Delhi: Oxford University Press, Date: 31.8.1942.
40 Vinay Lal (2000), 'Nakedness, Nonviolence, and Brahmacharya: Gandhi's Experiments in Celibate Sexuality'. *Journal of the History of Sexuality*, 9:1, pp. 105–136, 118–9.
41 S. Gopal (1975), *Jawaharlal Nehru: A Biography, vol 1*, London: Jonathan Cape, pp. 196.
42 Rudrangshu Mukherjee (2023), 'Life with the Mahatma', *The India Forum*. Available: https://www.theindiaforum.in/article/diary-manu-gandhi [Accessed: 3.5.23].
43 Renuka Ray (1982), *My Reminiscences: Social Development During Gandhian Era and After*, New Delhi: Allied, pp. 64.
44 Geraldine Forbes (1996), *Women in Modern India*, Cambridge: Cambridge University Press, pp. 134.

45 Sarojini Naidu (2020), *Speeches and Writings of Sarojini Naidu*, Ragged Hand, pp. 146.
46 Geraldine Forbes (1988), 'The politics of Respectability: Indian Women and the Indian National Congress', in D.A. Low (Ed.), *The Indian National Congress: Centenary Hindsights*. Delhi: Oxford University Press, pp. 80-1.
47 B.R. Nanda (1962), *The Nehrus: Motilal and Jawaharlal*, The John Day Company, pp. 201.
48 Suruchi Thapar-Bjorkert (2006), *Women in the Indian National Movement: Unseen Faces and Unheard Voices, 1930-42*, New Delhi: Sage Publishing.
49 Promilla Lalhan (1973), *Kamala Nehru*, Digital Library of India, pp. 103.
50 Roshani Rai (2016), 'Role of Women With Special Reference to Swarup Rani and Kamala Nehru in the Political Life of Jawaharlal Nehru', *International Journal of Research in Humanities and Social Studies*, 3:5, pp. 69–72, 69.
51 Shashi Tharoor (2003), *Nehru: The Invention of India*, New York: Arcade, pp. 90.
52 Kamaladevi Chattopadhyay (1986), *Inner Recesses, Outer Spaces: Memoir*, New Delhi: Navrang, pp. 152.
53 Nico Slate (2012), *Colored Cosmopolitanism: The Shared Struggle for Freedom in the United States and India*, Harvard University Press, pp. 1.
54 Durgabai Deshmukh (1980), *Chintaman and I*, New Delhi: Allied, pp. 10.
55 Meryl Sebastian (2022). 'Accamma Cherian: Why India forgot this freedom fighter from Kerala', *BBC News*. Available: https://www.bbc.co.uk/news/world-asia-india-62559091 [Accessed: 7.12.22]
56 Dinyar Patel (2021), 'Khurshedben Naoroji: The singer who preached nonviolence to bandits', *BBC News*. Available: https://www.bbc.co.uk/news/world-asia-india-57523456 [Accessed 19.2.23].
57 Nitika Bajpayee (2009), 'A Patriot Speaks: An Interview with Satyavati Devi', *Harmony India*. Available: https://web.archive.org/web/20140527214759/http://www.harmonyindia.org/hportal/VirtualPageView.jsp?page_id=10510&index1=1 [Accessed: 21/3/23].
58 Forbes (1996), pp. 148–9.

Partners and Politicians

59 M. Reza Pirbhai (2017), *Fatima Jinnah: Mother of the Nation*, Cambridge University Press, pp. 121.
60 Kanji Dwarkadas (2011), *Ruttie Jinnah: Story of a Great Friendship*, Karachi: Virsa, pp. 164.

61 Shagufta Yasmeen (2011), *Ruttie Jinnah: Life and Love*, Karachi: Royal Book Company, pp. 25.
62 Sheela Reddy (2017), *Mr and Mrs Jinnah: The Marriage that Shook India*, Gurgaon: Penguin, pp. 152.
63 Saad S. Khan & Sara S. Khan (2020), *Ruttie Jinnah: The Woman Who Stood Defiant*, Haryana: Penguin, pp. 112.
64 Kiran Doshi (2015), *Jinnah Often Came to Our House*, New Delhi: Westland, pp. 211.
65 Khan & Khan (2020), pp. 206.
66 Khwaja Razi Haider (2010), *Ruttie Jinnah: The Story, Told and Untold*, Karachi: Oxford University Press, pp. 110.
67 Pirbhai (2017), pp. 129.
68 Vijaya Lakshmi Pandit (1966), 'Vijaya Lakshmi Pandit on Gandhi's Influence', Alpha Press: BBC Sound Archive, *The British Library*. Available: https://www.bl.uk/collection-items/vijaya-lakshmi-pandit-on-gandhi [Accessed: 8.4.23].
69 Vijaya Lakshmi Pandit (1966), 'Vijaya Lakshmi Pandit on the Amritsar massacre', Alpha Press: BBC Sound Archive. *The British Library*. Available: https://www.bl.uk/collection-items/vijaya-lakshmi-pandit-on-amritsar-massacre [Accessed: 8.4.23].
70 Asghar Ali and Shahnaz Tariq (2002), 'Begum Jahanara Shahnawaz and the socio-cultural uplift of Muslim women in British India', *Journal of the Research Society of Pakistan*, 45:2, pp. 115–133, 124.
71 Jahanara Shahnawaz (2002), *Father & Daughter: A Political Autobiography*, Oxford University Press, pp. 192.
72 Nabeela Jamil (2018), 'Abadi Bano Begum AKA Bi Amma: The Burqa Clad Freedom Fighter', *Feminism in India*. Available: https://feminisminindia.com/2018/10/12/abadi-bano-begum-a-k-a-bi-amma-the-burqa-clad-freedom-fighter-indianwomeninhistory/ [Accessed: 29.12.22].
73 'Abadi Bano Begum (Bi Amma)', *Government of India*. Available: https://www.indianculture.gov.in/node/2794863 [Accessed: 29.12.22].
74 Rakhahari Chatterji (2013), *Gandhi and the Ali Brothers: Biography of a Friendship*, India: Sage Publishing, pp. 53.
75 Durriya Kazi (2021). 'Remembering Amjadi Bano Begum'. *Dawn*. Available: https://www.dawn.com/news/1615005 [Accessed: 13.9.23].
76 Rinchen Norbu Wangchuk (2018). 'Meet India's First Woman CM: A Freedom Fighter & Feminist From Uttar Pradesh', *The Better India*. Available: https://www.

thebetterindia.com/138291/india-first-woman-cm-freedom-fighter-sucheta-kriplani/ [Accessed: 5.4.23].

77 *Constituent Assembly of India – Volume VIII* (1949). Available at: https://web.archive.org/web/20170131083907/http://parliamentofindia.nic.in/ls/debates/vol8p8b.htm [Accessed: 13.12.22].

78 Prasar Bharati Archives, '1947 – Hansa Mehta's Constituent Assembly Speech on Aug 15', *YouTube*. Available: https://www.youtube.com/watch?v=CFC6_5yqM-U [Accessed: 16.1.23].

Bibliography

'India: I and My Government'. *TIME Magazine*, 8 February 1932. Available: https://time.com/vault/issue/1932-02-08/page/17/ [Accessed: 21.3.2023].

'Kalpana Dutt Caught At Last', *The Indian Express* (Free Press of India, Chittagong, 19 May 1933).

Ali, Asghar and Tariq, Shahnaz (2002). 'Begum Jahanara Shahnawaz and the socio-cultural uplift of Muslim women in British India'. *Journal of the Research Society of Pakistan*, 45:2, pp. 115–133.

Anand, Anita (2015). *Sophia: Princess, Suffragette, Revolutionary*. London: Bloomsbury.

Atwal, Priya (2020). *Royals and Rebels: The Rise and Fall of the Sikh Empire*. London: Hurst.

Banerjee, Sikata (2005). *Make me a Man! Masculinity, Hinduism, and Nationalism in India*. New York: State University of New York.

Banjan, Meghna (2022). 'Gulab Kaur: The Sikh Woman Who Fought For India's Freedom From Manila'. *Feminism in India*. Available: https://feminisminindia.com/2022/05/10/gulab-kaur-the-sikh-woman-who-fought-for-indias-freedom-from-manila-indianwomeninhistory/. [Accessed: 12.1.23].

Butalia, Urvashi (2000). *The Other Side of Silence: Voices from the Partition of India*. Duke University Press.

Chaudhurani, Saralaedbi and Banerjee, Sikata (Trans.) (2011). *The Scattered Leaves of my Life: An Indian Nationalist Remembers*. New Delhi: Women Unlimited.

Constituent Assembly of India - Volume VIII (1949). Available at: https://web.archive.org/web/20170131083907/http://parliamentofindia.nic.in/ls/debates/vol8p8b.htm [Accessed: 13.12.22].

Dasgupta, Priyanka (2019). 'At 14, my mother had shot dead a British district magistrate. She said it was the need of the hour: Sunita Choudhury's daughter.' *The Times of India*. Available: http://timesofindia.indiatimes.com/articleshow/67689187.cms?utm_source=contentofinterest&utm_medium=text&utm_campaign=cppst [Accessed: 21.03.23].

Dey, Arunima (2016). 'Women as Martyrs: Mass Suicides at Thoa Khalse During the Partition of India', *Indi@logs*, 3, pp. 7–17.

Doshi, Kiran (2015). *Jinnah Often Came to Our House*. New Delhi: Westland.

Dutt, Kalpana (1945). *Chittagong Armoury Raiders: Reminiscences*. Bombay: People's Publishing House.

Dwarkadas, Kanji (2011). *Ruttie Jinnah: Story of a Great Friendship*. Karachi: Virsa.
Edwardes, Michael (1975). *Red Year: The Indian Rebellion of 1857*. London: Cardinal.
Forbes, Geraldine (1996). *Women in Modern India*. Cambridge: Cambridge University Press.
Forbes-Mitchell, William (1910). *Reminiscences of the Great Mutiny 1857-1859*. London: Macmillan and Co.
Ghosh, Durba (2013). 'Revolutionary Women and Nationalist Heroes in Bengal, 1930 to the 1980s'. *Gender & History*, 25:2, pp. 355–375.
Government of India. 'Jhalkari Bai'. *Indian Culture*. Available: https://www.indianculture.gov.in/node/2790247 [Accessed: 17.1.23].
Grewal, Herpeet Kaur (2010). 'Rebel Queen – a thorn in the crown'. *The Guardian*. Available: https://www.theguardian.com/lifeandstyle/2010/dec/31/rebel-queen-thorn-crown [Accessed: 12.5.23].
Guhathakurta, Meghna and Schendel, Willem van (Eds.) (2013). *The Bangladesh Reader: History, Culture, Politics*. Duke University Press.
Gupta, Charu (2007). 'Dalit 'Viranganas' and Reinvention of 1857'. *Economic and Political Weekly*, 42:19, pp. 1739–1745.
Haider, Khwaja Razi (2010). *Ruttie Jinnah: The Story, Told and Untold*. Karachi: Oxford University Press.
Karim, Elita (2010). 'A Long Walk to Freedom'. *The Star Magazine*, 9:8. Available: https://archive.thedailystar.net/magazine/2010/02/03/cover.htm [Accessed: 16.3.23].
Kazi, Durriya (2021). 'Remembering Amjadi Bano Begum'. *Dawn*. Available: https://www.dawn.com/news/1615005 [Accessed: 13.9.23].
Keay, John (2010). India: A History: From the Earliest Civilisations to the Boom of the Twenty-first Century. London: Harper Press.
Khan, Saad S. & Khan, Sara S. (2020). *Ruttie Jinnah: The Woman Who Stood Defiant*. Haryana: Penguin.
Khan, Yasmin (2017). *The Great Partition: The Making of India and Pakistan*. Hampshire: Yale University Press.
Malcolm, John (1824). *A Memoir of Central India, Including Malwa, and Adjoining Provinces: With the History, and Copious Illustrations, of the Past and Present Condition of that Country*. United Kingdom: Kingsbury, Parbury, & Allen.
Mandal, Tirtha (1991). *The Women Revolutionaries of Bengal 1905-1939*. Minerva Associates.
Menon, Parvati (2012). 'Captain Lakshmi Sahgal (1914-2012) – A Life of Struggle'.

The Hindu. Available: https://www.thehindu.com/news/national/captain-lakshmi-sahgal-1914-2012-a-life-of-struggle/article3672666.ece [Accessed: 9.01.23].

Mukhoty, Ira (2017*). Heroines: Powerful Indian Women of Myth and History*. New Delhi: Aleph.

Nehru, Jawaharlal (1946/1985). *The Discovery of India*. Calcutta: Rajiv Gandhi.

Pal, Sanchari (2016). 'Remembering Madam Bhikaiji Cama, the Brave Lady to First Hoist India's Flag on Foreign Soil.' *The Better India*. Available: https://www.thebetterindia.com/69290/madam-bhikaji-cama-flag-stuttgart-india/ [Accessed: 29.12.22].

Pandit, Vijaya Lakshmi (1966). 'Vijaya Lakshmi Pandit on Gandhi's Influence'. Alpha Press: BBC Sound Archive. *The British Library*. Available: https://www.bl.uk/collection-items/vijaya-lakshmi-pandit-on-gandhi [Accessed: 8.4.23].

Pandit, Vijaya Lakshmi (1966). 'Vijaya Lakshmi Pandit on the Amritsar massacre'. Alpha Press: BBC Sound Archive. *The British Library*. Available: https://www.bl.uk/collection-items/vijaya-lakshmi-pandit-on-amritsar-massacre [Accessed: 8.4.23].

Pati, Biswamoy (2012). 'India "Mutiny" and "Revolution," 1857-1858'. In Kaushik Roy (Ed.), *Military History*, Oxford Bibliographies.

Pirbhai, M. Reza (2017). *Fatima Jinnah: Mother of the Nation*. Cambridge University Press.

Prasar Bharati Archives. '1947 – Hansa Mehta's Constituent Assembly Speech on Aug 15'. *YouTube* Available: https://www.youtube.com/watch?v=CFC6_5yqM-U [Accessed: 16.1.23].

Puri, Kavita (2020). *Partition Voices: Untold British Stories*. London: Bloomsbury.

Reddy, Sheela (2017). *Mr and Mrs Jinnah: The Marriage that Shook India*. Gurgaon: Penguin.

Sahgal, Lakshmi (2012). 'My days in the Indian National Army by Lakshmi Sahgal'. *NDTV*. Available: https://www.ndtv.com/india-news/my-days-in-the-indian-national-army-by-lakshmi-sahgal-493887 [Accessed: 9.1.23].

Sahgal, Manmohini Zutshi (1993). *An Indian Freedom Fighter Recalls Her* Life. USA: Library of Congress.

Sarala, Srikrishnan (1999). *Indian Revolutionaries 1757-1961 (Vol-1): A Comprehensive Study*. Prabhat Prakashan.

Shahnawaz, Jahanara (2002). *Father & Daughter: A Political Autobiography*. Oxford University Press.

Wangchuk, Rinchen Norbu (2018). 'Meet India's First Woman CM: A Freedom

Fighter & Feminist From Uttar Pradesh'. *The Better India*. Available: https://www.thebetterindia.com/138291/india-first-woman-cm-freedom-fighter-sucheta-kriplani/ [Accessed: 5.4.23].

Yasmeen, Shagufta (2011). *Ruttie Jinnah: Life and Love.* Karachi: Royal Bok Company.

Acknowledgements

My biggest thanks must go to everyone at Pen & Swords Book but especially to my commissioning editor, Kerrin Wilkinson, not just for approaching me to write this book in the first place but for her patience and support throughout the process and for making my oldest and biggest dream come true.

The most important acknowledgement to make is that the stories in this book are not mine to tell and that as a white British woman I can truly never understand the struggles these women overcame. Nonetheless, it has been an honour to get to know them while researching this book and I – and all the world – owe them a huge debt for the legacies they left behind. Please use the bibliography to read more about them in their own words, for I could never truly do them justice.

I'd also like to acknowledge with gratitude all the Desi women in my own life, who prove that the formidable spirit embodied by the women in this book lives on. Thank you for letting this *gori* tell your story.

I am extremely grateful to Dr Naomi Appleton, my role model and university supervisor who was patient enough to let me write this book at the same time as my PhD and who has supported me through three degrees, making me a better writer and a better scholar.

Thank you to my (s)heroic leader at the Remedial Herstory Project, Kelsie Brook Eckert, for the amazing opportunities she has given me but more importantly, for showing me that Herstory is not just a hobby but a vocation and a moral duty. Someday, somebody will be writing a book about how she changed the world too.

It has been my greatest blessing that on both sides, I was born into a family of amazing, strong, inspiring women who showed me that success has many faces and that women are more powerful than anyone gives us credit for (especially ourselves). The stories of my mother, grandmothers, aunties, and cousins are written on my bones and guide me wherever I

Acknowledgements

go and whatever I do, reminding me that there is nothing that can't be conquered when you tap into the enduring strength of womanhood and support each other. However, there is no one to whom I owe more than my mum, Karen Jenner. In every possible way, I wouldn't be here without her. No words could ever do justice to everything she has done for me, or to her kindness, patience, intelligence, and passion. She taught me always to be myself and to only care what the right people think. Everything she is, is everything I someday hope to be. I would also like to thank my Babar, whose daily chats have been the one constant in my life and who has been my biggest protector and confidante. So many of the things that I value most about myself, I inherited from her, and if she is proud of me then nothing else matters. Honourable mention to my Auntie Dawn, whose love of antiques and stately homes was my gateway to history and my love of all things old and beautiful.

Men were few and far between in my family but that made those I did have more special. My Grandad, Len Jenner, was an incredibly kind man; he taught me that education is the one thing that can never be taken away. Being his granddaughter will always be the thing of which I am most proud. My Grandpa, Jim Gardner, the gentle giant who always cut the crusts off my sandwiches and turned every car ride into a game, served in India during the Second World War. I would give anything to swap stories with him now, but I hope this book does some justice to the land he so adored. My dad, Jimmy Gardner, sadly passed away while this book was being written, but he has inspired me to make the world a better place, and always will. I'd also like to thank my uncles, Bobby and Billy. Bobby inspires me to learn more about the world through his stories of his time on the seven seas. Billy made my childhood a joy and my future a dream come true.

My friendships are my greatest treasures, and I am exceedingly grateful to Sarah, Kim, and all those who have put up with and supported me in every stage of my life. While I cannot name everyone individually, I hope they know who they are and how much I cherish them. I do, however, need to say a special thank you to my oldest friend, *meri behen aur meri rooh*, Rabia Khan. She and her mum were the first to show me the beauty of Pakistani culture and the strength of South Asian women, but those are only two of the many, many things Rabia has taught me over the years, and I can never repay her. Likewise, thank you to Euan Meston, the brother I never had and the friend I could never live without. He has done more for me than he can ever know.

My deepest thanks go to Bharati and Mohan Sharma, for always loving and supporting me as their own, and for all they have taught me about their languages, their religion, and their lands – and about life in general. My mother-in-law, Bharati, is the embodiment of *shakti*. It is a joy and an honour to know her, love her, and learn from her. My father-in-law, Mohan, is a force of nature who inspires me to be the best version of myself with no excuses. Shubham and I could not ask for better role models as we embark on our own marriage, and I will spend my life trying to earn the privilege of being a Sharma.

Last, but definitely not least, thank you to my better half, Shubham Sharma, without whose support, love, and relentless faith in me I could not have written this book. The first present he gave me was a fountain pen with the inscription: 'Keep writing with your heart and the world will read it'. But if I really wrote with my heart all I'd ever write about is him.

Index

Ahimsa – see nonviolence
Ahmed, Hajrah, 251-253
Alcohol (boycotting of), 129, 147, 174, 194
Ali, Aruna Asaf, 119-121, 256
Ali, Shareefa Hamid, 253,
All-India Muslim League (AIML), 20, 22, 155, 159, 222-3, 226-9, 237, 239-42, 246, 248-9, 252-3, 258-9
All-India Trade Union Congress (AITUC), 218-9
All-India Women's Conference (AIWC), 121, 153, 155-6, 161-2, 167, 186, 235, 237, 246, 252-3, 260,
Ambabai, 194-5
Amritsar Massacre – see Jallianwala Bagh Massacre
Anglo-Sikh Wars, 51, 53
Ashram/s, 35, 134, 146, 168, 174, 208, 233,
Assassination, 18, 52, 86-7, 92, 102, 105, 109, 139, 147, 206, 266
   of Charles Stephens, 102, 105
   of Mohandas Gandhi, 18, 139, 147, 206, 266
   of the Governor of Bengal (attempted), 86-7, 89
Bajaj, Jankidevi, 198-9
Bandyopadhyay, Nanibala, 82-3,
Bangladesh, 91, 98, 100, 102, 159,
Bano, Abadi, 245-8
Bano, Amjadi, 248-50
Bedi, Freda, 17
Begum, Asghari, 81
Bengal, 21-2, 82, 86, 89, 91, 96-9, 98, 100-5, 119, 151-2, 155-6, 158, 165, 167, 170-2, 172, 190, 192, 235, 254, 256
   Bengal Famine, 21-2, 96, 155-6, 165, 235
Besant, Annie, 17, 45, 160, 233, 246
Bethune College, 86, 91, 94, 98,
Bhago, Mai, 116, 213
Bharatiya Janata Party (BJP), 109
Bhoodan Movement, 199, 213
Bhutto, Benazir, 266
Bi Amma – see Abadi Bano
Boer War, 127
Bombay, 18, 107, 110, 149-50, 160-1, 176, 182-3, 186-7, 189, 194, 204, 208, 218, 226-7, 229, 251, 260
Bose, Latika, 170-2
Bose, Prabhabati, 170

Bose, Subhas Chandra (S.C.), 86, 98, 100, 123-5, 127, 136, 152, 170, 172, 175
Boycott, 19, 135
Brahmin, 14-15, 61, 82, 91, 119, 149, 185-6, 200, 254,
Brahmo Samaj/ Brahmosim, 86, 119, 151, 190
British conquest of India (Origins of) 13-20, 22-5, 27, 37-8
British East India Company (BEIC), 13-14, 16, 45-6, 48-9, 51, 53, 58, 65, 72, 75
British imperial ideology, 14, 24-5, 37, 52-3, 56, 58, 61, 73, 78, 127, 155-7, 183-4, 251
British Indian Army (BIA), 22, 123, 125
Burqa, 237, 242, 245-6, 249-51, 258
Calcutta, 55, 72, 83, 86, 90, 94, 96-7, 99, 102-4, 109, 151, 154-6, 172, 190, 193
Caliphate Movement (see Khilafat Movement)
Cama, Bhikaiji Rustom, 107-11
Cambridge (University of), 159
Caste, 14-15, 18, 23, 25-8, 38, 41, 47, 58, 61, 69-71, 77-9, 88, 94, 96, 115, 122, 135, 151, 159, 163-5, 169, 173, 196, 198-9, 205-7, 231, 251, 262-3, 265, 267
and gender, 25-6, 28, 88
Brahmin, 14-15, 61, 82, 91, 119, 149, 185-6, 200, 254,
Casteism/caste discrimination, 15, 25, 27-8, 79, 122, 151, 163, 196, 198, 205-6,
Caste-oppressed, 15, 18, 25, 58, 69-70, 78-9, 115, 169, 205, 207
Dalit, 14-15, 28, 43, 47, 69-70, 77-80, 122, 134, 192, 198-9, 251, 263
Dominant caste, 15, 25, 27, 47, 38, 61, 88, 94, 122, 163,173, 260, 262,
Efforts to end caste discrimination, 28, 96, 122, 135, 151, 159, 163, 165, 169, 196, 198-9, 205-6, 265, 267, 231
Erasure of caste oppressed, 25-6, 47, 70, 77, 80, 263,
Intersection with class, 14-15, 25-6, 163,
Origins of, 14-15, 18, 25
Privilege from, 15, 38, 262-3, 115, 163, 265,
Unity between, 135, 164-5, 199, 231, 251,

Celibacy, 76, 132, 129, 142-3, 147-8, 255,
Chattopadhyay, Kamaladevi, 147, 185-189
Chauhan, Subhadra Kumari, 205-207
Chennamma, Rani Kittur, 48-49
Cherian, Accamma, 203-4
Child marriage, 44, 82-3, 96, 116, 122, 131, 134, 149, 169, 180, 182, 185, 192, 194, 196, 198, 200-1, 245, 251, 266
Child Marriage Act, 180, 251-2
Choudhury, Suniti, 102-6
Christian/ity, 15, 25, 56, 82, 112, 114-5, 133, 136, 167, 169, 183, 203
Churchill, Winston, 22, 155, 158
Civil Disobedience Movement, 18-19, 129, 133, 167-8, 180, 182, 192, 196, 241

Index

Communism, 95-7, 104-5, 108-10, 121
  Communist Party of India (CPI), 96-7, 105
Constituent Assembly of India, 101, 157, 168, 201, 235, 256, 259, 261,
Court of Wards, 58
Cousins, Margaret, 17, 186
Dalhousie, Lord James-Broun, 48, 62-3
Dalit, 14-15, 28, 43, 47, 69-70, 77-80, 122, 134, 192, 198-9, 251, 263
Dandi March (see Salt March)
Das, Bina, 86-90
Delhi (New Delhi), 63, 114, 119, 120-1, 125, 144, 146-7, 155, 168-9, 173, 188, 214, 229, 240, 247, 249, 254, 256
Desh Sevika Sangha (DSS), 150, 180-2, 204
Deshmukh, Annapurnabai G. V., 183
Deshmukh, Gammiḍidala Durgabāi, 200-2
Devadasis, 169, 200
Devi, Kadambini, 190
Devi, Mahabiri, 79-80,
Devi, Satyavati, 211-4,
Doctrine of the Lapse, 48, 62
Dowry, 151, 205, 211, 122, 185
Dutt, Kalpana, 92, 94-97
Dyer, General Reginald, 17, 233-4
Empress of India – see Queen Victoria
Famine, 21, 27, 96, 107-8, 155-6, 165, 235
First Round Table Conference, 161, 226, 238, 248-9
First World War, 16, 21, 110, 177, 187, 233,
  Indian involvement in, 16, 21, 177, 187, 233,
  Opposition to, 16, 110
Flag, 84-5, 95, 108-10, 119, 149, 157, 172, 187, 193, 209, 213, 242, 261
Gandhi, Indira, 147, 173-4, 177, 235-6, 266
Gandhi, Kasturbai, 131-42, 144, 146, 148, 159, 174
Gandhi, Manu (Mridula, Manuben), 139-45
Gandhi, Mohandas K., 18-22, 29, 38, 41, 89, 96, 100, 104, 113, 115, 119-21, 129-49, 151-4, 156-7, 159-61, 166-8, 170, 173-4, 177, 180, 182, 186, 188, 192-4, 198, 201, 203, 206, 208-9, 211-2, 216, 229, 233, 245-6, 248, 251-2, 255-6, 260, 263, 266,
  Ideology, 18-22, 29, 89, 113, 115, 119-20, 129-30, 149, 151-3, 157, 168, 170, 177, 180, 182, 186, 188, 196, 198, 208-9, 211, 216, 255-6,
  Views on and treatment of women, 29, 131-8, 142-4, 152, 173-4, 248, 255, 263,
  Celibacy tests, 142-4, 146-7
  Assassination of, 18, 139, 144-7, 206, 266
  Opposition to, 20, 142, 148
  Role in mobilizing women, 120, 151-3, 161-2, 186-7, 192-4, 196, 198, 201, 203,

283

208-9, 211-2, 233, 246, 255,
Gangopadhyay Jyotirmayee, 190-1
Ghose, Santi, 102-6
Gokhale, Avantikabai, 146-7, 186
Gokhale, Gopal Krishna, 149, 167
Gupta, Kamala Das, 86-7,
Hazra, Matangini, 192-3
Hindi, 14, 109, 124, 151, 200-1, 206-7, 211, 217, 263
Hindu, 13-15, 18, 20-1, 24-7, 31, 33, 35, 44, 48, 61-3, 65, 71, 74, 76, 86, 99, 111, 115, 135-6, 141-3, 161, 163, 165, 171, 176, 178, 182-3, 186, 194, 196, 198, 202-3, 209-12, 215-6, 222, 225, 235, 243, 247-8, 252-5, 261, 264
    Hindu nationalism, 15, 21, 35, 71, 76, 99, 109, 111, 115, 163, 171, 182, 216, 264
    Hinduism, 13-15, 21, 25-6, 31, 33, 62-3, 65, 86, 141-3, 171, 176, 183, 186, 194, 196, 261
    Hindu concepts of gender, 25-6, 31, 35, 143, 171, 202, 212, 235
Hindu-Muslim relations, 18, 20, 135, 156, 163, 165, 209, 210, 222, 225, 243, 247, 252-3, 255, 264
Hobhouse, Emily, 127
Holkar, Ahilya Bai, 44-5
Hunger strikes, 19, 83, 119, 140, 206, 213
Indian Mutiny – see 1857 War of Indian Independence
Indian National Army (INA), 123, 125-7, 191
Indian National Congress (INC), 18, 20-3, 45, 84, 86, 89, 100, 104-5, 107, 119-21, 133, 151, 153, 155, 159-61, 167-8, 171-2, 177-8, 183, 190, 192-4, 203-4, 209, 213, 222-3, 228, 233, 240, 246, 251-2, 255-7
Indian Republican Army (IRA), 91, 94, 152
Jagmohandas, Lady, 182
Jain, 182
Jallianwala Bagh Massacre (1919), 17, 20, 160, 167, 219, 233, 254
Jewellery, 55, 124, 132, 152, 174, 177, 200-1, 233, 245
Jhalkaribai, 69-70
Jhansi, Rani Lakshmibai of, 61-71, 75, 91, 94, 121, 123-6, 203, 205, 207
Jinnah, Fatima, 223, 225-232, 241-2
Jinnah, Mohammad Ali, 19-21, 38, 166, 173, 217-32, 240, 249, 265
Jinnah, Rattanbai (Ruttie, Maryam), 20, 217-24, 226
Kali, 26, 143
Kaur, Gulab, 116-8
Kaur, Jindan 50-7
Kaur, Rajkumari Amrit, 167-9
Khadi, 19-20, 94, 129, 134-5, 149, 178, 180, 192, 198, 200, 211, 214
Khilafat Movement, 245-6, 248
Koh-i-noor, 55

Kolkata (see Calcutta)
Kriplani, Sucheta, 254-7
Lahore, 32, 52, 56, 117, 176, 213, 227-8, 230, 237, 239, 241-3, 249, 254, 258
Lahore Resolution, 227, 239, 249
Legislative Assemblies, 89, 97, 104, 147, 183, 186, 206, 239, 259,
Lodhi, Rani Avantibai, 58-60
Lucknow, 20, 63, 71-2, 160, 167, 227, 235, 249, 256
Lucknow Pact (1916), 20, 160
Madam Cama – see Bhikaiji Rustom Cama
Mahal, Begum Hazrat, 71-7
Mahatma Gandhi – see Mohandas Gandhi
Martyr/martyrdom, 19, 30-1, 60, 70, 78-9, 84-5, 87-9, 91-3, 95, 103, 105, 136, 191, 193, 246
Maulana, Mohammad Ali Jouhar and Maulana, Shaukat Ali, 245, 247-8
Mehta, Hansa, 157, 260-1
Missionaries, 15, 82, 112, 115
Mitra, Surama, 86
Mother India, 25, 59, 88
Mountbatten, Lady Edwina, 32, 173, 229-31
Mountbatten, Lord Louis, 229-30.
Mughal Empire, 13, 26, 44, 116, 163
Mumbai – see Bombay
Munshi, Lilavati, 182-4,
Muslim, 13-14, 18-21, 24-8, 31, 33, 35, 40, 53, 71, 74-6, 81, 107, 119-20, 135-6, 139, 156, 161, 163, 209-10, 215-6, 222-3, 226-7, 229-31, 237-53, 258-9, 264
  Islam, 18, 25, 28, 31, 35, 109, 212, 217, 225, 237, 245, 253, 258,
  Islamic concepts of gender, 28, 35, 227, 337-8, 243, 258,
  Islamophobia, 18, 20, 24, 26, 111, 240, 264
  Muslim nationalism, 19, 21, 25, 156, 209, 222, 227, 239, 242, 245, 247-8, 252, 258-9 (see also All-India Muslim League)
  Muslim state (agitation for), 21, 222, 227-8, 240-2, 253 (see also Pakistan)
  Muslim-Hindu relations – see Hindu-Muslim relations
  Muslim League Women's Sub-Committee (MLWSC), 227
  Muslim National Guard (MNG), 240-1
  Mughal Empire, 13, 26, 44, 116, 163
Nachiyar, Rani Velu, 44-8
Naga, 112-115
Naidu, Sarojini, 159-66, 186, 233, 252, 260,
Naoroji, Khurshedben, 208-10
Nayyar, Dr Sushila, 146-8
Nehru, Jawaharlal, 21-2, 38, 45, 114-5, 121, 147, 161, 168, 173, 175-9, 183, 188, 201-2, 229, 233, 242, 252-3, 256, 265

Nehru, Kamala, 144, 173-7
Nehru, Swarup Rani, 176-9
Nepal, 54, 74-5
Nimbkar, Krishnabai Rau, 180-1
Nivedita, Sister, 17
Noakhali, 100, 156, 256
Non-cooperation movement, 18-19, 84, 113, 134, 151, 160, 174, 177, 186, 190, 205, 260
Non-violence, 19, 120, 129, 132, 135, 182, 191, 209, 256,
Oxford (University of), 167, 170, 245
Pakistan, 19, 21, 27, 32-5, 37-40, 126, 146, 157, 208, 216, 222-5, 227-32, 240, 242, 249, 253, 263-6
Pakistan Resolution – see Lahore Resolution
Pamei, Rani Gaidinliu, 112-5
Pandit, Vijayalakshi, 176, 233-6
Parsi, 107, 110, 208, 217, 223
Partition (of India), 23, 27-40, 101, 126, 157, 165, 213, 228, 230-1, 234, 242-3. 247, 256, 259, 266
  Aftermath, 37, 157, 266
  British involvement in, 27, 37-8, 157
  Case for, see Muslim state
  Movement against, 101, 157,
  Relief efforts, 126, 213, 243, 256
  Violence during, 27-30, 35, 157, 165, 230, 243, 247
Pasi, Uda Devi, 77-8
Phukanani, Bhogeshwari, 84-5
Prisons, treatment within, 49, 53, 82-3, 87, 95-6, 104, 109-10, 117, 119, 127, 130, 132-3, 136, 178, 194, 196, 206, 208, 212-3, 235, 242, 256
Punjab, 27, 50-1, 53, 55-6, 116, 119, 160, 211, 237-40, 242, 258
Punjabi, 92, 110, 116, 237, 240
Purdah, 24, 51, 59, 61-2, 72, 134, 151-2, 154, 160, 164-5, 169, 196, 198, 205, 211, 225-8, 231, 237, 242, 245-6, 249-51, 258, 262-3, 265
  Meaning of, 24, 59, 72, 198, 262
  Adherence to, 72, 151, 154, 164-5, 211, 226-8, 242, 246, 258, 262-3, 265
  Rejection of, 51, 61-2, 152, 198, 205, 211, 225, 227, 237, 242, 251, 258, 263
  Movement against, 134, 169, 196, 198, 205, 227, 231, 237, 242, 251, 258, 263
  British violation of, 154, 160
Queen Victoria, 14, 50, 54-6, 74-5
Quit India Movement, 22, 84, 89, 100, 119, 146, 154-5, 165, 168, 190, 197, 204, 206, 235, 256
Rashtriya Stree Sangha (RSS), 160
Rasul, Qudsia Aijaz, 258-9

Ray, Renuka, 151-8
Refugees, 37, 100, 126, 147, 188, 213, 231, 242-3
Rioting, 37, 87, 100, 136, 156-7, 206, 228, 256
Roy, Leela, 98-101,
Sabarmati *ashram,* 149, 208
Sahgal, Captain Lakshmi, 122-8
Salt March – see Salt Satyagraha
Salt Satyagraha, 119, 149, 161, 167-8, 178, 182, 186-7, 192, 194, 197, 201, 257
Sanskrit, 15, 19, 60, 79, 98, 186, 211
Sarda Act (Sharda Act, Child Marriage Act)
Sati, 25, 31, 44,
Satyagraha, 19, 26, 119, 129-30, 160, 170, 177, 190, 194, 201, 203, 205, 233, 255-6
Satyagrahi, 19, 119, 129-215, 220, 254
Sayani, Kulsum, 252
Second Round Table Conference, 161
Second World War, 16, 21-3, 89, 117, 119-20, 122-7, 154-6, 239-40, 256,
   Indian involvement in, 16, 21-2, 122-7, 155, 239-40
   Opposition to, 22, 119-20, 123, 127, 156, 239, 256
Sen, Surya, 91-2, 94-5,
Sengupta, Nellie, 17
Sex workers, 71, 75, 200, 221,
Shahnawaz, Jahanara, 237-244
Sikh, 13, 18, 25-8, 30-1, 33, 50-6, 116-8, 169, 213, 240
Simon Commission, 170
Singh, Bhagat, 38, 117, 213
Sita, 35
Slade, Madeline. 17
Socialism, 108-10, 121,
Spinning, 134, 140, 151, 192, 198, 220, 233
Suicide, 29-31, 47, 93, 171
Tamil, 46, 124, 201
Third Round Table Conference, 161, 238
Torture, 17, 30, 65, 82-3, 117, 104, 132, 140, 191, 212, 235
   Of prisoners by British, 17, 82-3, 104, 117, 140, 191, 212, 235
   Of civilians by British, 17, 65, 191
   Of women during Partition – see violence against women
Travancore State Congress (TSC), 203-4
Trials, 89, 96, 103, 113, 125-6, 146-7, 194, 219
   Indian National Army trials, 125-6
   Of Ambabai, 194
   Of B.G. Horniman, 219
   Of Gandhi's assassins, 146-7

Of Kalpana Dutt, 96
Of Kalyani Das, 89
Of Rani Gaidinliu Pamei, 113
Of Santi Ghose and Sunita Choudhury, 103
United Council for Relief and Welfare (UCRW)
United Nations (UN), 235, 240, 253, 260,
Urdu, 46, 201, 211, 217, 237-8, 251
Veiling – see purdah
Viceroy, 13, 23, 32, 154, 215, 220-1, 229, 238-9
Violence against women, 25, 27-37, 39-40, 67, 100, 103, 131, 140, 147, 156, 160, 178, 182-4, 191-3, 211, 242, 65-6
  By the British, 17, 67, 82-4, 103-4, 117, 140, 160, 178, 182-4, 191-3, 211-2, 235, 242
  Domestic abuse, 131, 147, 266
  During partition, 25, 27-37, 39,
  Women's resistance to, 37, 40, 265,
  Rape, 25, 29-30, 32, 35, 67, 100, 103, 156, 183, 265
  Honour killings, 27-35, 39, 266
Waddedar, Pritilata, 7, 91-5, 99
War of Indian Independence, (1857) 14, 58, 63-9, 71-3, 75, 77-9, 81-2, 156, 207, 211, 245
  Causes of, 74-5, 77
  Women's involvement in, 58-81
  British retaliation for, 65, 72-3, 81, 156, 245
Widows/widowhood, 25, 28, 31, 62, 68, 82-3, 151, 185-6, 189, 193-4, 196-7, 202, 235, 249, 263
Women's education (advocation for), 16, 37, 98-9, 148, 153, 161, 164-6, 168, 171, 190, 199, 202, 212, 231, 237-9, 251-2, 262, 265
Women's Indian Association (WIA), 160, 237
Women's National Guard (WNG), 230, 243
Women's suffrage, 56, 109-10, 159-60, 168-9